WITHDRAWN

Project Decisions

THE ART AND SCIENCE

Second Edition

Lev Virine
Michael Trumper

BERRETT-KOEHLER PUBLISHERS, INC.

Berrett-Koehler Publishers, Inc.
1333 Broadway, Suite 1000
Oakland, CA 94612-1921
Tel: (510) 817-2277
Fax: (510) 817-2278
www.bkconnection.com

ORDERING INFORMATION

Quantity sales. Special discounts are available on quantity purchases by corporations, associations, and others. For details, contact the "Special Sales Department" at the Berrett-Koehler address above.

Individual sales. Berrett-Koehler publications are available through most bookstores. They can also be ordered directly from Berrett-Koehler: Tel: (800) 929-2929; Fax: (802) 864-7626; www.bkconnection.com.

Orders for college textbook / course adoption use. Please contact Berrett-Koehler: Tel: (800) 929-2929; Fax: (802) 864-7626.

Distributed to the U.S. trade and internationally by Penguin Random House Publisher Services.

Berrett-Koehler and the BK logo are registered trademarks of Berrett-Koehler Publishers, Inc.

Printed in the United States of America.

Berrett-Koehler books are printed on long-lasting acid-free paper. When it is available, we choose paper that has been manufactured by environmentally responsible processes. These may include using trees grown in sustainable forests, incorporating recycled paper, minimizing chlorine in bleaching, or recycling the energy produced at the paper mill.

Library of Congress Cataloging-in-Publication Data

Names: Virine, Lev, 1964– author. | Trumper, Michael, 1963– author.
Title: Project decisions : the art and science / Lev Virine, Michael Trumper.
Description: Second edition. | Oakland, CA : Berrett-Koehler Publishers, [2019] |
    Includes bibliographical references and index.
Identifiers: LCCN 2019017127 | ISBN 9781523085446 (print pbk. : alk. paper)
Subjects: LCSH: Project management—Decision making. | Project management. |
    Decision making.
Classification: LCC HD69.P75 V568 2019 | DDC 658.4/04—dc23
LC record available at https://lccn.loc.gov/2019017127

Second Edition

25 24 23 22 21 20 19   10 9 8 7 6 5 4 3 2 1

Book producer: Westchester Publishing Services
Text designer: Westchester Publishing Services
Cover designer: Dan Tesser, Studio Carnelian

Contents

Preface

Project management is the art of making the right decisions. To be effective, a project manager must be conversant on the following questions:

- How do we make rational choices in project management?
- How can we improve our ability to make these choices?
- Which tools are available to help us during this process that will enable us to make better decisions?

In most cases, the answers to these questions are not trivial. In managing projects, we deal with multiple objectives, multiple risks and uncertainties, and multiple stakeholders. And the underlying framework of project management problems can be quite complex.

Fortunately, a set of practical methods and tools—called decision analysis— can help solve these problems. A unique aspect of decision analysis is that it involves two seemingly separate disciplines: (1) the psychology of judgment and decision-making and (2) mathematics and statistics. Psychologists try to understand the underlying mental processes we use when we make decisions. Mathematicians try to apply their knowledge and use the numbers involved in project management to assess and evaluate options. In this manner, both psychologists and mathematicians are looking to develop methodologies that will improve our ability to make good decisions despite the inherent limitations of our mental capabilities.

In recent years, decision analysis has become a practical tool in many disciplines. Companies routinely base their major investment strategies on the results of decision analysis and, in industries such as energy or pharmaceuticals, never proceed with major projects before performing a comprehensive, structured decision analysis. Decision analysis is used to analyze mergers and acquisitions, capital investments, reorganizations, and new product development. Governments apply decision analysis to policy development, attorneys use it to assess complex litigation that may have an uncertain outcome, and medical professionals use it to help them make correct diagnoses and prescribe the most effective treatments.

Coming to project management from a decision science background, we believe that project management is a primary candidate for the application of decision analysis. We have discovered, however, that most organizations use only a few components of the decision analysis process. In addition, many project managers are not familiar with the decision analysis approaches that are in wide use in other industries; if they happen to be aware of the processes, they do not believe that the processes are applicable to their own industry or organization. When we started to make presentations about the psychology of judgment and decision-making in project management, we found that it was an eye-opening experience for many project managers. At that point, we decided that the best way to get our message out to the widest audience would be to publish a book that provides a short, practical introduction to decision analysis.

Project management is all about processes. Decision analysis provides processes that will help project managers improve their ability to make good decisions. In Part 1 of this book, we outline the project decision analysis process. The subsequent four parts describe each phase of the process in detail, including a review of both its psychological aspects and various quantitative methods. We have tried to avoid complex mathematical discussions because we believe in the maxim "Knowledge of geography is unnecessary as long as there are taxi drivers." In other words, complex mathematics and statistics are implemented in the myriad software applications you use as a project manager—you don't need to know every last one of the details.

Instead, in this book we concentrate on the psychology of decision-making, which we think is terra incognita for many project managers. Decision-making is a fundamental skill of project management that can be improved by training. If project managers can avoid known mental traps and follow certain thinking processes, they can significantly improve the quality of their project decisions.

We hope this book will be useful, even perhaps entertaining, for everyone involved in the project management process: managers, members of project teams, and project sponsors. As part of this effort, we have tried to map our discussion of the decision analysis process to the project management process described in the *Project Management Institute's A Guide to the Project Management Body of Knowledge (PMBOK® Guide)*.

This is the second edition of the book that was originally published in 2007. We have included references to new research in the areas of decision analysis and project management, have devised more examples, and have increased our focus on psychology of judgment and decision-making.

Finally, technical books are a lot like exercise machines. You can make a resolution to get in shape by losing weight and buying an exercise machine, which you then use religiously for a couple of weeks. When you see a few results—when you look down and your toes are visible for the first time in years—your interest flags, tedium sets in, and eventually the treadmill is collecting dust in the basement. The same thing happens with most technical books. You use them for a few weeks and are able to make a few small improvements, but the reading is so tedious and boring that you would rather poke yourself in the eye than read the next chapter. We devoutly hope that this is not an issue with our book!

Lev Virine, Michael Trumper
Calgary, Alberta, Canada

Test Your Judgment

Here is a quiz to test your judgment as a project manager. This is *not* an IQ test, and it is definitely *not* some sort of psychological experiment to stress-test your brain. *This is a test of your intuition; you do not need to do any calculations.*

Consider this exercise an introduction to the book. We will discuss the problems from the test along with other issues throughout the book.

1. You are a project manager working on a movie called *Pirates of the Caribbean–24*. Your project is to produce and deliver a prop for the set: a treasure chest. You estimate that manufacturing the chest in China and filling it with gold will take between 10 days (you have 10% confidence in this estimate) and 40 days (90% confidence), using normal distribution. Delivery time should be the same in all cases. The film's director has requested that you come up with an estimate with 90% confidence for both manufacturing and shipping the treasure chest.

    Which of the following is your estimate?

    A. ~80 days   B. ~50 days   C. ~63 days.

2. You are an artist drawing a wedding portrait of a royal couple: Prince Garry and Princess Eden. You have two strategies:

    (1) Draw both of them at the same time. This strategy will take 20 days. However, if, at any time during the 20 days, Eden and Garry decide that they do not like the portrait, you have to start all over. The probability of their not liking your work is 60%.

    (2) Draw Eden first and then Garry. This strategy will take 10 days for each of them. If at any time during these 10 days Eden or Garry decides that they do not like their portraits, you will need to restart your 10 days of work. The probability that either of them will not like your work is 30%.

Which strategy should you use to complete the portrait faster (on average, taking into account potential delays)?

   A. Both strategies will lead to the same duration.

   B. Strategy B is 17% faster than strategy A.

   C. Strategy B is 70% faster than strategy A.

3. Assume that you selected strategy 2 from the previous question. There could be two scenarios: (a) Eden's and Garry's art preferences are similar, so if Eden doesn't like the portrait, Garry probably won't like it either; or (b) Eden's and Garry's preferences are different. What is the project duration (on average, taking into account potential delays)?

   A. Situation A leads to a 50% faster completion of the portrait than situation B.

   B. Situation B leads to a 50% faster completion than situation A.

   C. Portrait completion times in situation A and B are about the same.

4. Billionaire Mike Zukkerfield decided to invest in a new software venture. He has three choices:

   A. A social network site for dogs and cats, so they can meet and enjoy themselves. Cost to develop is $200 million, and the probability of success is 50%.

   B. A computer game called "You Are Doomed" for current and prospective criminals. Cost to develop is $400 million, and the probability of success is 25%.

   C. A mobile app to determine less mosquito-infested spots for camping. Cost to develop is $300 million, and the probability of success is 80%.

   In which venture should Mike Zukkerfield invest?

5. You are in Anchorage, Alaska, to film the new *National Lampoon's* "Vacation in Hawaii" movie starring Chevy Chase. If snow starts falling while filming a beach scene, you will have to restart 10 days of shooting. The chance of snowfall is 30%, and the official weather forecast says that there is an equal probability of snowfall for each of the 10 days. However, you think that it is most likely to snow close to the end of filming rather than at the beginning. Assuming that both forecasts are equally accurate, which situation will result in the longest time to complete filming, taking into account potential delays?

   A Your forecast will lead to a 5% longer filming time than the official weather forecast.

   B. The official forecast will lead to a 5% longer filming time than your forecast.

   C. Filming will take about the same time regardless of the forecast.

6. You are involved in a project to promote rapper MC Uglyface. Despite spending $1 million for ads, video clips, and marketing promotions, MC Uglyface is still at the bottom of the charts. Which option would you choose?

    A. One more $50,000 ad campaign, because similar campaigns for other rappers were successful in 50% of the cases.

    B. One more $100,000 ad campaign, because similar campaigns for other rappers were successful in 75% of the cases.

    C. Give up on MC Uglyface and start promoting the rapper BadPosture.

7. You meet a young actress who you believe can become an A-list actress and a celebrity in a few years, so you offer to be her future divorce lawyer. What is the chance that you will earn millions in attorney fees from her if there is a 10% chance that she will become a celebrity, a 100% chance that she will be married, a 100% chance that she will be divorced, and a 10% chance that she will choose you to be her divorce lawyer?

    A. 10%   B. 1%   C. 0.1%   D. 100%

8. You are a screenplay writer trying to figure out what type of screenplay will have the best chance of being produced. As part of this decision, you have reviewed historical data related to all the screenplays you know and have put them in the table below. Which type of screenplay will have highest probability of *not* being produced?

	Screenplay not produced	Screenplay produced
A. Action	20 times	4 times
B. Love stories	11 times	2 times
C. Children stories	15 times	3 times

9. Your project is to buy new clothes for the fall season. You read a number of fashion magazines and see that most experts agree that a mixture of bright and pale tones will be in style during the fall. A few magazines also stress the revival of a historical theme. In addition, some articles emphasize a trend to pink and blue colors. Which description do you think will be the most probable?

    A. Bright hues mixed with pale tones.

    B. Bright hues mixed with pale tones, combined with the purity of pink and blue colors.

    C. Bright hues mixed with pale tones, combined with the purity of pink and blue colors that bring a sense of energy and refinement to historical and classic themes.

10. You are a stunt double in a Western movie. Despite all your skills, you fall from your horse in 16% of all the shots. The occurrence of these falls appears to be completely random; it does not seem to have any correlation to how hard you try, which horse you use, the weather conditions, the filming locale, or anything else. In this movie, you have already fallen from your horse 7 times out of 35 shots. Are you going to be lucky the next time around? How many times do you estimate you will fall from the horse in the remaining 25 shots?

A. 5 times   B. 2 times   C. 4 times

Answers to Judgment Quiz

1. The correct answer is **C** (63 days). You cannot add together high estimates (40 days + 40 days = 80 days) to get the duration of the project with two activities associated with 90% confidence. It cannot be 50 days (2 × (10 days + 40 days) ÷ 2), which is the mean duration. The actual calculation can be performed using quantitative analysis tools based on Monte Carlo simulations. For more information, please read chapter 16, "What Is Project Risk? Monte Carlo Method."

2. The correct answer is **B** (Strategy B is 17% faster than strategy A). A similar example is discussed in chapter 20, "Adaptive Project Management." Splitting a risky project into smaller phases usually accelerates the project, but not as significantly as 70%. An actual calculation can be performed using Event chain methodology.

3. The correct answer is **C** (portrait completion times in situations A and B are about the same). The correlation between risk events plays a significant role only if probabilities are relatively high. In this case, the probability that Eden or Garry will not like the portrait is 30%; therefore, correlations will not have a significant effect on the results. See chapter 14, "Choosing What Is Most Important: Sensitivity Analysis and Correlations."

4. The correct answer is **C**. This question relates to the notion of expected value. Expected value is a probability-weighted average of all outcomes that is calculated by multiplying each possible outcome by its probability of occurrence and then summing the results. Probability multiplied by outcome is lower in C ($300 M × 80% = $240 M). We will learn about expected value in chapter 4, "What Is Rational Choice? A Brief Introduction to Decision Theory."

5. The correct answer is **A** (your forecast will lead to a 5% longer filming time than the official weather forecast). The moment of risk (when the

snow falls) may significantly affect duration. See chapter 17, "'A Series of Unfortunate Events,' or Event Chain Methodology."

6. Whatever money you have already invested in MC Uglyface's career is a sunk cost. The high success rate of the ad campaign applies to other rappers, and there is evidence that more ad campaigns will not help MC Uglyface. We recommend answer **C** (give up with MC Uglyface and start promoting the rapper BadPosture). For more information about sunk cost, read chapter 2, "'Gut Feel' vs. Decision Analysis: Introduction to the Psychology of Project Decision-Making" and chapter 20, "Adaptive Project Management."

7. The correct answer is **B** (1%.) You need to multiply all probabilities: 0.1 (become celebrity) $\times$ 1 (married) $\times$ 1 (divorced) $\times$ 0.1 (choose lawyer) = 0.01.

   This question is related to the bias called "overestimating the probability of conjunctive events": people tend to choose much higher numbers. See appendix B, "Heuristics and Biases in Project Management."

8. The correct answer is **B** (love stories). This question is related to the covariation assessment effect. People tend to pay more attention to high absolute values than they do to relative indicators of success or failure. The relative chance that the screenplay will be produced is higher for love stories (11 $\div$ 2 = 5.5). See chapter 14, "Choosing What Is Most Important: Sensitivity Analysis and Correlations."

9. The correct answer is **A** (short descriptions such as "Bright hues mixed with pale tones" are more general and therefore more probable). The more conditions that you add to a description, the less likely that all of them will be met. This question is related to the representativeness heuristic, and particularly to the conjunction fallacy. These are discussed in chapter 2, "'Gut Feel' vs. Decision Analysis: Introduction to the Psychology of Project Decision-Making."

10. The correct answer is **C** (4 times). The probability always remains the same: 16% (25 trials $\times$ 16% = 4 times). This question is related to the gambler's fallacy. See appendix B, "Heuristics and Biases in Project Management."

Now score yourself and see where you fall on the table below.

Number of Correct Answers	Means That . . .	Some Advice
9 – 10	You are an ace of project management.	Your intuition as a project manager is outstanding. (The bad news is that this book may not improve your excellent mental abilities!.)
4 – 8	You are a king or queen of project management.	Your intuition is very good. But you can still improve your decision-making skills by reading this book.
0 – 3	You are part of the general population of project managers.	Don't worry. Most people have difficulties answering these questions without running a computer analysis. In this book you will find answers to these and many other questions.

PART 1

Introduction to Project Decision Analysis

CHAPTER 1

Project Decision Analysis
What Is It?

Most of us believe we are pretty good at making decisions, yet we continue to make poor ones. And over time our poor decisions become a burden that we impose on each other, especially when the decisions we make as managers are connected to large-scale projects that affect many people. The process known as structured decision analysis—which is described in detail in this book—can improve our ability to make better decisions, particularly in project management, where the decisions can be complex. Indeed, today many organizations in both the public and private sectors use decision analysis to solve their project management problems.

The Burden of Poor Decision-Making

In the summer of 2017, several South Carolina utility companies decided to halt the construction of two new nuclear reactors on the V.C. Summer nuclear project (Plumer 2017). The project was originally planned to be completed in 2018 and cost $11.5 billion. In 2017 it was determined that the reactors would not begin generating electricity before 2021 and could cost as much as $25 billion. The companies had spent over $9 billion before canceling the project, and the reactors were only 40% completed. The reactors were meant to be the vanguard of a nuclear comeback as the United States had built no nuclear reactors since the 1970s. Instead, the halting of this project was a major setback for U.S. ambitions to reinvigorate the nuclear power industry. Currently, the Alvin W. Vogtle Electric Generating Plant, in Georgia, remains the only nuclear power plant under construction in the country, and it too faces enormous cost overruns and delays.

So, "What went wrong?" This question should always be asked in such cases. First, utility companies selected an advanced reactor design from Westinghouse Electric Company, the AP1000. However, when construction started, new features were incorporated into the design that caused significant re-engineering. In addition, since no new reactors had been built for some 40 years, supply chain and engineering expertise had been lost. In the resulting mess, Westinghouse, the company responsible for the plant's design and construction, filed for bankruptcy and the utilities companies decided to accept the losses rather than pass on the costs to consumers.

We all remember that our parents always told us to "think before you do something." Apparently, the people who sanctioned, planned, and executed this nuclear project failed to think about all the possible implications before making their decisions. Perhaps this was an isolated incident, or perhaps it was an emerging trend, never before seen? Here is another example:

In 2004–2005, Governor Arnold Schwarzenegger of California was involved in a complex decision-making process. He was not considering a role for his next action movie after he left office, nor was he selecting a new energy weapon to blast villains in a sci-fi movie. This was something more serious: the governor involved himself in the design process for a new bridge in San Francisco (Cabanatuan 2005).

This was not just any bridge. The $6.3 billion project (figure 1-1) was to replace the existing Bay Bridge. The original plans called for the section of the bridge east of Yerba Buena Island to include a huge suspension span. Although the construction of the foundations for the suspension span had started a few years earlier, the governor's office insisted that a simple viaduct would be cheaper and faster to build. Transportation officials did not agree, believing that a design change from a suspension span to a viaduct would slow construction.

Wrong decisions are a burden that we impose on each other.

Early in 2005 the governor's side appeared to have prevailed: work on the foundation was halted, and the contract was terminated. A few months later, however,

Figure 1-1. San Francisco Bay Bridge Construction (Photo by Oleg Alexandrov)

following a detailed analysis, both sides agreed to follow the original design, which included the suspension span. In the end, the fight over the bridge design cost $81 million.

If you do not live in Northern California, you may not be directly affected by the Bay Bridge cost overrun. However, directly or indirectly, at some time you will pay for somebody's wrong decision—regardless of where you live or what you do. This is because, for example:

- Costs related to problems in developing new drugs are passed on to consumers in the form of higher prices for medications.
- Dry wells lead to increased costs for oil and gas exploration and production, leading in turn to higher prices at the gas pump.
- Governments sometimes implement ill-considered policies that can adversely affect your taxes.
- You yourself occasionally make wrong decisions. The cheap brand of deck coating that you used to save a couple of dollars is already peeling off and you will have to paint your deck again next year (next time with a better brand).

Problems result from poor decision-making, whether the person making the decision is the manager at the pharmaceutical company, the geologist making a bad choice of where to drill for oil, the ineffective government bureaucrat or legislator making policy for the wrong reasons, or even you yourself, trying to save a few bucks by buying a low-priced deck coat.

We human beings have been making poor decisions since we first developed the ability—and the necessity—to make choices. In the modern world, however, due to the complexity and cost of projects, the price we pay for poor decisions has significantly increased. The overall cost of wrong decisions is very hard to estimate, but it is undoubtedly enormous. Say, for example, we design a multibillion-dollar oil pipeline but make a poor decision on the path it will follow through a particular location. Because of that poor decision, we now have to move it—a step that might increase the project costs by millions of dollars. Who pays that cost? It is passed on to somebody—investors, consumers, or the government.

Poor decision-making in the medical field can have expensive, even fatal, results. The causes of medical mistakes differ. Sometimes the cause is a flaw in a hospital procedure. Most medical mistakes, however, are related to errors in human judgment. In the United States, more than 250,000 deaths per year are the result of medical errors (Makary and Daniel 2016). As a comparison, according to the Centers for Disease Control, in 2013 a total of 611,105 people died of heart disease, 584,881 of cancer, and 149,205 of chronic respiratory disease—the top three causes of death in the nation.

Why Do We Make Wrong Decisions?

Lawrence Phillips, a prominent decision analysis expert, cites a curious paradox: although the ability to make right decisions is considered a main indicator of project-management professionalism, many project managers are unwilling to try to improve the quality of their decisions (Goodwin 2014). Phillips suggests that many people consider decision-making to be merely an automatic process, as natural as breathing. And if we don't need to learn how to breathe, why do we need to learn how to make better decisions? With such a blasé attitude, many project managers don't make the effort to understand decision analysis, or perhaps they believe that it is just a theoretical discipline with no practical use in their work.

If you were asked to rate your decision-making ability, most likely you would rate yourself as "better than average." The "better-than-average effect," where people tend to rate themselves as above average when asked to characterize their abilities, is a common psychological bias (Massey, Robinson and Kaniel 2006) that is applicable not only to self-assessments of decision-making but also to other activities. But, if we believe that we are such good decision-makers, why do we often make poor ones?

The answer resides in the fact that most of today's important project-management decisions are complex. Without proper analysis, it is hard to make choices between alternatives. Every day, project managers make numerous decisions. Most of them are trivial and do not require sophisticated analysis. If a component for your construction project is delayed, you might decide to call the supplier. Obviously, in making this choice, you can rely on common sense. You do not need to perform an advanced analysis, solve a few differential equations, or run a complex simulation model. However, if you need to select a new supplier, the situation is quite different. A great deal is at stake, and a wrong decision could be very costly. In addition, you likely have many alternatives. So, now you realize that relying solely on your intuition may not be enough; you probably should perform a decision analysis.

Why is decision-making so complicated? It's true for a number of reasons:

- **Most problems in project management involve multiple objectives.** Tesla's Model 3 was planned to be an affordable, reliable, sporty, fuel-efficient, high-tech, luxurious, and practical mass-produced electric car (Grinshpun 2018). Production of such an ambitious product faced many challenges: the supply chain management needed to be built from scratch, new manufacturing processes needed to be developed, and distribution and delivery processes required implementation. Finally, costs had to be kept under control. That is quite a list of objectives that Tesla needed to achieve in a very short time frame. Because of these objectives, some hiccups were encountered along the way, particularly in regard to delays in reaching production goals and cash flow concerns. Decision analysis would help to prioritize multiple objectives.

- **Project managers deal with uncertainties.** Predicting the future is not an easy task. Selecting alternatives is the primary objective of decision analysis. Decision analysis offers tools to help project managers deal with uncertainties.

- **Project management problems can be complex.** The number of alternatives you face in managing a project can be significant. Decisions are usually made sequentially, based on previous decisions. Moreover, understanding how each decision will affect subsequent ones is difficult.

- **Most projects include multiple stakeholders.** Project managers deal with clients, project team members, project sponsors, and subcontractors, among others. All these stakeholders have different objectives and preferences.

Decision Analysis as a Process

Having explained what decision analysis encompasses, we still must ask: What is it, really? First, decision analysis is a tool to solve problems. It is a "practical framework of methods and tools to promote creativity and help people make better decisions" (Keeney 1982).

As a project manager, you don't need to know every last detail about these methods and tools, some of which can be extremely complicated. It *is* important, however, that you know two basic things that affect how decisions are made:

- **We are all subject to common psychological pitfalls.** People come hardwired with psychological constructs that can mislead them when they make project decisions. If you are estimating projects costs, identifying possible risks, selecting viable alternatives, or identifying the most important project objectives, you can make predictable mental mistakes. A basic knowledge of these pitfalls and how they can affect decision-making will help you avoid them.

- **We can use decision analysis techniques to avoid those pitfalls.** These techniques will improve your ability to make better decisions. Moreover, most of these techniques can be applied in other areas of practice, such as financial analysis.

What you really need to know in general is that project decision analysis is a scalable and flexible process that is both practical and effective. In addition, it is important to understand that decision analysis is *not* a process that creates an additional level of bureaucracy. It can be integrated into other processes that are defined in the *PMBOK® Guide* (Project Management Institute 2018). We strongly recommend that you begin to establish this process by improving your own thinking processes rather than setting it up at the organizational level.

The process includes four major phases (which are discussed in the following parts of this book):

1. Decision-framing, or structuring the problem (Part 1)

2. Modeling the situation (Part 2)

3. Quantitative analysis (Part 3)

4. Implementation, monitoring, and reviews of the decisions (Part 4)

Each phase of the process involves several steps, which we will cover in our discussions of each phase.

Often, project managers believe that decision analysis is a type of cost-benefit analysis. That is a technique used to compare the various costs associated with a project with the benefits that it is intended to return. In comparison, decision analysis is a much broader process that takes into account many parameters and uncertainties. It focuses on developing a more complete analysis of a project and on understanding the ramifications of the possible choices facing a project manager.

Normative and Descriptive Decision Theory

The foundation of decision analysis is *decision theory*, which is the study of how to make better choices when faced with uncertainties. Normative decision theory describes how people should make decisions; descriptive decision theory describes how people actually make their decisions.

To distinguish between the normative and the descriptive approaches, let's look at decisions related to recovering a hidden treasure. The movie *National Treasure* (2004), starring Nicolas Cage, follows a team of treasure hunters as they methodically and logically unravel a series of extremely convoluted clues. This is an example of normative decision theory, because it shows how people should behave if they want to recover a treasure. Stanley Kramer's movie *It's a Mad, Mad, Mad World* (1963) is an example of descriptive decision theory, for it shows how people actually behave when they try to recover a treasure. In trying to find the treasure, instead of acting logically, the characters behave spontaneously and irrationally. Chaos and hilarity ensue, yet no treasure is found.

Driving Forces behind Project Decision Analysis

Realizing that poor decision-making in large-scale projects can both result in high costs and even cause harm, governments and private businesses alike are increasingly recognizing the importance of instituting decision analysis techniques.

The U.S. Government Performance Results Act of 1993 states that "waste and inefficiency in Federal programs undermine the confidence of the American people in the Government and reduce the Federal Government's ability to address adequately vital public needs." The first stated purpose of the act is to "improve the confidence of the American people in the capability of the Federal Government, by systematically holding Federal agencies accountable for achieving program results."

The act mandates that all major decisions made by government agencies be properly justified in the public interest. One of the main outcomes of the act is a much wider adoption of decision analysis and risk management in government organizations.

Private companies also understand the importance of decision analysis to justify their decisions. It is not enough for a company's management to report to shareholders and Wall Street analysts that the company just spent X million dollars on research and development and Y million on capital projects. Investors need to see assurances that their money was spent wisely. Therefore, many companies have started to establish structured decision analysis processes. Many organizations use decision support tools such as Enterprise Resource Management or Project Portfolio Management systems to improve their efficiencies. SixSigma is a proven methodology to improve decision-making related to quality. One of the main areas of improvement, especially in the area of new product development, is the ability to successfully select which projects should go forward.

Government regulations and pressure from investors have become the driving forces behind the wider adoption of decision analysis. As government agencies and large companies implement the process, more information about decision analysis is becoming available, more experience with the technique is being accumulated, and more businesses are using it to improve the efficiencies of their projects.

A Little Bit of History

The fathers of decision analysis had lofty goals. In the 1700s, the French-born mathematician Abraham de Moivre and the English Presbyterian minister and mathematician Thomas Bayes tried to apply mathematics to prove the existence of God. Their work made important contributions to probabilities and statistics. In 1718, de Moivre published *The Doctrine of Chances*, in which he presented the concept of relative frequency for probabilities. De Moivre became one of the fathers of the "frequentistic" approach to the theory of probabilities and statistics. Bayes came up with a different concept, one that would later become the foundation for the Bayesian theory in the field of probabilities. Around the same time, a Swiss mathematician and physicist, Daniel Bernoulli, came up with idea of decision-making based on analyzing various possible outcomes of given events. Their work became the foundation of decision analysis.

The publication of *Theory of Games and Economic Behavior* in 1944, by John von Neumann and Oskar Morgenstern, was another significant step in decision science. After their theory was published, a number of scholars developed expansions and variations on it (Savage 1954; Luce 1959; Fishburn 1984; Karmarkar 1978; Payne 1973; Coombs 1975). Contemporary decision theory was introduced in the 1960s by Howard Raiffa and Robert Schlaifer of the Harvard Business School, who introduced the framework of decision analysis methods and tools (Raiffa 1968; Schlaifer 1969). The advent of the computer over the past few decades has also had a strong influence, and today decision and risk analysis software has become a useful tool for practitioners.

Interestingly, in 2002 the Nobel Prize for economics was awarded to a psychologist rather than an economist. Daniel Kahneman was awarded the prize for "having integrated insights from psychological research into economic science, especially concerning human judgment and decision-making under uncertainty" (Sveriges Riksbank Prize 2002). The research, which Kahneman conducted with Amos Tversky and other psychologists, outlined the basic psychological foundation behind decision-making, which has significantly changed our understanding of human behavior. It affected not only our understanding of economics but also other areas, including project management. Kahneman later wrote a popular book called *Thinking, Fast and Slow* (Kahneman 2013), which is a comprehensive, easy-to-read overview of the psychology of judgment and decision-making as well as of Kahneman's own research.

In 2017 Nobel Award in economics was awarded to Richard Thaler for his contribution to behavioral economics, which is directly related to decision analysis. Thaler is a professor of behavioral science and economics at the University of Chicago, Booth School of Business. In 2015, he served as president of the American Economic Association. He is probably most well-known for authoring, with Cass Sunstein, the best-selling book *Nudge: Improving Decisions about Health, Wealth, and Happiness* (Thaler and Sunstein 2009).

Decision Analysis Today

Built on the work of many scholars in numerous fields, decision analysis has now become a practical framework that helps to solve a huge variety of problems in various disciplines, including project management. The methodology is widely used by many companies—General Motors, DuPont, Boeing, Eli Lilly, AT&T, Exxon Mobil, Shell, Chevron, BP, Novartis, Baxter Bioscience, Bristol-Myers Squibb, and Johnson & Johnson, to name a few—as well as in U.S. government agencies such as the Department of Defense, Department of Homeland Security, and NASA. Because easy-to-use, decision analysis software tools have become widely available, the adoption of decision analysis methods in all types of organizations, even down to small- and medium-sized companies, has accelerated (see appendix A).

Many universities, including Stanford, Harvard, Duke, the London School of Economics and Political Science, University of California–Los Angeles, and the University of Massachusetts, offer courses in decision analysis. And a substantial number of scientific papers, textbooks, and reference works on the subject have been published in recent years.

Experts in decision analysis have joined together in a number of professional organizations, one being the Decision Analysis Society. That society is a subdivision of the Institute for Operations Research and the Management Sciences (INFORMS, for short). It publishes the journal *Decision Analysis* and holds group meetings in conjunction with INFORMS annual meetings. Another professional group, the Decision Analysis Affinity Group (DAAG), focuses mostly on practical aspects of decision analysis. The Society for Judgment and Decision-Making (SJDM) focuses mostly on the behavioral aspects of decision theory.

Wrong decisions are a heavy burden that people working in numerous industries impose on each other—and on society.

- Making decisions related to real-life problems is a complex process as a result of multiple objectives, complex structures, multiple risks and uncertainties, and multiple stakeholders.
- The advocacy-based approach to decision-making often involves an intuitive assessment of the problem and does not necessarily lead to better decisions; the alternative to this approach is the decision analysis process.
- Government regulations and industry pressure are the main driving forces behind the active integration of decision analysis into organizational processes.
- Decision analysis is based on extensive research in mathematics, logic, and psychology; today, decision analysis is a framework of methods and tools that help people as well as organizations make quality decisions.

CHAPTER 2

"Gut Feel" vs. Decision Analysis
Introduction to the Psychology of Project Decision-Making

The purpose of psychology is to give us a completely different idea of the things we know best.

—PAUL VALERY, FRENCH POET (1871–1945)

The root cause of almost all project failures is human error or misjudgment. These errors are hard to prevent, for they stem from human psychology. But decision-making is a skill that can be improved by training. By understanding how psychological heuristics and biases can affect our judgment, it is possible to mitigate their negative effects and make better decisions.

Human Judgment Is Almost Always to Blame

In his paper "Lessons Discovered but Seldom Learned or Why Am I Doing This if No One Listens" (Hall 2005), David C. Hall reviewed a number of projects that had failed or had major problems. Among them were:

- Malfunctions in bank-accounting software systems, which cost millions of dollars

- Space programs, including the Mars Polar Lander, Mars Climate Orbiter, and Ariane 5 European Space Launcher, that were lost

- Defense systems, including the Patriot Missile Radar System and the Tomahawk/LASM/Naval Fires Control System, which had serious problems

Hall listed the various reasons why projects are unsuccessful:

- Sloppy requirements and scope creep
- Poor planning and estimation
- Poor documentation
- Issues with implementation of new technology
- Lack of disciplined project execution
- Poor communication
- Poor or inexperienced project management
- Poor quality control

Hall's list includes only the results of human factors; he did not find any natural causes—earthquakes, say, or falling meteorites or locust attacks—for project failures in these cases. In his paper he also described a recent study by the Swiss Federal Institute of Technology. The study analyzed 800 cases of structural failures where engineers were at fault. In those incidents 504 people were killed, 592 injured, and millions of dollars of damage incurred. The main reasons for failures were:

- Insufficient knowledge (36%)
- Underestimation of influence (16%)
- Ignorance, carelessness, and neglect (14%)
- Forgetfulness (13%)
- Relying upon others without sufficient control (9%)
- Objectively unknown situation (7%)
- Other factors related to human error (5%)

Extensive research on why projects fail in different industries leads to the same conclusion: human factors are almost always the cause (Johnson 2016; Rombout and Wise 2007). Furthermore, one fundamental reason for all these problems can be attributed: poor judgment. Dave Hall asks, "Why don't more people and organizations actually use history, experience, and knowledge to increase their program success?" The answer lies in human psychology.

All project stakeholders make mental mistakes or have biases of different types. Although the processes described in the *PMBOK® Guide* and many project management books help us to avoid and correct these mental mistakes, we should try to understand why these mistakes occur in the first place. In this chapter we will review a few fundamental principles of psychology that are important in project management. In subsequent chapters we will examine how each psychological pitfall can affect the decision analysis process.

Blink or Think?

Malcolm Gladwell, a staff writer for *The New Yorker,* published a book titled *Blink: The Power of Thinking without Thinking* (Gladwell 2005), which instantly became a best seller. Gladwell focused on the idea that most successful decisions are made intuitively, or in the "blink of an eye," without comprehensive analysis. In a very short time, Michael LeGault wrote *Think! Why Critical Decisions Can't Be Made in the Blink of an Eye* (LeGault 2006), as a response to Malcolm Gladwell. LeGault argued that in our increasingly complex world people simply do not have the mental capabilities to make major decisions without doing a comprehensive analysis. So, who is right—Gladwell or LeGault? Do we blink or do we think?

Both authors raised a fundamental question: What is the balance between intuitive ("gut feel") and controlled (analytical) thinking? The answer is not straightforward. As the human brain evolved, it developed certain thinking mechanisms—ones that are similar for all people regardless of their nationality, language, culture, or profession. Our mental machinery has enabled us to achieve many wondrous things: architecture, art, space travel, and cotton candy. Among these mechanisms is our capacity for intuitive thinking. When you drive a car, you don't consciously think about every action you must make as you roll down the street. At a traffic light, you don't think through how to stop or how to accelerate. You can maintain a conversation and listen to the radio as you drive. You still think about driving, but most of it is automatic.

Alternatively, controlled thinking involves logical analysis of many alternatives, such as you might perform when you are looking at a map and deciding which of several alternative routes you are going to take (after you've pulled over to the side of the road, we hope). When you think automatically, and even sometimes when you are analyzing a situation, you apply certain simplification techniques. In many cases, these simplification techniques can lead to wrong judgments.

People like to watch sci-fi moves in part because by comparing ourselves with aliens we can learn how we actually think. The Vulcans from the *Star Trek* TV series and movies are quite different from humans. They are limited emotionally and arrive at rational decisions only after a comprehensive analysis of all possible alternatives with multiple objectives. In many cases, Vulcan members of *Star Trek* crews like Spock from the original *Star Trek* (figure 2-1), T'Pol from *Enterprise,* or Tuvoc from Voyager help save the lives of everybody on board. However, in

> Project managers should resist the temptation to make an intuitive choice when they feel there is a realistic opportunity for further analysis.

Figure 2-1. Spock from *Star Trek* had the ability to think rationally
(Credit: NBC Television, 1967)

a few instances, especially those involving uncertainties and multiple objectives, human crew members were able to find a solution when Vulcan logic proved fallible. In the "Fallen Hero" episode of *Enterprise*, the Vulcan ambassador V'Lar noted that the human commander Archer's choice was not a logical course of action when he decided to fly away from an enemy ship. Archer replied that humans don't necessarily take the logical course of action. Ultimately, in this episode, Archer's choice proved to be the best one.

The balance between intuitive and analytical thinking for a particular problem is not clear until the decision-making process is fully examined. Significant intellectual achievements usually combine both automatic and controlled thinking. For example, business executives often believe that their decisions were intuitive; but when they are questioned, it can be demonstrated that they did in fact perform some analysis (Hastie and Dawes 2009).

When people think consciously, they are able to focus on only a few things at once (Dijksterhuis et al. 2006). The more factors involved in the analysis, the more difficult it is to make a logical choice. In such cases, decision-makers may switch to intuitive thinking in an attempt to overcome the complexity. However, they always have the option to use different analytical tools, including decision analysis software, to come up with better decisions.

So, coming back to our original question—do we blink or think?—it is important not to dismiss the value of intuitive thinking in project management. Ever since there have been projects to manage, managers have been making intuitive decisions, and they will continue to do so. Intuition can work well for most short-term decisions of limited scope.

Because project managers rarely have enough time and resources to perform a proper analysis, and since decision analysis expertise is not always available, project managers are always tempted to make intuitive decisions. Even if you have experience with and knowledge of a particular area, some natural limitations to your thinking mechanisms can lead to potentially harmful choices. In complex situations, intuition may not be sufficient for the problems you face. This is especially true for strategic decisions that can significantly affect the project. In addition, intuitive decisions are difficult to evaluate: when you review a project, it is difficult to understand why a particular intuitive decision was made.

Cognitive and Motivational Biases

Let's imagine that you are a campaign manager for a U.S. senator. You organized a few very successful meetings with voters in local day care centers, distributed one million "My Opponent Is a Degenerate" flyers, and released $3 million worth of negative ads exposing your opponent's scandalous behavior when he was five years old. After all your hard work, you estimate that your senator has the support of at least 55% of the decided voters. Unfortunately, your estimate happens to be wrong: in reality you have only 40% support. So, what is the cause of this discrepancy (figure 2-2)? This is not only a mistake in your estimate of the poll numbers; there is also the question of whether you ran your campaign (project) correctly.

> Bias is a discrepancy between someone's judgment and reality.

Why did you make this mistake? There might be a number of explanations:

- You were overconfident, and your expectations were greater than what was actually possible.

- You did not accurately analyze your own data.

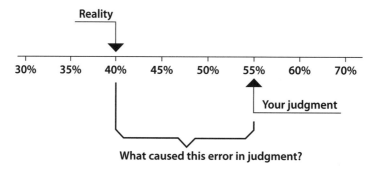

Figure 2-2. Bias in Estimation of Poll's Results

- You were motivated to produce such positive estimates because you didn't want to be fired if the poll numbers were not good enough.
- Your boss, the senator, told you what your estimates should be.

We can explain the discrepancy in your poll numbers, and perhaps other problems in the campaign, by looking at some of the biases in your thinking. Don't worry—we're not picking on you. These are biases that can occur in anyone's thinking.

There are two types of biases: cognitive and motivational.

COGNITIVE BIASES

Cognitive biases show up in the way we process information. In other words, they are distortions in the way we perceive reality. Many forms of cognitive bias exist, but we can separate them into a few groups:

Behavioral biases influence how we form our beliefs. An example is the illusion of controlling something that we cannot influence. For example, in the past some cultures performed sacrifices in the belief that doing so would protect them from the vagaries of the natural world. Another example is our tendency to seek information even when it cannot affect the project.

Perceptual biases can skew the ways we see reality and analyze information. Probability and belief biases are related to how we judge the likelihood that something will happen. This set of biases can especially affect cost and time estimates in project management.

Social biases are related to how our socialization affects our judgment. It is rare to find anyone who manages a project in complete isolation. Daniel Defoe's classic novel *Robinson Crusoe* may be the only literary example of a project carried out in complete isolation (aside from the occasional requirement raised by the threats from the local island population where he was living and writing). The rest of us are subject to varying biases about how people communicate with each other.

Memory biases influence how we remember and recall certain information. An example is hindsight bias ("I knew it all along!"), which can affect project reviews.

An example of one of the more common perceptual biases in project management is overconfidence. Many project failures originate in our tendency to be more certain than we should be that a certain outcome will be achieved. Before the disaster of the space shuttle *Challenger,* NASA scientists estimated that the chance of a catastrophic event was 1 per 100,000 launches (Feynman 1988). Given that the disaster occurred on the *Challenger's* tenth launch (NASA 2018), the 1 in 100,000 estimate now appears to be wildly optimistic. Overconfidence is often related to judgment about probabilities, and it can affect our ability to make accurate estimates. Sometimes we can be overconfident in our very ability to resolve a problem successfully (McCray et al. 2002).

Another example of biases that is extremely common in project management is *optimism bias* or planning fallacy. Optimism bias, among other things, affects how project managers perform their estimations. We will discuss this bias in details in chapter 11.

Appendix B lists cognitive biases that are particularly related to project management. The list is not a comprehensive set of all possible mental traps that pertain to project management. Instead, we offer it as a tool that can help you understand how such traps can affect you and your projects.

MOTIVATIONAL BIASES

The personal interests of a person expressing an opinion cause what we call motivational biases. These are often easy to identify but difficult to correct, as you must remove the motivational factors causing the bias. If an opinion comes from an independent expert, removing the bias will not be too difficult because, by definition, such an expert has no vested interest in the project outcomes. If, however, you suspect that a member of the project team is biased, corrective actions can be difficult to accomplish, as it is hard to eliminate the personal interests of team members or managers from the project without removing the individuals themselves. Motivational biases are like an illness: you know that you have the flu, but there is very little you can do about it.

Perception

Consider a situation in which you and your manager are in the midst of a heated disagreement. You believe that your project is progressing well; your manager thinks that it is on the road to failure. Both of you are looking at the same project data, so you and your manager obviously have different perceptions of the project. Who is right?

Most people believe themselves to be objective observers. However, perception is an active process. We don't just stand back passively and let the real "facts" of the world come to us in some kind of pure form. If that were so, we'd all agree on what we see. Instead, we reconstruct reality, using our own assumptions and preconceptions: what we see is what we *want* to see. This psychological phenomenon is called selective perception. As a project manager, you will have a number of expectations about the project. These expectations have different sources: past experience, knowledge of the project, and certain motivational factors, including political considerations. These factors predispose you to process information in a certain way.

Psychologists try to understand how the process of making judgments actually works. One of the tools that can be used to model mental activities associated with project management is the lens model. Invented by Edon Brunswik in 1952 (Hammond and Stewart 2001), the lens model is not a comprehensive theory about how judgments are made, but rather a conceptual framework that models how judgments are made under uncertain conditions.

For example, let's assume that you are working for a national intelligence agency and are involved in a project to capture some terrorists. Occasionally they issue a new tape that could provide some information about their whereabouts. Your task is to analyze the tape to discover the location of his hideout. We can assess your task by applying the lens model.

The lens model is divided in two: the left side represents the "real world"; the right side represents events as you see them in your mind (figure 2-3). You try to see a true state of the world (the terrorist's location) through the lens of cues or items of information. On the right side of the diagram, information is conveyed to you by cues in the form of estimates, predictions, or judgment of the value of the input parameter. If, for example, you have an audiotape supposedly from the terrorists, you could try to listen for some external sounds specific to a geographical location, certain features of the speaker's voice, the content of the speech, or anything else that might give an indication regarding the location. A videotape might give you more information or cues. However, the way that you interpret these cues is predicated on the lens through which you view them.

For example, if a video came in showing a group of "Islamic-appearing" men drinking tea, the intelligence officer might immediately infer that they are meeting to discuss political matters, perhaps planning a future attack somewhere in the Pakistan–Afghanistan border area, and will start to look for clues to confirm this perception. The reality may be that they are merely discussing family matters in an entirely different location.

This "lens of cues" is a certain mind-set that predisposes you to see information in a certain way. These mind-sets are unavoidable: it is impossible to remove our own expectations from our prior judgments. Moreover, these mind-sets are easily formed but extremely hard to change. You can come to an assumption based on very little information (such as your certainty of a terrorist network in Pakistan) but, once formed, it is hard to change the perception

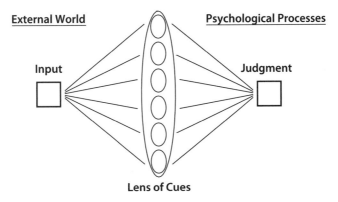

Figure 2-3. Lens Model of Judgment

unless solid evidence to the contrary is provided. Therefore, if your intelligence manager has come to an opinion about the project (for instance, she already believes that terrorists are plotting something in Pakistan) based on inaccurate or incomplete information, it is hard to change this opinion. You probably know about this phenomenon with regard to first impressions; when you judge people or somebody judges you, original impressions are quite difficult to change.

A project manager will manage a project based on how he or she perceives the project. When a manager believes that everything is going well in spite of evidence to the contrary, he or she will not see the need to take corrective actions. In these cases, selective perception can lead to biases—and eventually to wrong decisions. A common upshot of this bias is a premature termination of the search for evidence: we tend to accept the first alternative that looks like it might work. We also tend to ignore evidence that doesn't support our original conclusion.

Before making a decision, therefore, it is important to pause and consider these questions:

- Are you motivated to see the project in a particular way?
- What do you expect from this particular decision?
- Would you be able to see the project differently without these expectations and motivational factors?

Bounded Rationality

Why, you may wonder, do our cognitive abilities have limitations? Herbert Simon suggested the concept of bounded rationality (Simon 1956)—that is, we humans have a limited mental capacity and cannot directly capture and process all the world's complexity. Instead, people construct a simplified model of reality and then use this model to come up with judgments. We behave rationally within the model; however, our model does not necessarily represent reality. For example, when you plan a project, you have to deal with a web of political, financial, technical, and other considerations. Moreover, reality has a lot of uncertainties that you cannot easily comprehend. In response, you create a simplified model that enables you to deal with these complex situations. Unfortunately, the model is probably inadequate, and judgments based on this model can be incorrect.

Heuristics and Biases

According to a theory that Daniel Kahneman developed with Amos Tversky (Tversky and Kahneman 1971), people rely on heuristics, or general rules of thumb, when they make judgments. In other words, they use mental "shortcuts." In many cases, heuristics lead to rational solutions and good estimates. In certain situations, however, heuristics can cause inconsistencies and promote cognitive biases. Kahneman and Tversky outlined three main heuristics.

AVAILABILITY HEURISTIC

Assume that you are evaluating project-management software for your company. You did a lot of research, read a number of detailed reviews, used a number of different evaluation tools, and concluded that Product X is a good fit for your organization. Then, just after you finished your report, you went to a conference and met a well-known expert in the industry who had a different opinion: "Product X is a poor choice. It is slow and difficult to use." You feel relieved that you had this conversation before you handed in your recommendations, but your real mistake may be in throwing out your original recommendations. On the basis of the opinion of one individual, you are ready to scrap the findings in your well-researched and comprehensive report. You are giving too much weight to this opinion because of the manner and the timing in which it was presented to you. This is an example of a bias that is related to the *availability heuristic*.

According to the availability heuristic, people judge the probability of the occurrence of events by how easily these events are brought to mind. When we try to access the probability of a certain event or recall all instances of an event, we initially recall events that are unusual, rare, vivid, or associated with other events, such as major issues, successes, or failures. As a result, our own assessment of probabilities is skewed because the ease with which an event can be recalled or imagined has nothing to do with actual probabilities of the event's occurring.

When you see a slot machine winner holding up a poster-sized multimillion-dollar check, you might assume that you yourself have a reasonable chance of winning at the casinos. This belief can be formed because you have received a vivid image or information related to a rare (and desirable) event: winning the lottery. Add to this what you read and see in the media, and you have all necessary means to misjudge your probability (or hope) of winning. If the government really wanted to fight gambling, based on what we know about the availability heuristic, it should erect huge billboards listing personal bankruptcies and showing broken families in front of casinos. How would you feel about your chances of winning if each time you went to the casino you saw this sign:

Welcome to Our Friendly Casino
This year 168,368 people lost $560 million here!
5% of our guests divorced, 1% became alcoholics,
and 0.4% committed suicide

You might have second thoughts about your chances of winning the jackpot. Advertisers, politicians, salespeople, and trial lawyers use the power of vivid information all the time. Biases associated with availability heuristic are extremely common in project management, primarily when we perform project estimations. We will review the psychology of estimating in chapter 11.

(Here is a suggestion: if you want your project idea to be accepted, use many colorful images and details in your presentation! When the time comes for management to decide which projects should go forward, they will have an easier time remembering your presentation.)

So, how do you mitigate the negative impact of any availability heuristics? One suggestion is to collect as many samples as you can of reliable information and include it with the analysis. For example, if you estimate a probability of a risk of "delay with receiving components," ask your procurement department for records related to all components. Are they delayed or not?

REPRESENTATIVENESS HEURISTIC

Take a look at figure 2-4. What brand is this car and where is it produced? Is it a Mazda, Toyota, or Kia? In fact, it is a Malaysian-designed Proton, assembled in Bangladesh. You probably don't associate very nice-looking and well-built cars with Malaysian *or* Bangladesh design and production.

Here is another example: let's assume that you want to estimate the chance of success for a project with the following description:

The project is managed by a project manager with ten years of industry experience. He has PMP designation and actively uses processes defined in the PMBOK Guide *in his management practices.*

Based on this description, you categorize this as a well-managed project. You will judge the probability of success of the project based on the category this project represents (Tversky and Kahneman 1982). In many cases this *representativeness heuristic* will help you to come up with a correct judgment.

Figure 2-4. What brand is this car, and where was it produced? (Photo by Areo7)

However, sometimes it causes major errors. For example, we may believe the software of a new startup is unproven and potentially unreliable and, therefore, we choose to avoid dealing with their products even if they are of very high quality.

One type of bias related to this heuristic is the *conjunction fallacy*. Here is an example of a conjunction fallacy: a company is evaluating whether to upgrade its existing network infrastructure and is considering two scenarios:

A. New networking infrastructure will improve efficiency and security by providing increased bandwidth and offering more advanced monitoring tools.

B. New networking infrastructure will be more efficient and secure.

Statement A seems to be more plausible, and therefore more probable, than the more general statement B. However, in reality, the more general statement B has a higher probability of occurring. The conjunction fallacy states that people tend to believe that scenarios with greater detail are also more probable. This fallacy can greatly affect your ability to manage projects, because if you must select one project from a number of proposals, you may tend to pick those proposals with the most details, even though they may not have the best chance of success.

Another bias related to representativeness is *ignoring regression to mean*. People expect some extreme events to be followed by similar extreme events. This is extremely common in investing and sales. If you have a huge return on investment or a significant sales deal, you expect that it will repeat again and become part of a trend. However, it may be just a single event and everything will come back to its normal state.

So, how can you mitigate the negative effect of representativeness? You may try to think about different methods to categorize processes or objects. For example, you have to estimate how long it might take to do excavation during construction. That particular task could belong to different categories: excavation of foundation for a residential building, excavation for utilities, and so on. This way, you can make your estimates based on similar tasks for each different category.

ANCHORING HEURISTIC

How often have you gone to a store and found that an item you want is on sale? For example, the suit you want is priced down from $399 to $299 with a "sale" label attached to it. "What a great bargain!" you think, so you buy the suit. However, from the store's point of view, the original price of $399 served as a reference point or anchor, a price at which they would probably never actually attempt to sell the suit. But by posting $399 and a "sale" sign on it, the store is able to sell a lot of suits at $299. By fixating on only a single piece of information, the price of $399, you probably did not stop to consider whether the asking price of $299 was a good value for your money. Further research might show, for example, that other stores

> **Anchoring is the human tendency to rely on one trait or piece of information when making a decision.**

sell the same suit for $199, or that other suits in the first store priced at $299, but not "on sale," are better values.

We always use a reference point when we try to quantify something. This is called the *anchoring heuristic*, which can be very helpful in many cases. Unfortunately, as with the other heuristics we have mentioned, it often causes biases that are difficult to overcome. One of them is related to an *insufficient adjustment* after defining an initial value. Once we have determined a certain number or learned about a certain reference point, we don't significantly deviate from this value when we research a problem.

Another bias related to anchoring is called the "focusing effect" (Schkade and Kahneman 1998). The focusing effect occurs when decision-makers place too much importance on one aspect of an event or process. For example, people often associate job satisfaction with salary and position, while in fact job satisfaction is determined by many factors, including working environment, location, and so on.

The problem with the anchoring heuristic is that it very difficult to overcome. Our suggestion is to use more than one reference point during your analysis of an issue. When you buy suit, for instance, try to assess prices using not just the suit from the department store as a reference, but also suits that you can find at Walmart or other less expensive outlets. When you think about project cost, use more than one example as a reference.

Behavioral Traps

Let's say that you are managing a software project that includes the development of a component for creating 3-D diagrams. Four team members are slated to work on this particular component for at least a year. The development of the component could easily cost more than $1 million when you add up the salaries and expenses such as travel, computers, the holiday party, and other sundries. (If you are lucky, the team members are sitting in cubicles somewhere in rural Montana. If they develop this component in Manhattan, development costs will probably triple.) As luck has it, the project progresses on time and within budget, and everything appears to be going extremely well. Inadvertently, though, while browsing an industry website you discover that you could have purchased a similar component off the shelf, one that not only has better performance but also costs only $10,000. At this point, your project is 90% complete, and you have spent $900,000. Should you halt your project and switch to the off-the-shelf solution—or continue your project with the added $100,000 investment?

When psychologists asked people a similar question, 85% chose to continue with the original project (Arkes and Blumer 1985). But when the original investment was not mentioned, only 17% of people chose to continue the original project. This is a classic case in which you are asked to either "cut and run" or "stay the course."

This phenomenon is called the "sunk-cost effect," and it is one of many behavioral traps (Plous 1993). These traps occur when you become involved in rational activity that later becomes undesirable and difficult to extricate yourself from. A number of different categories of behavioral traps can be found in project management. The sunk-cost effect belongs to the category of investment traps. Walter Fielding, played by Tom Hanks in the 1986 film *Money Pit*, experienced an investment trap when he purchased his dream house. His original investment was quite small, but the incremental cost of the required renovations proved to be his undoing. A rational person would have walked away, once the real cost of the house became apparent.

The following are a few other types of traps that you will want to avoid.

TIME DELAY TRAPS

One type of trap, the *time delay trap*, occurs when a project manager cannot balance long-term and short-term goals. If you want to expedite the delivery of a software product at the expense of the software's architecture, unit testing, and technical documentation, you will jeopardize the long-term viability of the software, even though you get the first (and possibly flawed) generation of it out to your customers on time. All project managers are aware of this trade-off but often ignore long-term objectives to meet short-term goals. In these cases, project managers usually blame organizational pressure, customer relationships, and so on, when the problem is really a fundamental psychological trap. It's like when you postpone your dental cleaning appointment to save a few bucks or because it's inconvenient, and a few years later you end up needing to have major dental work done. Or when you use your credit cards for your holiday shopping and end up with an even larger debt.

DETERIORATION TRAPS

Similar to investment traps, *deterioration traps* occur when the expected cost and benefits associated with the project change over time. During the course of new product development, costs may grow substantially. At the same time, because of a number of unrelated marketing issues, fewer clients may be willing to buy the product. In this case, the results of the original analysis are no longer valid.

Deterioration traps are common in processes involving the maintenance of "legacy" products. Should the software company continue releasing new versions of its old software or develop completely new software? Releasing new versions of the old product would be cheaper. Over time, however, it can be more expensive to delay the new product. Should automakers continue with an old platform or invest hundreds of millions of dollars to develop a new one?

Frames and Accounts

As a project manager, you are probably a frequent flyer. Oil prices go up and down, so airlines often impose fuel surcharges. They can do it in two ways:

1. Announce a fuel surcharge of, say, $20 per flight when fuel prices go up.

2. Advertise prices that already include a fuel surcharge, and announce a sale ("$20 off!") when fuel prices go down.

The consumer actually finds no financial difference between these two methods of advertising, but tends to perceive them differently. Tversky and Kahneman (1981) call this effect *framing*. They proposed that decision frames are the ways in which we perceive a problem. These frames are controlled by contrasting personal habits, preferences, and characteristics, as well as the different formulation or language of the problem itself.

We apply different frames not only to our choices but also to the outcomes of our choices. In the example that follows, consider three scenarios:

Scenario 1: You are involved in a construction project worth $300 million and have discovered a new approach that would save $1 million. It will take you a lot of time and effort to do the drawings, perform structural analysis, and prepare a presentation that will persuade management to take this course. Would you do it?

Scenario 2: You are involved in an IT project worth $500,000 and have discovered a way to save $80,000. You need to spend at least a couple of days for researching and putting together a presentation. Would you do it?

Scenario 3: You are involved in the same construction project as in scenario 1 and have found a way to save $80,000 (by replacing just one beam). You need to spend several days on research and the presentation. Would you do it?

Most likely you would *not* bother with an $80,000 improvement for a $300 million project (scenario 3) but would pursue your ideas in scenarios 1 and 2. This is because people have different frames and accounting systems for different problems. When we purchase a home, we don't worry if we overspend by $20 because it comes from our "home buying" account and $20 is a tiny part. However, when we purchase a shovel, we are really concerned about an extra $20 because it comes from our "home tools" account and $20 is a significant amount. Both accounts operate according to different mental rules, even though everything technically comes from the same bank account.

Training for Project Decision-Making Skills

The CN Tower in Toronto (figure 2-5) was the world's tallest building at 1,815 feet (553 meters) until 2007. A glass-floored outdoor observation deck is located at a height of 1,122 feet (342 meters). There, you can walk on a glass floor and see what is directly below your feet—the ground, more than a thousand feet below (figure 2-6). At first, you would probably be afraid to step out onto the floor. But as you realize that the glass is extraordinarily strong (you might bounce a little to see how rigid it is), you walk a few steps away from the edge. Finally, as you overcome your anxiety, you start walking more or less freely. Still, you can see that more people stay on the edge of the glass than actually walk out on it.

All of us have inherited a fear of heights. We are afraid to fall, and this is a natural fear. This property of our mental machinery saves as from a lot of trouble. At Toronto's CN Tower, you have started to teach yourself to overcome this particular bias as your instinctive fear of heights is gradually replaced with the logic that there is no danger in this particular case.

This example illustrates a very important point. Decision-making is a skill that can be improved with experience and training (Hastie and Dawes 2009).

Figure 2-5. CN Tower (Photo by Wladyslaw)

Figure 2-6. View from CN Tower glass floor (Photo by Franklin.vp)

Remember the Vulcans from the *Star Trek* series we discussed earlier? They are used to juxtapose their extreme rationality with how human emotions cause the other main characters to act irrationally. But according to *Star Trek* lore, this was not always the case. In the past, Vulcans were much more like *Star Trek*'s human characters, though in response to severe internal conflicts they taught themselves to be more rational and less emotional. Could you follow the Vulcans' footsteps?

Project managers can teach themselves to make better choices by overcoming common mental traps. Many biases are hard to overcome, and it requires concerted effort and some experience to do so. As a first step, you need to learn that these biases exist.

- The fundamental reason for failed projects is poor judgment expressed by all project stakeholders.
- Intuitive thinking is an important mechanism that helps us solve many problems. However, such thinking may lead to poor judgments when dealing with complex problems.
- Decision-makers make predictable mental mistakes called biases. Understanding different cognitive and motivational biases helps to reduce their negative effect.

- Our perception of a problem depends on our preferences and expectations. As a result, "we see what we what to see." This phenomenon is called selective perception.
- When people deal with complicated problems, they use certain simplified mental strategies, or heuristics. In many cases, heuristics lead to fairly good estimates. But in certain situations heuristics can cause predictable biases.
- Decision-making is a skill that can be improved with experience and training.

CHAPTER 3

Understanding the Decision Analysis Process

The Americans will always do the right thing . . . after they've exhausted all alternatives.

—WINSTON CHURCHILL

We want to make rational choices, we would like a transparent decision-making process, and we want a mechanism for correcting mistakes. These goals can be accomplished through the decision analysis process: decision-framing, modeling, quantitative analysis and implementation, and finally monitoring and reviewing of decisions. Decision analysis is simple and fully adaptable to different types of project decisions.

Example of Decision Analysis Process

An example of applying decision analysis to a complex project can be seen at the National Aeronautics and Space Administration (NASA). The U.S. Congress mandated that NASA be more accountable when it evaluates its advanced technology projects. As a public agency, NASA is concerned about maximizing the value it gets from its expenditures and measures of cost reduction. But taking risks is inherent in all space exploration, so eliminating *all* risk would mean eliminating NASA's very purpose. (From another perspective, what do you think was the primary objective of the Wright brothers—maintaining a healthy net present value or getting an airplane to fly?) To manage its inherent risk, many NASA divisions are today applying decision analysis methods to improve their ability to select the best courses of action (Williams-Byrd et al. 2016).

For example, NASA exploration mission directorates need to determine which capabilities and technologies will enable human exploration. NASA developed a decision analysis process that looks at multiple functional capabilities:

- Autonomous Systems and Avionics
- Communication and Navigation
- Cryogenic Fluid Management
- Environmental Control and Life Support System
- Entry, Descent, and Landing
- Extravehicular Activity (Spacewalks)
- Fire Safety
- Human Research and Crew Health & Performance
- Plus quite few others

NASA's process involves elicitation of judgments from subject matter experts (the scientific term for "we ask experts about their opinion"), as well as mathematical modeling that takes into account experience from previous missions. Using decision analysis, NASA is trying to determine the risks associated with different missions and technologies, as well as how much would they would cost. The result of the process is a selection of technologies that will be used in future human space missions, as well as an allocation of investment funds in the development of new technologies.

When Decision Makers Go Bad

Everybody wants to make good decisions, but in reality many project decisions turn out to be wrong. For example:

- Why did a company decide to develop a product that it could not actually sell?
- Why did its project team decide to use supplies of poor quality?
- Why did its management appoint a project manager who clearly does not understand the business?

You might say that the company did not really want a product it could not sell, did not really wish to use poor-quality materials, and did not really intend to appoint an incompetent project manager. But it *did* make those decisions, using its own decision-making process.

The process that leads to such decisions is often cloaked. Decisions are frequently made behind closed doors, so it is difficult to know how, when, where, and why a decision that results in dire consequences was made. And once people make a decision, they tend to stick to it, even in the face of mounting evidence that it is wrong. This is a known psychological bias. People tend to be consistent, even if it means behaving irrationally; they don't want to admit that they made a bad decision. As a result, poor decisions tend to take on a life of their own, which can exacerbate an already bad situation.

But there is a better way—decision analysis.

The Decision Analysis Manifesto

Here are three basic things you should want from a decision analysis process. We call it the Decision Analysis Manifesto:

- **You want rational decisions.** Quality decisions should lead to maximizing project value while minimizing expenditures. Good decisions should be based on an unbiased assessment of all possible alternatives. They should benefit the whole business, not just the interests of a specific individual or group.

- **You want transparent decision-making.** You want to know how decisions are made, who made them, and who should be accountable if a decision is wrong. You want to be able to participate in decision-making.

- **You want a mechanism for correcting mistakes.** If a problem is found with the original decision, you should be able to recognize it and take corrective actions in a timely manner.

In sum, what you want is a *process*. As with many other business processes, decision analysis has identified a set of procedures and tools that an organization can readily follow.

The "3C" Principle of Project Decision Analysis

Decision analysis is not a single, fixed process, but rather an adaptable framework that an organization can tailor to meet its specific needs.

There is no exact recipe for how to structure a decision analysis process. Different processes can be adopted for various companies, types of projects, and the types of decisions required. Your organization may already have, if not a fully established process, at least some components of decision analysis. For example, how do you review project risks and uncertainties? How are decisions made at product launch meetings?

> The decision analysis process is an integrated set of procedures, rules, preferences, and tools that help the organization make a rational choice.

But what does a "fully established decision analysis process" imply? Any established or mature decision analysis process is based on three main rules, which we call the "3C" principle: consistency, comprehensiveness, and continuity (figure 3-1).

CONSISTENCY

The decision analysis process should be standardized for similar kinds of problems and opportunities. Inconsistency in decision-making can cause projects to change directions unnecessarily, which can lead to failure. This necessitates

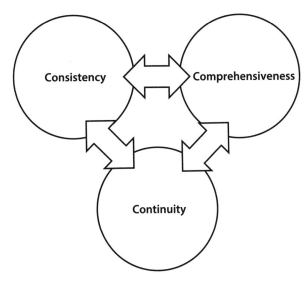

Figure 3-1. "3C" Principle of Project Decision Analysis

that organizations must have the same set of rules and preferences for making decisions in all similar types of projects.

Suppose, for example, an oil company has numerous offices around the world evaluating exploration prospects. The company does not have enough resources to drill everywhere at the same time, so it must make choices. The evaluations on potential drilling prospects are forwarded from the various outlying offices to the corporate planning headquarters, where decisions about resource allocation are made. One of the main difficulties that the corporate planners face is that this information is submitted by different groups looking to develop their prospects in different locations, which are often in different countries. The planners don't want to compare apples with oranges, as the saying goes, so the company tries to ensure that the methods used to generate the data regarding prospects are consistent across the organization. Otherwise it would be impossible to make a comparison of potential oil reserves and then make decisions on which prospects to develop (Rose 2001).

COMPREHENSIVENESS

Decision analysis processes should include a comprehensive assessment and analysis of the business situation. Missing or incomplete information can lead to incorrect decisions.

Let's say that your manager approaches you and shows you a project schedule. He says, "We performed a comprehensive analysis on all of our possible alternatives and have decided to go ahead with this particular one."

After a brief look at the schedule, you say, "Looks like it's a very tight schedule. Did you account for any risk events? Where is the contingency time?"

"Don't worry about contingencies," he replies. "We covered everything. If you recall, we have done some similar projects in the past and didn't have any problems. Plus, the decision has come down from up high, so it's out of our hands."

Two days into the project, a major event occurs—and the project is delayed.

Did upper management perform a comprehensive decision analysis, as claimed? No, because they relied simply on their experience of some past projects and did not include risks and uncertainty. The analysis was not comprehensive, and therefore it was flawed.

CONTINUITY

Decision analysis is a continuous process of evaluating and refining decisions during the course of a project. High-quality results can be achieved only through constant and consistent *adaptive management.*

Here's an example of failing to use adaptive management:

You recently completed a project and presented it to your client. Unfortunately, the client is not very happy with it. Why? A couple of years ago, when the project was initiated, somebody made an incorrect decision that appears to have reduced the value of the project as a result of huge cost overruns. The person responsible for that decision is no longer on the team, so it will be difficult to understand the basis for it. And why were no corrective actions taken when it became obvious that the evaluation of cost was flawed?

Upon further investigation, you discover that it is not a common practice in your organization to revisit a decision once it has been made. In addition, when the problem surfaced, a great many resources had already been expended, and there was great reluctance at that point to change course. The final result is that your project failed to meet its requirements because the team did not adapt to changing circumstances.

Decision Analysis Process versus the PMBOK *Guide's Project Risk Management Process*

You may question how decision analysis differs from what is described in the *PMBOK Guide*, chapter 11, "Project Risk Management." Decision analysis and risk management both deal with uncertainties, but they do so from different perspectives. So, are both processes required? Could you imagine a country with two presidents—one responsible for decision-making and the other for managing risks?

> In many aspects, decision analysis enriches the project management process described in the *PMBOK Guide.*

Just think: two White Houses, two sets of Secret Service agents, and two White House chefs. This might not be the end of the world, for we have a lot of redundant government agencies and we could probably survive with two White Houses. However, the two presidents would have a difficult time with their appointed roles, since you can't make a decision without risk analysis, and conversely you can't manage risks without making decisions.

The good news is that you do not need two (or more) business processes to manage related issues. You can integrate decision analysis into your overall project management process, as described in the *PMBOK Guide*. Decision analysis and risk management processes have a significant overlap. A good decision analysis should include risk analysis. In other words, decision analysis is a broader exercise than merely risk analysis.

In this book we do not discuss the *PMBOK Guide* processes in detail. (A number of very good books on risk management are listed in the Future Reading section.) We will, however, show you how the *PMBOK Guide*'s risk-management processes parallel the decision analysis. We will mention all of the *PMBOK Guide*'s risk-management processes, so you will have a complete, logical picture of how the two approaches relate to each other.

Phases of the Decision Analysis Process

The decision analysis process includes a number of phases, each one containing a number of steps. We can illustrate the process with a project you may be familiar with from your childhood, an incident involving Winnie the Pooh:

As you may recall, Pooh dropped in on Rabbit one day and ended up jammed in Rabbit's doorway after helping himself to all of Rabbit's honey. For Pooh, it was supposed to be a very short project: (1) visit Rabbit; (2) consume honey; and (3) go home. But Pooh, being Pooh, ate too much honey during the "consume honey" activity. This is a good example of the psychological bias of overconfidence. As a result of this event, the trivial activity ("go home") could not be accomplished as scheduled, for Pooh was firmly wedged in the doorway. Now Pooh and his friends had a decision to make: they had to select the best alternative to solve this problem (figure 3-2).

Let's examine how a decision analysis process (figure 3-3) would help identify the best solution for the problem facing Rabbit and Pooh.

PHASE 1: DECISION-FRAMING

Decision-framing helps decision-makers identify potential problems or opportunities; assess business situations; determine project objectives, trade-offs, and success criteria; and finally identify uncertainties. The project manager defines the scope of the decision. Depending on the situation, a project manager alone, an independent expert, or a team of experts can perform the decision-framing. The processes of risk-management planning and risk identification described in the *PMBOK Guide* can be accomplished along with decision-framing.

Figure 3-2. Using Decision Analysis to Resolve Complex Problems

Step 1.1. Identifying Potential Problems and Opportunities In some cases it is difficult to identify problems and opportunities, especially when they are related to a strategic decision. For example, what causes different projects within the organization to be consistently late?

In our Pooh example, the problem was clear: Pooh was stuck and was not happy about it (neither was Rabbit). Both of them need Pooh to be removed from Rabbit's house as soon as possible.

Step 1.2. Assessing the Business Situation Before making a decision, it is important to assess the business environment and define the constraints related to the problem. Business environments can influence resource availability as well as costs. The assessment may also include an analysis of markets, competition, prices, or anything else that can be related to the problem or opportunity. During this step, it is important to list all external factors that may have an impact on the problem.

Who or what could be used to get Pooh out of his predicament? Of course, it could be Christopher Robin and Pooh's other friends. Wise Owl also had some project management experience. In addition, Gopher had the expertise and tools to provide some engineering work.

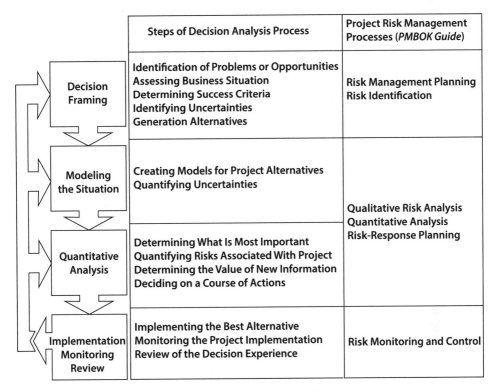

	Steps of Decision Analysis Process	Project Risk Management Processes (*PMBOK Guide*)
Decision Framing	**Identification of Problems or Opportunities** **Assessing Business Situation** **Determining Success Criteria** **Identifying Uncertainties** **Generation Alternatives**	**Risk Management Planning** **Risk Identification**
Modeling the Situation	**Creating Models for Project Alternatives** **Quantifying Uncertainties**	**Qualitative Risk Analysis** **Quantitative Analysis** **Risk-Response Planning**
Quantitative Analysis	**Determining What Is Most Important** **Quantifying Risks Associated With Project** **Determining the Value of New Information** **Deciding on a Course of Actions**	
Implementation Monitoring Review	**Implementing the Best Alternative** **Monitoring the Project Implementation** **Review of the Decision Experience**	**Risk Monitoring and Control**

Figure 3-3. Decision Analysis Process

Step 1.3. Determining Project Objectives, Trade-Offs, and Success Criteria Projects usually have multiple objectives and therefore multiple criteria for decision-making, which can make the analysis very complex. Decision-making criteria include project duration, cost, scope, quality, and safety, among other parameters. Project managers should find the right balance between these objectives and make trade-offs when necessary.

In Pooh's situation the success criteria were:

- *Remove Pooh from the doorway as soon as possible*
- *Do not harm Pooh during this process (safety concern)*
- *Do not damage Rabbit's dwelling*

Step 1.4. Identifying Uncertainties Understanding uncertainties is the key to the decision analysis process. In the decision-framing step, risks and uncertainties should be identified. Uncertainties can be found in a project's cost, scope, duration, quality, safety, or environment.

In this project—removing Pooh—we primarily have uncertainties in time, as well as uncertainties in cost.

Step 1.5. Generating Alternatives In decision-framing, it is important to generate key alternatives. First, you must identify what cannot be changed—that is, what the constraints are in the particular decision analysis. Then you can determine potential alternatives.

Pooh needed to be removed, one way or another. He could not be stuck in Rabbit's doorway forever. Therefore, project scope was a constraint. There was, however, the possibility of bringing in additional resources to accelerate the project. As a result, we have three potential project scenarios:

- *External contractor Gopher digs out Pooh*
- *Gopher blasts Pooh out with dynamite*
- *Christopher Robin's suggestion—waiting until Pooh loses enough weight and is slim enough to slip through the doorway*

PHASE 2: MODELING THE SITUATION

A mathematical model can help to analyze and estimate future events. For example, to understand how a structure withstands particular loads, engineers perform structural analysis on buildings, using mathematical models. They don't want to find out that a particular beam cannot bear a load after it has been put in place, because by then it may be too late to change it. The same situation exists with any other projects.

Step 2.1. Creating Models for Each Project Alternative Project managers constantly create mathematical or valuation models of projects. In most cases, it is simply the project schedule. A more comprehensive model of a project includes a breakdown of resources, costs, and other project variables.

Sometimes, quite elaborate models are required. For example, in the analysis of a product's life cycle, comprehensive models will include not only product development but also marketing and sales efforts.

Each model includes input and output variables, as well as a calculation algorithm. In the case of a project schedule, input parameters are tasks with their start and finish times, costs, and resources, as well as the relationships among all the tasks. Outputs include project cost, duration, start and finish times, critical tasks, resource allocation, and other parameters.

Modeling the situation in general, and project scheduling in particular, can be a highly complex process. A model should be created for each project scenario; in most situations, however, these models are variations of a single base model.

In the Pooh removal project, a schedule for each alternative was needed.

Based on Owl's request, Gopher estimated the duration of the excavation alternative. He did a review of the site and performed some exploratory excavation.

He estimated that the work would take two or three days. He also performed a cost analysis. He based his calculation on his hourly rate and estimated project duration. He also added overtime and 10% for contingency.

Gopher estimated that using dynamite would lead to a quick removal of Pooh, but with uncertain effects on Rabbit's doorway and Pooh's rear end.

The slimming alternative, suggested by Christopher Robin, seemed to have the least risk and cost, but the longest duration.

Step 2.2. Quantifying the Uncertainties The uncertainties in a project, identified through the decision-framing process, should be quantified. One of the ways to quantify uncertainties is to define ranges for their parameters. For example, define low (optimistic), base (expected), and high (pessimistic) duration or cost estimates for each task.

Another way to define uncertainties is to list all the potential events that could affect the project schedule, then quantify their probabilities and impact.

The *PMBOK Guide*'s steps for risk management recommend using a qualitative risk-analysis process to assign probability and impact.

- *Gopher estimated the uncertainty in duration of the excavation as a range (between two and three days).*
- *The blasting alternative had minimal uncertainties in estimating duration.*
- *There were several uncertainties with the last alternative (Pooh's slimming down). Nobody knew for certain how long before Pooh's stout frame would melt away enough to free him from the door. They were also faced with the prospect that Pooh would continue to eat (on the sly) during the course of the project. That risk, which should be given both a high impact and a high probability, could significantly increase project duration.*

PHASE 3: QUANTITATIVE ANALYSIS

After the mathematical model is ready, the analysis may include a number of steps, depending on the situation. It is possible to apply simulation techniques to analyze the project. These techniques can usually give project managers enough data to make an informed decision.

Even with the most advanced analytical tools and techniques, interpretation of the results of an analysis is performed subjectively by project managers; therefore, it is subject to the types of mental traps discussed in chapter 2. For example, quantified analysis may show that the chance that a project will be completed on time equals 80%. Is this acceptable? It may be in some projects, but not in others. In addition, the results of quantitative analysis must be communicated properly to decision-makers to minimize the potential for biased decisions.

Quantitative methods such as sensitivity analysis, Monte Carlo analysis, and decision tree analysis are described in chapter 11 of the *PMBOK Guide*.

Step 3.1. Determining What Is Most Important A model of a project may include a considerable number of variables: large numbers of tasks, resources, risks, and other parameters. Some of these parameters may significantly affect the course of the project. For example, certain risks will cause failure of the project, whereas other risks will have no noteworthy effect. It is impossible for a project manager and a project team to concentrate their efforts on mitigating all possible risks. The team should therefore focus first on mitigating critical risks.

To determine which project parameters are the most critical, project managers can use sensitivity analysis, which is described in detail in part 4 of this book.

In the Pooh situation, the risk associated with feeding Pooh would probably have the most effect on the project duration and was therefore a critical risk. To mitigate this risk, Rabbit set up a poster, warning "Do Not Feed Bear."

Step 3.2. Quantifying Risks Associated with the Project Uncertainties associated with input parameters were already quantified during the modeling step. Now you need to analyze how the combination of all these uncertainties could affect the project. The goal of this analysis is to create a "risk profile" of the project. You may need to know the following information:

- The chance that the project will be completed within a certain period and on budget
- The project's success rate, or the chance that it will be completed
- The low, average, and high estimates for duration, cost, and other project parameters.

Again, a number of analytical techniques can be applied to this analysis.

Here is the result of the analysis of Pooh's project, based on the success criteria identified during the decision-framing stage. Three alternatives had been identified:

- *"Excavate Pooh." There was a 100% chance of damaging Rabbit's home, a significant chance of harming Pooh, and a very significant chance that the project would be completed within a few days.*
- *"Blast out Pooh." There was a 100% chance of damaging Rabbit's home, a very significant chance of harming Pooh, and a very significant chance that the project would be completed almost instantly.*
- *"Slim down Pooh." There was zero chance of damaging Rabbit's home, zero chance of harming Pooh (although he might have an extended period of relative deprivation), and large uncertainties in the project duration.*

Step 3.3. Determining the Value of New Information A useful decision analysis technique is to assess the value of new information.

For example, Gopher needed to estimate the duration of the excavation project to remove Pooh from the doorway. Gopher could perform exploratory excavation, but it could be costly and time-consuming. This analytical technique helps establish the value of new information—how much money can be saved if additional information is obtained through an exploratory excavation.

Step 3.4. Deciding on a Course of Action In some cases, it is easy to select the most efficient alternatives, based on the results of risk analysis. The best alternative based on selected success criteria may be obvious and can be easily selected without further steps.

In many situations, however, the selection between the alternatives is not so easy. Sometimes, different scenarios are executed only if certain conditions exist. In many cases, decisions are made using numerous criteria, which complicates the selection of the most efficient alternative.

In the Pooh example, the decision was based on multiple criteria. The safety of Pooh was the first priority; therefore, the blasting alternative had to be rejected. The excavation alternative was also rejected because it did not provide adequate safety and could cause substantial damage to Rabbit's house. Therefore, despite concerns about project duration, the slimming-down alternative was selected. Interestingly, in a Russian cartoon version of the same Pooh story, made in the early 1970s, Pooh's friends and Pooh himself decided that he would not be able to withstand the deprivation imposed by the slimming alternative, so they just yanked him out, causing a great deal of structural damage to Rabbit's house in the process. Does this say something interesting about the differences between Western and Soviet psychology? Or perhaps the producers of the cartoon were on a limited budget and decided that having the characters forcefully dislodge Pooh was cheaper to produce and therefore a better choice.

PHASE 4: IMPLEMENTATION, MONITORING, AND REVIEW

Phase 4 involves two steps.

Step 4.1. Project Implementation and Monitoring Now the decision has been made, and the selected course of action is under way. But what if, in the middle of the project, an unforeseen event occurs, causing the plan to deviate? Luckily, a valuation model of the selected project alternative is available (created in step 1.5), so the project manager can update that model, perform a new analysis, and then make a decision. It is very important to track project performance constantly and analyze all potential pitfalls and opportunities. In many cases, a new decision-framing step will be required if a new decision within the same project is required.

Tracking project performance helps you to forecast what could happen to the project, even if some activities are only partially completed. Before the project started, you had only one source of input information for the decision analysis process: historical data, which either is objectively defined based on certain records or is the result of expert judgment based on past experience. Now the project manager can also use actual project performance to make decisions. This process for continually improving decisions by learning from the outcomes of earlier ones is one reason that adaptive management is so powerful.

Pooh's friends continually checked Pooh's slowly shrinking girth, trying to estimate when he would be slim enough to pop out. Eventually, when their measurements indicated that the time was ripe, they managed to extract Pooh without damage to either Rabbit's home or Pooh himself.

Step 4.2. Review of the Decision Experience You need to know whether your analysis and decisions were correct. Otherwise, you will make the same mistakes all over again.

Apparently, in this situation, the decision was correct. Some small things could have been done better, however. For example, the sign "Do Not Feed Bear" could have been installed at the beginning of the project rather than after Gopher's offer of food to Pooh.

Big and Small Decisions

When we ask project managers why a decision analysis process has not been implemented in their organizations, they usually give some form of the following replies:

- We don't know what the decision analysis process means
- We already have processes, such as project management, and we don't need to introduce yet one more
- Decision analysis processes are not suitable for our organization or our types of projects
- Our projects are small, so we make decisions based on our experience and intuition
- We are planning to implement the process in the future, but we are too busy right now
- Decision analysis processes require significant resources, including training that we don't want to invest in at the moment

Interestingly, most project managers use a number of answers from this list instead of just one. However, the third answer ("Decision analysis processes are not suitable for our organization or our types of projects") happens to be most

---

Rule number one in project decision analysis: the process must be simple.

---

common. Most managers believe that decision analysis is suitable only for large projects. In their opinion, intuitive decision-making is sufficient for small projects. But what differentiates a small project from a large one? Is drilling one well that costs $2 million a small project for a large oil company? Maybe. But a $2 million software project is definitely a large project. So, it is all relative to the particular industry or organization.

We agree that small projects probably do not require as complex an analysis as large ones. Yet we strongly advise against relying purely on intuitive decision-making for a project of any size.

Table 3-1. Decision Analysis Process for Various Types of Projects

Type of Decision	Suitable Decision Analysis Process	Some Comments
Small tactical decisions during the course of projects	Try to process information logically by answering a few simple questions: • What is the problem? • What do we want to achieve? • What are the uncertainties? • What are the alternatives? • What will happen if each alternative is implemented?	You may use any components of the process described in this chapter that you find both easy to implement and useful. For example, you may start with decision-framing with some simple analysis.
Important decisions concerning small projects or tactical decisions in large projects	You may use some components of the process described in this chapter, if you find them easy to implement and useful. For example, you may start with decision-framing with some simple analysis.	This is the first step toward a formalized decision analysis process in the organization.
Strategic project decisions	Apply the decision analysis process described in this chapter for a comprehensive evaluation of alternatives.	If the complete project depends on this decision, a full decision analysis process will be useful.
Strategic enterprise-wide decisions	Use a consistent, continued, and comprehensive decision analysis process for all project decisions within a portfolio.	Enterprise-wide decisions should be made based on a comprehensive analysis of alternatives, with continued monitoring of results.

The decision analysis process shown in figure 3-3 was developed for strategic decision-making. Making strategic or individual decisions is different than making project decisions. The process should be tailored for project management. In subsequent chapters of the book we will show practical steps how to apply various steps of the decision analysis process to projects. Table 3.1 offers some advice on how you can tailor the decision analysis process to different types of decisions.

In any case, remember that the process should be as simple as possible. If you suggest a full-blown process for your organization, but your organization is not ready for it, it will kill the whole idea (and any hope we have of selling more books to your colleagues!). In addition, remember that in 99% of cases, project decision analysis is simply an exercise in rational thinking.

- The decision analysis process is an integrated set of procedures and tools that help project managers make rational choices. Decision analysis is not a single, concrete prescriptive process, but rather an adaptable process framework that can be tailored to the specific needs of an organization.
- Decision analysis can be integrated with other business processes, including project management.
- The fundamental principles of decision analysis are comprehensiveness, continuity, and consistency. Decision analysis implies a comprehensive, repeatable analysis of the business situation plus an evaluation of alternatives.
- The four main phases of the decision analysis process are (1) decision-framing, (2) modeling the situation, (3) quantitative analysis, and (4) implementation, monitoring, and review of the decision.

CHAPTER 4

What Is Rational Choice?
A Brief Introduction to Decision Theory

Different organizations and individuals use different preferences and principles to select policy alternatives. We call those preferences and principles their "decision policies." An important part of an organization's decision policy is its attitude toward risk.

In this chapter we look at what it means to make rational decisions. We examine the concept of expected value and the normative *expected utility theory*, which provides a set of axioms, or rules, for how rational decisions should be made. Finally, we look at prospect theory, which is a descriptive approach to understanding decision-making.

Decision Policy

A decision policy is the set of principles or preferences that an organization uses when selecting its policy alternatives. The organization's attitude toward risk is a key component of its decision policy.

Every decision policy reflects the attitude of an organization toward its objectives. The policy is a function of many parameters, such as client requirements, corporate culture, organizational structure, and investor relationships. In most cases, decision policies are not written; instead, they are an unwritten understanding that evolves over time with organizational changes, and they are understood by the managers. However, even though decision policies are usually an informal understanding, they are very difficult to change, even if directed by executive management.

> The art and science of decision-making is applying decision policy to make rational choices.

In addition to an organization's attitude toward risk, a decision policy includes attitudes toward cost, customer satisfaction, safety, quality, and the environment, among other parameters. When an organization makes its choices, it

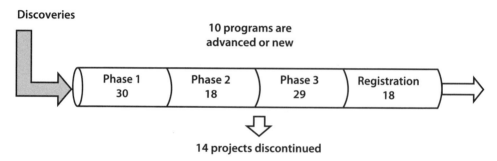

Figure 4-1. Pfizer Project Pipeline as of January 30, 2018

puts a premium on some parameters and downplays others. The problem is that different objectives often conflict. For example, maximizing shareholder value in the short term may conflict with a long-term research and innovation agenda.

How much risk should an organization take? How to protect against it? How to balance risk-taking with other organizational goals? Consider the example of Pfizer, one of the world's largest pharmaceutical companies.

Figure 4-1 shows the actual Pfizer project and product pipeline as of January 2018 and tells how many drugs are at various phases of the trial and registration process (Pfizer 2018). The development process for new drugs is rife with risks and uncertainties. Only a small percentage of medications that are pursued by researchers actually reach consumers. They all must undergo numerous tests, clinical trials, and finally a complex Food and Drug Administration (FDA) approval process. The FDA is under intensive public scrutiny and therefore is very risk-averse. Normally, if there is any indication of significant side effects, new medications do not pass the FDA approval process, an outcome that can dramatically affect the pharmaceutical company's bottom line.

> A decision policy is a set of principles or preferences used for selecting alternatives.

In the Pfizer example, different companies were willing to take on varying levels of risk depending upon their *decision policy*. For the most part, the decision policy regarding tolerable risk levels is motivated by a desire to create wealth; however, a business may want to achieve other objectives.

The drug-approval process, of course, does not apply to the production of other goods, such as axes or shovels. Risks and uncertainties are present in every business, but some involve much more risk than others. Designing and manufacturing garden tools has some risks, yet they are relatively much smaller—there is no Axe and Shovel Administration to approve your tool. To guide a medicine from a research proposal through the final approval requires a pharmaceutical company to invest significant time and money. Alternatively, if few potential drugs are in the pipeline, a pharmaceutical company like Pfizer can purchase a business with promising projects by paying a very hefty price.

Different companies have contrasting attitudes toward risk. Junior pharmaceutical companies are often less risk-averse than more established ones. But the established companies may have the means to pay the companies that assumed this risk.

For another example, here are the basic components of the decision policy of Don Corleone's enterprise in Mario Puzo's novel *The Godfather*. This design policy would include a strong emphasis on:

- Profitability
- Security of its own employees, with a special concern for management
- Organizational structure, including clear definitions of roles, responsibilities, and reporting
- Fostering good relationships with the local community

And a low regard for:

- The safety of adversaries
- Legal rules and regulations

What was Don Corleone's decision policy? That is, what was his attitude toward risk? Was he a risk-taker or a risk-averse leader?

Which Choice Is Rational?

All decision-makers try to make rational decisions. Before we can describe how you can make rational decisions, though, let's first try to understand what the term "rationality" means.

Reid Hastie and Robyn Dawes (2009) define rationality as "compatibility between choice and value" and state that "rational behavior is behavior that maximizes the value of consequences." Essentially, rational choice is an alternative that leads to the maximum value for the decision-maker. It is only through the prism of an organization's decision policy that we can judge whether or not a decision is rational. Because decision policies can vary greatly, your rational decision can appear completely irrational to your friend who works in another company. This holds true not only for organizations but also for individuals, project teams, and even countries. It is very important to remember that when you work with a project team, decisions should be made based on a consistent decision policy.

Returning to our *Godfather* example, were Vito Corleone's decisions rational or irrational? Our answer is that he was a rational decision-maker because, according to our definition of "rationality," he followed the decision policy of his enterprise. In other words, he always followed the fundamental rules on which his organization was based. What this analysis does not tell us is whether, from the rest of society's point of view, this was a good decision policy.

Expected Value

One method of evaluating multiple alternatives is to apply the concept of expected value. Let's begin our discussion of this concept with a simple example of a decision driven by a single objective. Consider that a big pharmaceutical company has two choices:

1. It can continue to develop a drug in which it has invested $200 million in research and development. The chance that it will get FDA approval is 80%. If the drug is approved, the company will earn $800 million in profit (80% chance). But if it fails, the company will have lost the $200 million in development costs (20% chance).

2. It can buy another company that has already developed an FDA-approved drug. The estimated profit of this transaction is $500 million.

This problem can be represented by using a decision tree (figure 4-2). There is a simple procedure to calculate the indicator. You simply multiply the probability by the outcome of the event. In the first case, the company has an 80% chance (the probability that the FDA will approve the drug) of earning $800M: therefore, the expected value is $800M × 80% = $640M. If the FDA rejects the drug (20% chance), the expected value will be $-200M × 20% = $-40M. From a probabilistic viewpoint, the company can expect to receive $600M from developing its own drug: $640M − $40M = $600M.

> Expected value is a probability-weighted average of all outcomes. It is calculated by multiplying each possible outcome by its probability of occurrence and then summing the results.

This number ($600M) is the expected value of the drug development project. Now we can compare this value to the alternatives. The expected value if the company develops its our own drug ($600M) is higher than the profit forecasted if it buys the other company ($500M). If the objective is to maximize revenue, the choice is clear; the company should develop its own drug. The arrow on figure 4-2 represents that choice. Outcomes can also be expressed as duration, cost, revenue, and so on. If the outcome is defined in monetary units, expected value is called expected monetary value, or EVM.

Basically, we combined two outcomes, using the probability of their occurrence. Because we cannot have a drug that at the same time is and is not approved by the FDA, expected value does not represent actual events. It is a calculation method that allows us to integrate risks and uncertainties into our decision analysis of what might happen.

In the real world, drug companies perform a quite similar process. Of course, the underlying valuation models they use are much more complex with more

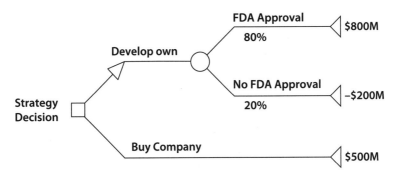

Figure 4-2. Decision Tree

alternatives, risks, and uncertainties, so their decision trees can become quite large. We will cover quantitative analysis using decision trees in chapter 15.

The St. Petersburg Paradox

Almost 300 years ago, the Swiss scholar Nicolas Bernoulli came up with an interesting paradox. He proposed a game, which looked something like this:

1. You toss a coin and if tails come up, you are paid $2.

2. You toss the coin a second time. If you get tails again, you are paid $4; otherwise, you get nothing and the game is over.

3. If you get tails a third time, you are paid $8; otherwise, you get nothing and the game is over.

4. The fourth time you may get $16; the fifth time, $32; and so on.

In theory, you can continue indefinitely and might win a lot of money. In fact, according to the expected-value approach, you can win an infinite amount of money, as shown in table 4-1.

Table 4-1. Bernoulli's Coin-Tossing Game

Toss	Payoff	Probability	Expected Value	Total Expected Value of the Game: sum of the Expected Values after each turn
1	$2	50%	$1	$1
2	$4	25%	$1	$2
3	$8	12.5%	$1	$3
4	$16	6.25%	$1	$4
				Infinite amount of money

Would *you* play this game? In reality, most people are not willing to risk a lot of money when they play any game. If they win for a while and the payoff gets larger, it becomes less likely that they are willing to stay in the game. The paradox lies in the question of why people don't want to try to win an infinite amount of money if it costs them nothing to try. The only thing they risk is ending up back where they were before they started the game.

This kind of game probably sounds familiar, for it is the basis for the popular TV show *Who Wants to Be a Millionaire?* You can argue that the game is not the same because the answers are not random. But unless you are a genius or an extremely lucky guesser, as the payoff grows and the questions grow more difficult, you will probably need a wild guess to win. Sometimes people want to take a chance and give a random answer, but often they don't, so they take the money instead of continuing to play the game. People like to watch this game not only because of its interesting questions but also because of the way it highlights this particular aspect of human psychology.

In 1738 Nicolas's cousin Daniel Bernoulli proposed a solution to this problem in his book *Commentaries of the Imperial Academy of Science of Saint Petersburg.* This game was named the "St. Petersburg Paradox." Bernoulli suggested that we need to take into account the value—or utility—of money, to estimate how useful this money will be to a particular person. Utility reflects the preferences of decision-makers toward various factors, including profit, loss, and risk.

Utility is a highly subjective measure. What is the relationship between utility and objective measures, such as wealth or time? Bernouilli's idea was that "twice as much money does not need to be twice as good." The usefulness, or utility, of money can be represented on a graph as a curved line (figure 4-3). As you can see, the value of additional money declines as wealth increases. If you earn $1 million per year, an extra $10,000 will not be as valuable as it would be to somebody who earns $100,000 per year.

We need to be able to measure utility. The scale of the utility axis can be measured by arbitrary units called *utils*. It is possible to come up with a mathematical

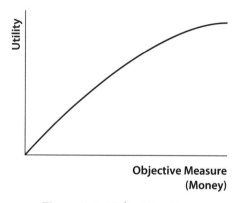

Figure 4-3. Utility Function

equation that defines this chart. The chart of the mathematical equation is called the utility function. The function represents a person's or organization's risk preferences, or their risk policy. Risk policy is the component of decision policy that reflects an attitude toward risk.

Risk-Taker versus Risk-Avoider

We have discussed how some companies and individuals can be risk-avoiders or risk-takers, depending on their risk policy, which is part of their general decision policy. We can now explain it using the utility function (figure 4-4).

1. A risk-avoider will have a concave utility function. Individuals or businesses purchasing insurance exhibit risk-avoidance behavior. The expected value of the project can be greater than the risk-avoider is willing to pay.

2. A risk-taker, such as a gambler, pays a premium to obtain risk. His or her utility function is convex.

3. A risk-neutral decision-maker has a linear utility function. His or her behavior can be defined by the expected value approach.

Most individuals and organizations are risk-avoiders when a certain amount of money is on the line and are risk-neutral or risk-takers for other amounts of money. This explains why the same individual will purchase both an insurance policy and a lottery ticket.

An example of an ultimate risk-taker is the fictional James Bond. When the world is about to be taken over by a villain, who are we most likely to see jumping into a shark-infested pond with only swim trunks and a pocketknife to save the day? Bond, James Bond, that's who. According to Bond's risk policy, the more dangerous the situation, the more likely he is to take the risk.

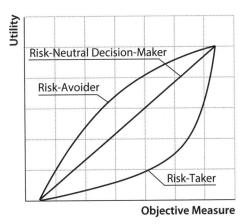

Figure 4-4. Using the Utility Function to Depict Risk Behavior

Expected Utility

Utility function can be used in conjunction with quantitative analysis to reflect a risk policy when selecting particular alternatives. Let's try to apply the utility function to the analysis of the strategic decision-making by the pharmaceutical company we discussed above (see the decision tree shown in figure 4-2).

The risk policy of the pharmaceutical company is represented by the utility function in figure 4-5. Using this chart, we can get a utility associated with each outcome. Arrows on the chart show how to get utility for the "buy company" outcome. The utility of the "buy" outcome of $500M ($500 million) equals 4.5. However, in most cases it is better to use a mathematical formula for the utility function rather than the chart.

Table 4-2 shows the results of each outcome.

Expected utility is similar to expected value, except instead of using the outcomes, it uses utilities associated with these outcomes. Expected utility is calculated by multiplying the utility associated with each possible outcome by the probability of occurrence and then adding the results. In our case the expected utility of the "develop own drug" alternative equals 0.50 (no approval outcome) + 3.68 (FDA approval outcome) = 4.18. The utility for the "buy company" alternative is 4.5. So, based on utility theory, we should buy the company.

In this example we see an interesting phenomenon: using the expected value approach, the company should select the "develop own drug" alternative. Using the expected utility approach, the company should select the "buy company" alternative. Why? This company is risk-averse, and the expected utility approach incorporated the company's risk profile. The company does not want to accept the risk associated with the potential loss that could occur if it attempted to develop its own drug.

Expected Utility Theory

Euclid, the Greek philosopher and mathematician, developed the postulates for plane geometry. They include all the necessary assumptions that apply in plane geometry, from which the entire theory was derived. John von Neumann and Oskar Morgenstern attempted to do a similar thing in decision science.

Table 4-2. Calculation of Expected Utility

Outcome Name	Outcome	Utility	Probability
Develop own drug (no FDA approval)	−$200	2.5	20%
Develop own drug (FDA approval)	$800	4.6	80%
Buy company	$500	4.5	

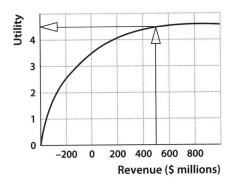

Figure 4-5. Using the Utility Function to Select an Alternative

In their book *Theory of Games and Economic Behavior*, von Neumann and Morgenstern proposed the expected utility theory, which describes how people *should* behave when they make rational choices. They provided a set of assumptions, or axioms, which would be the rules of rational decision-making. To a certain extent, they were trying to build a logical foundation beneath decision analysis theory. Their book is full of mathematical equations. To avoid mathematical discussions, we will cover just a few of their basic ideas:

> **Axioms of the expected utility theory are conditions of desirable choices, not descriptions of actual behavior.**

1. Decision-makers should be able to compare any two alternatives based on their outcomes.

2. Rational decision-makers should select alternatives that lead to maximized value in at least one aspect. For example, project A and project B have the same cost and duration, but the success rate of A is greater than the success rate of B. Therefore, project A should be selected.

3. If you prefer a 10-week project as opposed to a 5-week project, and a 5-week project to a 3-week project, you therefore should prefer a 10-week project to 3-week project.

4. Alternatives that have the same outcomes will cancel each other out. Choices must be based on outcomes that are different. If project A and project B have the same cost and duration but different success rates, the selection between the two projects should be based on the success rate—the only differing factor.

5. Decision-makers should always prefer a gamble between the best and worst outcomes to ensure an intermediate outcome. If project A has guaranteed revenue of $100 and project B has two alternatives—a complete disaster or revenue of $1,000—you should select project B if the chance of a complete disaster is 1/100000000000. . . .

Some of these axioms are just common sense, yet they are the necessary building blocks of decision theory. Von Neumann and Morgenstern mathematically proved that violation of these principles would lead to irrational decisions.

Extensions of Expected Utility Theory

A number of scientists have suggested that the axioms of von Neumann and Morgenstern unreasonably constrain the manner in which we make choices. In reality, people don't always follow the axioms, for a number of reasons:

- Often, people make rational decisions, but *not* as von Neumann and Morgenstern conceived them. They may not have complete or perfect information about the alternatives. In addition, people often cannot estimate the advantages and disadvantages of each alterative.

- Even if people make rational decisions, there are still a number of exceptions to the axioms.

In spite of these and other observations, since the publication of their book scientists have continued to come up with explanations for the expected utility theory and have developed a number of extensions to it. As a result, currently there is no single, accepted expected utility theory. Expected utility theory is now a family of theories explaining rational behavior.

Leonard Savage (1954) focused his extension of expected utility theory on subjective probabilities of outcomes. For example, he concluded that if a type of project has never been done, it is therefore hard to determine the probability of the project's success. However, according to Savage's theory, it makes sense to consider subjectively defined probability.

How to Use Expected Utility Theory

The axioms of expected utility theory were intended to serve as the definition of a rational choice. In reality, project managers will likely never use the set of axioms directly. If you need to select a subcontractor for a project, the last thing you are going to do is open the von Neumann and Morgenstern book, peruse a dozen of pages of mathematical equations, and after a couple of weeks of analysis come up with your conclusion (which still has a chance of being wrong!). Doing such a thing would in itself be absolutely irrational.

When you take a measurement of a building's wall, you don't think about Euclid's axioms, but you *do* use methods and techniques derived from his axioms. It is the same situation with expected utility theory when you are attempting to understand how to best maximize the value of your projects:

- You may read about best practices in one of the many project management books available.

- Your consultant may recommend some useful project management techniques.

- You may use the quantitative methods described in this book.
- You may try to avoid psychological traps when you make decisions.

Keep in mind that there is a foundation for all these activities. It is called decision science, of which the expected utility theory is one of the fundamental components.

Target Oriented Interpretation of Utility

What is the target-oriented utility, and how could that approach help project managers? The goal of project management is to meet certain targets or benchmark that clients set. For example, the goal is to develop software within a certain deadline and budget. At the same time, the client has not provided detailed requirements for the software. In other words, the probability of achieving this goal is very uncertain. It is the job of project managers to increase the probability that this goal is met. Maximizing expected utility is equivalent to maximizing the probability of meeting certain targets. This set of axioms also implies that project managers should select actions that maximize the probability of meeting an uncertain target (Castagnoli and Calzi 1996; Bordley and LiCalzi 2000; Bier and Kosanoglu 2015; Bordley et al. 2015). In the target-oriented approach, utility assessment is focused on identification of benchmarks or targets, which are easier to identify and track. It can be done using methods similar to what we will describe in chapter 13 (Bordley 2017).

Descriptive Models of Decision-Making

Von Neumann and Morgenstern considered expected utility theory to be a *normative theory* of behavior. As we noted in chapter 1, normative theories do not explain the actual behavior of people; instead, they describe how people should behave when they have made rational choices.

Psychologists have attempted to come up with *descriptive models* that explain the actual behavior of people. Herbert Simon proposed that people search for alternatives to satisfy certain needs rather than to maximize utility functions (Simon 1956). As a project manager, you probably will not review all your previous projects to select the subcontractor that seems to have the highest overall utility for your project. Instead, you will choose one that best satisfies your immediate requirements: quality of work done, reliability, price, and so on.

Daniel Kahneman and Amos Tversky developed a theory of behavior that helps to explain a number of psychological phenomena, which they called the *prospect theory* (Kahneman and Tversky 1979). They argued that a person's attitude toward risk is different from his or her attitude toward losses. Here is a question for you as a project manager. Would you prefer:

A. A project with an absolutely certain NPV of $100,000?

B. A project with a 50% chance of an NPV of $200,000?

Most likely you would select A. But let's reframe the question. Which would you prefer between these two:

A. A sure loss of $100,000?

B. A 50% chance of a loss of $200,000?

Most likely, you would prefer option B. At least, this was the most frequent answer from the people who participated in a survey.

This "loss aversion" effect can be demonstrated by using a chart (figure 4-6). Kahneman and Tversky replaced the notion of *utility* with *value*, which they defined in terms of gains and losses. The value function on the gain side is similar to the utility function (figure 4-3). But the value function also includes a steeper curve for losses on the left side compared with the curve for gains. Using the chart in figure 4-6, you can see that losses of $100,000 felt much stronger than gains of $100,000.

Unlike expected utility theory, prospect theory predicts that people make risk-averse choices if the expected outcome is positive, but make risk-seeking choices to avoid negative outcomes. Everything depends on how choices are framed or presented to the decision-maker.

Another interesting phenomenon explained by prospect theory is called the *endowment effect*, which asserts that "once something is given to me, it is mine." People place a higher value on objects they own than on objects they do not. In project management, these can be resources. It explains why most project man-

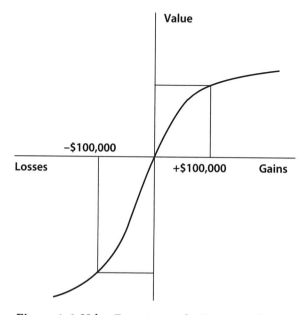

Figure 4-6. Value Function in the Prospect Theory

agers continue to use materials they have purchased, even though a better material may be available.

Prospect theory also explains zero-risk bias, which is the preference for reducing a small risk to zero, rather than having a greater reduction to a larger risk. Knowing about this bias is important in project risk analysis, because project managers usually like to avoid smaller risks rather than expend effort to mitigate more critical risks.

- Different organizations and individuals have different decision policies, or sets of preferences, for selecting alternatives.
- Rational choice is an alternative that leads to maximum value for the decision-maker. Rational choices should be made based on decision policy.
- Expected value helps you to make a choice between different alternatives. In many cases, it helps you come up with a good decision.
- Expected utility theory is the family of theories of rational behavior. Expected utility helps to incorporate risk profiles into the decision-making process.
- Kahneman and Tversky's prospect theory is the most widely accepted alternative to expected utility theory. It provides a more accurate description of how people actually make decisions.

CHAPTER 5

Creativity in Project Management

Creativity is the power to connect the seemingly unconnected.
—WILLIAM PLOMER, SOUTH AFRICAN AUTHOR (1903–1973)

Curiously, creativity is an essential component of successful project management. Psychologists have developed various theories explaining the process of creative thinking. Our ability to come up with creative solutions can be constrained due to creativity blocks, such as stereotyping, inability to see problems from another perspective, or fear of the "far-out" alternative. Cultural and organizational blocks such as those related to corporate culture can significantly constrain the creative process in project management.

Creativity and Decision-Making

As you know, this book is all about decision analysis processes, which we believe will help you make better project decisions. But where does creativity fit in? Does decision analysis prevent the discovery of original, nonstandard solutions or the selection of creative alternatives?

Creativity is related not only to technological innovations but also to the way we manage projects. Consider these problems:

- You have limited financial resources, but have been given an ambitious project development plan. How do you spend these resources wisely?

- How do you motivate a team that has gone through a number of painful project failures?

- How do you break a seemingly endless chain of client-driven changes without alienating your clients?

We usually think of creativity as if it related primarily to art, science, and technology. In this book, we are concerned only with how it relates to project management. We think that human creativity, also called "thinking outside the box," will improve the project-decision process.

Psychology of Creativity

How does creativity apply to project decision-making? Although it is hard to come up with a formal definition of creativity, it can be described as the ability to find an alternative way to perform a project that has at least three attributes: it should be (1) *new*, at least for the current project; (2) *feasible*; and (3) *useful*.

Understanding creativity is a new and growing field of inquiry in psychology. Scientists trying to explain it have come up with a number of theories. One of them explains creativity as a function of self-actualization. The psychologist Abraham Maslow (Maslow 1987; Davis 2004) developed a hierarchy of human needs, which is a model of wholeness and well-being. At the bottom of the hierarchy are the most basic needs for physical sustenance and safety.

At the top are esteem and self-actualization (figure 5-1). Basically, self-actualization is the drive to reach one's potential by fulfilling the desire to do something unique.

Some psychologists believe that creativity is related to our ability to make new mental associations with an object or concept. When people learn a new concept, their minds produce variations in which they associate the concept with something they already know. More creative people produce more of these variations. The range of variations depends upon a person's experience, knowledge, and environment, as well as some innate abilities.

As a project manager mulls over a problem, he or she typically comes up with a range of solutions (figure 5-2). These solutions can be generated by associating the problem with similar ones encountered in previous projects. Sometimes the solution can be related to personal experience, knowledge of other business areas, or even stories and anecdotes. (As you recall, we structured chapter 3 around the story of Pooh being stuck in Rabbit's door as a way of illustrating how choices are made.) The general idea is that the more variations that are available, the better the chance that creative alternatives will be found.

Figure 5-1. Maslow's Hierarchy of Needs

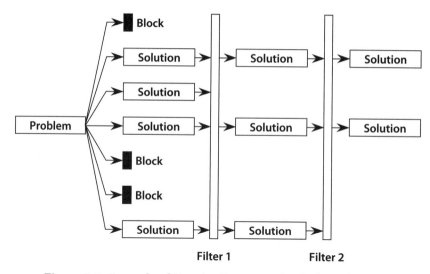

Figure 5-2. Example of Creative Process with Blocks and Filters

Can you have *too* many creative ideas—so many and so innovative that you lead your project, and maybe your company, right over the cliff? You can employ a number of techniques to channel and control creative alternatives. One of the more straightforward methods involves filters.

Assume that you managed to come up with many creative alternatives. For example, you have at least five ideas that address the problem of how to complete a project on time with your existing resources. In creative decision-making, a filter is a set of conditions used to test a proposed solution. If the solution does not satisfy these conditions, it will not pass through the filter and will not be considered during later stages of the analysis. Examples of these filters are:

1. Does this solution actually help to complete the project on time?

2. Is it possible to implement this course of action, given project constraints?

Individuals use a similar mental strategy to make intuitive choices. Psychologists call this "heuristic elimination by aspect" (Tversky 1972), which is discussed in chapter 19. The difference between elimination by aspect and the filter method is that the filter technique is a formalized analytical approach. Filters need to be set up very carefully to avoid blocking potentially good solutions.

A great example that demonstrates the process of creative thinking is Dan Brown's best seller *The Da Vinci Code* (2003). In the book, the fictional symbologist Robert Langdon is involved in a project to uncover ancient secrets. What is so interesting about his creative process?

- Langdon uses creative analogies to come up with a significant number of alternatives. Some of them are "far-out"; however, Langdon still considers them before making a final judgment.

- Langdon applies certain filters. He tests the solutions when he solves the puzzles. In these tests, he analyzes whether these solutions actually make sense.
- Langdon has the capability to come up with so many creative alternatives because he relies on his extensive knowledge and experience as a symbologist.
- Langdon's creative abilities are stimulated by the considerable stress brought about by the police and various shadowy figures who are pursuing him. In his case, finding creative solutions is not an exercise in curiosity, but a matter of survival. (figure 5-3).

Creativity Blocks

Despite our natural penchant as human beings to come up with creative solutions, our ability to do so is often blocked. Certain creativity blocks will simply not allow us to come up with innovative solutions. One way to enhance our creativity is to remove or at least weaken some creativity blocks. Clemen and Reilly (2013) classified the blocks this way:

1. FRAMING AND PERCEPTUAL BLOCKS

The following types of blocks affect how we perceive an original problem.

Figure 5-3. Finding Creative Solutions

1.1 Stereotyping A Microsoft Corporation staff photo, taken in 1978, surfaced and made the rounds on the Internet several years after it was shot. In it were 11 of the original Microsoft staff, including cofounders Bill Gates and Paul Allen. Most of them were very young and long-haired, so the group did not look like a very promising commercial enterprise, something like what is shown in figure 5-4. The title of the photo was "Would you invest in this company?" Typically, we try to fit all potential solutions into a standard category. If we cannot fit something into an existing category, we may block potentially good solutions. If you were an investor in those early days, would the staff at Microsoft have fit into your mental picture of a potentially successful company? Probably not, and because they didn't fit into a preconceived idea of what successful entrepreneurs look like, many investors likely ignored Microsoft as a possible investment opportunity.

1.2 Tacit Assumptions Let's suppose that you are managing a software project. You are naturally concerned about the software's performance, so you spend the majority of your efforts to make it run faster than that of any of your competitors. However, performance may not be the appropriate consideration. Hardware performance is improving all the time, and there is a good chance that by the time you complete the project most people's computers will be so powerful

Figure 5-4. "Would You Invest in This Company?"

that differences in the software's speed will be negligible. In this case you made an assumption—speed is the most important thing—that might not have been appropriate.

1.3 Not Seeing the Forest for the Trees As managers, we have to deal with a large volume of paperwork involving various organizational and management functions. While some of it may be unnecessary, in many cases the pile of papers contains a huge number of important project details that you absolutely need to know. Unfortunately, the amount of information you need to analyze may be so great that you cannot see the creative alternatives.

1.4 Inability to See the Problem from Another Perspective Many project managers approach a problem from their own perspective. Even if they think they are doing everything possible to satisfy their client's requirements, they may not be. Different project stakeholders have different objectives as well as their own ideas to contribute, and truly creative solutions should satisfy as many of these as possible. However, if you are not able to understand what other parties on your project really want, you will be blocked from finding creative solutions.

2. VALUE-BASED BLOCKS

These types of blocks are related to our personal and professional values and preferences. In some cases, these values block our ability to find creative solutions.

2.1 Fear of the "Far-Out" Alternative Very often we block a good alternative because we consider it too risky or impossible to implement. Sometimes we are even afraid to come up with an alternative ourselves because we do not want to look silly. But our not offering risky or "far-out" alternatives can interfere with our ability to think creatively. Proposing risky alternatives is a technique that can help us better understand and frame a problem.

2.2 "Do-Nothing" Bias Many people have an inherited bias toward the status quo. Basically, this is another way of describing inertia. However, decision-making implies that at least one alternative that is different from the status quo or "do-nothing" should be considered; otherwise, there is no need for a decision at all. Considering alternatives to the status quo is part of the continuous improvement process, which is one of the foundations of good project management.

2.3 Response to Criticism After spending considerable time and effort, you came up with what you thought was a good suggestion, but your boss dismissed it, saying, "What a silly idea!" How would you react? If you are like most of us, you probably will not bother with such a "creative" suggestion again. Unfortunately, whether it was a bad suggestion or not, your own reaction to this criticism may mean that your creative process becomes blocked, not only for this particular project but also for the many projects that you will be part of in the future.

First of all, you should not block your creative thinking as a result of criticism. If possible, continue to work with your idea. Add supporting information and improve your presentation. Also, ask your manager or your boss for more detailed information about why your idea was rejected. Let them know that you are willing to consider constructive criticism and will learn how to use it to improve your creative process. Failing to do so may indefinitely block your creativity.

3. CULTURAL, ORGANIZATIONAL, AND ENVIRONMENTAL BLOCKS

In his book *Think!* (2006), Michael LeGault mentioned a curious phenomenon—that Americans often make judgments based on Hollywood influences, which is not necessarily the best way to see things. In another example, the novelist Dan Brown overcame cultural blocks or taboos when he talked about particular issues related to Christianity (i.e., Jesus as a husband and a father) in *The Da Vinci Code*. His book is definitely controversial; however, its success was based on its creative views on some highly controversial issues.

The environment in which we live and work affects our creative thinking and in some cases can block the selection of creative alternatives. In project management, the environment is primarily the corporate culture. A company's environment can stimulate or block creativity. Lack of trust between coworkers, communication difficulties in project teams and between different project stakeholders, and excessive bureaucracy can all significantly limit the abilities of project contributors to conceive creative alternatives. Implementing decision analysis processes as merely another bureaucratic procedure can actually have an opposite effect by blocking creativity in organizations. We will discuss the role of corporate culture in decision-making in chapter 7.

In science fiction movies, time or space travelers often travel to another parallel universe or another dimension, where the inhabitants are unable to see their own true reality. Unfortunately, this type of "bounded reality" effect occurs not only with characters in science fiction movies but also with members of project teams. If a project manager and the team members have worked together in a company for a long time, they can develop "blind spots" where they work in a type of bounded reality. These blind spots prevent them from seeing the bigger picture. In other words, they are unable to see creative solutions because they have become enmeshed in a certain routine.

This effect is similar to selective perception, where new data is assimilated into existing mental images rather than understood for what it really means. A similar effect can be associated with different project stakeholders: clients, different project teams, or project sponsors, among others. At its worst, an organization's management can live in one reality and everybody else in another.

Bringing in external consultants, promoting people, or allowing mixed roles in project teams will help remove such creativity blocks.

Another block related to our organizational environment is called *premature closing* (Heuer 2016). Often, project managers must make decisions quickly— sometimes within days, sometimes within hours, sometimes almost instantly. In these cases, the project managers do not have the time or information to make a proper analysis and generate a creative alternative. Frequently, after the project manager has made the initial decision, new information that affects the original decision arrives.

In many cases, the project manager does not revise the decision, because the organization applies pressure to maintain a consistent project plan and vision. For example, could you imagine a situation in which you have just asked your manager for more resources to complete your project, but on the very next day you come up with a creative idea that doesn't require the extra resources? Would you approach your manager again to release the resources? Probably not, in which case a creative alternative has been blocked. Corporate environments that support creative thinking encourage changes for the right reasons, even if that means reversing a previous decision.

- Finding creative project alternatives is one of the fundamental skills of project managers.
- Creativity theories use various psychological processes, including the notion of self-actualization, preconscious mental activities, and the generation of mental associations of concepts.
- Creativity blocks prevent decision-makers from finding a creative solution to a problem.
- By setting up various creativity blocks, corporate culture can significantly affect your ability to make creative project decisions. Among these blocks are premature closing and blind spots.

CHAPTER 6

Group Judgment and Decisions

Group judgments can be different from individual judgments. Although the basic heuristics and biases that apply to individuals also apply at the group level, a number of biases are specific to groups. Group discussions such as brainstorming may lead to better decisions than those made by individuals. Game theory is a mathematical theory of human behavior in competitive situations, such as project management, in which players interact.

Psychology of Group Decision-Making

Project managers do not operate in a vacuum, and important decisions in project management are rarely made individually. They usually involve a number of people and are the result of discussions between various stakeholders. For example, project managers collaborate with project team members and communicate with clients to develop a balanced project plan.

If decisions are made in groups, are they subject to the same mental errors as those made by individuals? For example, do heuristics such as availability and representativeness, which we discussed in relation to individuals in chapter 2, work at a group level? Simply put, the answer is yes: individual heuristics and biases do continue to operate at a group level. Moreover, these biases can be even stronger in groups than in individuals (Plous 1993). For example, when estimating the duration of an activity, if you are working alone you may use a certain number as a reference point or anchor (say, four days) and then come up with the range of durations using a reference point of between three and five days (figure 6-1). This bias results from the anchoring heuristic (which we discussed in chapter 2). A group may use the same reference point (four days) but come up with a wider range (between two and six days).

A number of biases are specific to groups. One of them is called *group polarization* (Moscovici and Zavalloni 1969), in which people are more likely to advocate risky decisions after participating in group discussions. This effect has major implications in project management. Group polarization leads to greater

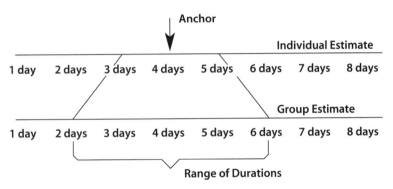

Figure 6-1. Developing a Range of Activity Durations

risk-taking on the part of the group than would occur with individuals. For example, project managers may be more inclined to agree to a risky extension of a project scope after a discussion with peers.

Group polarization affects more than risk-taking. Group discussions can amplify the preferences or inclinations of group members. If a project team member already had an opinion regarding a certain issue, after a discussion in a group he or she may have a much stronger opinion about the issue. In one experiment, simulated juries were presented with weak incriminating evidence. They became even more lenient after group discussion. At the same time, juries presented with strong evidence became even harsher (Myers and Kaplan 1976).

With this knowledge, it is fair to ask whether group discussions actually improve the quality of decisions. In other words, are several heads better than one? The psychologists' answer is a qualified "yes." The qualification is that it depends on the type and difficulty of the problem. Some problems are better handled in groups, while others are not. Reid Hastie (1986) reviewed three types of problems:

1. **Judgment of quantities** is related to the estimation of project cost, duration, and other parameters. Groups are usually more accurate than individuals in these types of decisions. Psychologists estimate that group judgments can be 23–32% more accurate than individual judgment (Sniezek and Henry 1989, 1990).

2. **Logical problems** are related (in project management) to finding solutions to complex business or technical issues. Groups perform better than the average individual; however, highly skilled or experienced team members who act alone usually outperform the team.

3. **Judgments in response to general knowledge questions** are related to finding factual data relevant to a project. Groups perform better than the average individual. Yet the best member of the team usually equals or surpasses the performance of the team.

Aggregating Judgment

Members of project teams often express differing opinions. Is it possible to mathematically calculate the judgment of a group, based on the judgments of its individual members? That is, can we average, say, the cost and duration estimates offered by different members of a group? And would doing so even be useful? Psychologists and decision scientists have extensively researched this problem (Goodwin 2014) and concluded that it is possible to do so if members of the group have similar expertise and work in the same environment. However, simple averaging of individual judgments can cause major errors. It is like the "average" body temperature in a hospital, which is always normal. Why? Because, while somebody may have a fever, there is also probably someone who is dead and therefore cold.

Is there a best way to come up with group judgments? The solution is to organize the discussion within a team in which the group as a whole makes a decision. For example, while the Supreme Court justices may have different opinions on a particular case, they deliver a common ruling in which they basically aggregate their judgments. The problem is that it is not always possible to come to a consensus as a result of a group discussion.

Group Interaction Techniques

Research in group judgment and decision-making confirms what we already know intuitively: group discussions can lead to better decisions. Now let's see what techniques can be used to facilitate these types of discussions. Based on how team members communicate with each other, these discussions can be separated into four categories:

1. **Consensus.** These are face-to-face discussions between group members where one judgment is eventually accepted by all members. This is one of the most common techniques in project teams. Team members meet regularly to discuss certain issues in anticipation that they will come to a consensus. The problem with this method is that some team members, who often happen to be managers, can monopolize the discussion and significantly influence the final judgment. This effect can be called the "We discussed and I decided" outcome.

2. **Delphi.** The Delphi process helps to protect against the "We discussed and I decided" effect. Group members don't meet face-to-face. Instead, they provide their opinions anonymously in a series of rounds until a consensus is reached. Delphi techniques require a facilitator, who sends out questionnaires to a panel of experts. Responses are collected and analyzed, and common and conflicting viewpoints are identified. The Delphi method was developed at the RAND Corporation, a

nonprofit global policy think tank, at the beginning of the Cold War to forecast the impact of technology on warfare. The name of the technique derives from the Oracle of Delphi.

3. **Dialectic.** In this technique, members are asked to discuss those factors that may be causing biases in their judgments. Group members who hold differing opinions on a specific topic try to understand each other and resolve their differences by examining contradictions in each person's position.

4. **Dictatorship.** This process uses face-to-face discussions that lead to the selection of one group member whose judgment will represent that of the group. Interestingly, according to Sniezek and Henry's research (1989), judgments produced by the dictatorship technique were more accurate than those produced by any of the other techniques. The dictatorship technique may be useful when a project team is trying to solve business or technical issues that require specific knowledge or expertise. In this case, it is important to identify the person with the best knowledge of the subject and discuss the issue under his or her guidance.

5. **Decision conferencing.** This technique has been proven to be effective for analysis of complex problems. Decision conferencing involves having experts get together for one to three days in face-to-face meetings that are moderated by a decision analyst. The analyst acts as a neutral observer and applies decision analysis methods and techniques during the meetings. The analyst creates a computer-based model that incorporates the judgment of the experts. It is extremely important that he or she does this in parallel to the discussions so that the experts can examine the results as the discussions progress. Through examination of the models, experts are able to create a shared understanding of the problem and then to come up with a decision. Essentially, the analyst is applying the decision analysis process described in this book: framing decisions, creating a model, and performing analysis in parallel with the decision conference.

Brainstorming

A good technique for creating a list that includes a wide variety of related ideas is brainstorming. In theory, brainstorming can be performed individually, but it is more effective if it is performed by a group. Brainstorming can be a very effective method in project management, to decide questions such as these: What is the best course of action in a complex business situation? What features of the new product can be developed first? What are the potential risks and opportunities for this project?

A number of techniques and tools are used for brainstorming (Clemen and Reilly 2013). The main goal of these techniques is to promote creative thinking among group members. All these techniques have the following rules:

1. Do not present detailed analysis of the ideas.

2. All ideas are welcome, even the absolutely "far-out" ideas; groups should come up with as many ideas as possible.

3. Group members are encouraged to come up with ideas that extend the ideas of other members.

Psychologists have discovered that brainstorming can be more effective if several people work on a problem independently and then share and discuss their ideas (Hill 1982). Many effective brainstorming techniques are built around this idea.

Figure 6-2 describes a brainstorming technique that we recommend as part of good project decision analysis. In it, each group member takes on a specific role. These roles are defined well before the meeting, so each participant can mentally prepare for the process. There are at least six roles, although some can be combined:

1. **Idea Generator:** develops as many ideas as possible but does not evaluate them

2. **Erudite:** provides more information about these ideas based on his or her own factual knowledge

3. **Devil's advocate:** criticizes the ideas presented

4. **Positive reviewer:** finds positive elements in the ideas

5. **Facilitator or Moderator:** organizes the discussion and makes sure that all participants follow their roles

6. **Scribe:** writes down the ideas and distributes them to group members in an easy-to-digest format

Two important rules should be followed when using this process:

1. Everybody has the right to occasionally move outside the boundaries of his or her role; however, it is important to stay within one's role for the discussion of a particular topic or for the duration of a brainstorming session.

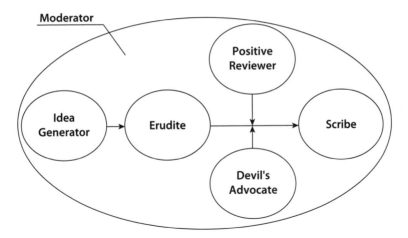

Figure 6-2. Brainstorming Technique

2. Two to four meetings, each with very a short time frame (15–30 minutes), are conducted with breaks of a day or two in between. The limited time frame is strictly enforced. Long breaks between meetings give participants the opportunity to think more about the ideas. Roles can be changed for the next meeting.

Another brainstorming method is called the nominal group method (Delbecq et al. 1975). At the beginning, each group member writes down as many ideas as possible. During the meeting the members present these ideas, the group evaluates the ideas, and the moderator records them. After the discussion every group member ranks the ideas. These rankings are then combined mathematically to select the best ideas.

> Effective brainstorming is an art. It takes practice to achieve good results.

If you and your team have not brainstormed before, you should not expect miraculous results from the first meeting. Don't be discouraged, for brainstorming requires a certain amount of practice. Therefore, if you believe that brainstorming would be useful for your projects, we recommend beginning by practicing on less important project issues before getting into complex problems. And the role of the moderator is important, for an inexperienced moderator can block good ideas. Good moderators set a positive tone for discussions and encourage creative ideas.

Tools for Facilitating Discussions

A number of tools can help with strategy planning, brainstorming, process improvement, and meeting management. During discussions you can record ideas and conclusions, create several diagrams and flowcharts, and share them among others regardless of the particular geographical locations of group members. In addition to analytical tools such as cause-and-effect diagrams and decision trees, tools are available that help to organize meetings by creating agendas and minutes, facilitating online discussions, defining team action items, and so on.

In recent years mind-mapping software tools have become popular in project management. Vendors of this software have sold hundreds of thousands of licenses, and we don't believe that this is a temporary trend; apparently project managers have realized the benefits of mind-mapping tools. A mind map is a diagram used to represent ideas, activities, risks, or other items linked to a central theme. In a mind map, the central theme is often illustrated with a graphic image. The ideas related to the main theme radiate from that central image as "branches." Topics and ideas of lesser importance are represented as "sub-branches" of their relevant branch. The mind map shown in figure 6-3 is based on a risk breakdown structure adapted from the *PMBOK Guide* (see appendix C).

A mind map helps you record ideas in a structured way and to review them later. You can find a list of vendors of these tools and other tools in appendix A.

When we think about project management tools, we mostly recall software tools, various paper templates, and checklists. But you don't need expensive or fancy software to facilitate discussions. A number of simple hardware tools are useful. In addition to traditional flipcharts or chalkboards, many project teams use electronic whiteboards, which automatically record information written on the whiteboard to a computer.

A Few Words about Game Theory

"Life is but a game," said Hermann, a character in Peter Tchaikovsky's opera *The Queen of Spades.* Today we can view decision analysis through the lens of modern game theory, a mathematical theory of human behavior in competitive

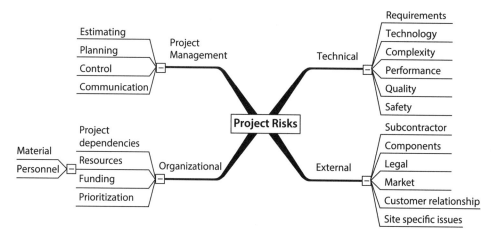

Figure 6-3. Mind Map of Project Risks

Game theory studies how an individual behaves depending on the choices of others.

situations that studies decisions made in an environment in which players interact. In other words, game theory studies how an individual selects optimal behavior when the costs and benefits of each option depend upon the choices of other individuals. While Hermann wasn't thinking about modern game theory, and was not even aware of it, he was right that "life is but a game." Game theory helps to analyze many processes in the common conflicts we deal with in our lives, such as stock market behaviors; political processes, including wars and elections; business activities, such as negotiations, auctions, mergers, and investments; and, yes, project management.

Game theory began with the classic book *Theory of Games and Economic Behavior*, by John von Neumann and Oskar Morgenstern (1947). The RAND Corporation used game theory to help define nuclear strategies. Do you remember the movie *A Beautiful Mind*? It is the biography of John Forbes Nash Jr., a mathematical genius who fell victim to schizophrenia after making amazing strides in game theory and economics. In 1994, Nash (figure 6-4) shared the Nobel Prize in economics with John C. Harsanyi and Reinhard Selten for their work in game theory. Eleven years later, Robert J. Aumann and Thomas C.

Figure 6-4. John Forbes Nash in 2006 (Photo by Peter Badge)

Schelling received the Nobel Prize, also in economics, "for having enhanced our understanding of conflicts and cooperation through game-theory analysis." And in 2012, the Nobel Prize in economics was awarded to Lloyd Shaple, of UCLA, and Alvin Roth, of Stanford University, also for their contribution to game theory.

Why do some projects succeed in promoting cooperation while others suffer from conflict between different stakeholders? Here is a very simple example of a situation in which you could apply game theory:

You are the manager of an IT project. Your client wants to make a change that he considers critical. You realize that this change will have major implications for your system and could significantly delay the project. Is this a source of potential conflict, or is there a way to compromise? Your decisions as a project manager are influenced by the choices and actions made by other stakeholders. Or, contrarily, the decisions of all project stakeholders are influenced by your decisions. The course of the project depends on the outcome of this "game."

Game theory offers mathematical mechanisms that can be helpful in solving these issues. Here are a few examples of simple games. Schelling (1971) described the "mattress problem," where there is a two-lane highway and one lane is jammed as people slow down to gawk at a mattress that has fallen from a car. The question is, who should stop to pick up the mattress? The people at the back of the traffic jam are only aware that there is a problem but do not know the cause. The people at the front can see the mattress but want to get out of the traffic jam as soon as possible. By the time they are at the mattress, they are at the end front of the traffic jam, and it will take them less time to ignore the mattress than to remove it. If they remove it, they will save everyone behind them a great deal of time—but at a cost to themselves.

The mattress dilemma can manifest itself in project management. If you have a software project for which your team cannot easily find the time to develop a testing tool, should you develop one anyway? You have completed your project, so you don't need the tool, and it will only be used to test someone else's software. When the application is done, why bother creating the testing tool, which can be used for future applications developed by somebody else? In psychology this effect is considered a mental trap, and this specific one is called the collective trap.

Another example of a game is deciding when to buy a ticket for a train. A limited number of trains will be leaving the station. If you arrive too late for the train for your destination, you may not get a ticket. If you arrive too early, you will have to stand in line for a long time. So, you will want to arrive at the station at a time when it maximizes your chances of getting a ticket while minimizing your wait standing in line. Your choice will depend upon when the other people decide to arrive. Game theory helps to find a mathematical answer to these types of problems.

One of the important concepts of game theory is called the "Nash equilibrium," named after John Nash. The Nash equilibrium is a solution to a game in which no player gains by unilaterally changing his or her own strategy. In other words, if each player has chosen a strategy and no player can benefit by changing his or her strategy while the other players keep theirs unchanged, then the current set of strategies with their corresponding payoffs constitutes a Nash equilibrium. A Nash equilibrium can be reached in the train ticket game, where everybody arrives at the station in such a way that all waiting times are minimized.

As a project manager, you will most likely *not* use game theory directly. Applications of game theory to project management are still under research, but we believe that practical solutions and tools will soon be available for project managers. If you want to read more about game theory, you will find some references in this book's Future Reading section.

- Psychological heuristics and biases that work at the individual level are applicable to groups of people.
- The group polarization bias is a tendency to advocate risky decisions after participation in group discussions.
- In many cases, group discussions lead to better decisions than those made by individuals.
- Brainstorming in project management helps us assess business situations, identify risks and opportunities, and select a better course of action.
- A number of software and hardware tools assist us in facilitating discussions; among them is mind-mapping software, used to record ideas in a structured manner.
- Game theory is a mathematical theory of human behavior in competitive situations in which players interact. Such situations frequently occur in project management.

CHAPTER 7

Are You Allowed to Make a Decision?

Or, About Decision Analysis and Organizational Culture

Our ability to make and implement project decisions depends on our professional environment—in particular, the corporate culture in which we work. In many organizations, project teams are unable to contribute to major decisions and are not properly rewarded for making good choices. This significantly undermines the productivity and quality of an organization's projects. We call this effect the Frustrated Employee Syndrome, or FES, a dangerous disease affecting corporate culture. It is hard to treat FES, mostly because senior management tends to recognize the problem only when it is very advanced.

What Is FES?

After reading this book, you may become an expert in project decision-making, but will you be allowed to apply your newfound expertise? Will your organization permit you to make

> FES is a disease that can afflict the corporate culture. It affects decision-making, efficiency, and productivity.

a decision, or at least will it heed your advice? In other words, will your manager continue to make decisions for you and your team, leaving you with only one choice: implement the project plan even if you disagree with it?

Projects always have constraints. Often, for technical reasons, you will be unable to perform certain tasks. Sometimes constraints are related to market conditions, safety, or environmental concerns. But all too often these constraints are artificial constructs imposed by upper management, and they make no practical sense. As a result, potentially superior alternatives are excluded from the decision-making process.

Such constraints are not an isolated problem but rather one of many symptoms of a disease that can infect an entire organization. FES affects the "central nervous system" of a company, which in essence is its corporate culture. FES manifests itself when managers and members of project teams are unable to contribute to major project decisions and are not properly rewarded for showing extra initiative and making good decisions. As a result, organizations lose the ability to produce high-quality, innovative projects at a reasonable cost.

By contrast, organizations that are free of FES display certain attributes:

- Project decisions are made at the lowest level possible; a consensus of project contributors is the optimal way of decision-making
- The environment is results-driven; the organization provides effective incentives (not necessarily financial) for valuable project contributions
- Members of a project team have a sense of autonomy
- Members are committed to their projects and share their visions and goals with others
- There is effective communication within the team, within the organization, and with clients; and there is mutual trust and mixed roles within a project team
- Team members have high levels of enjoyment

Is FES really that prevalent? One glib answer is that if FES were *not* prevalent, Scott Adam's *Dilbert* comic strip would not be so funny and popular. Unfortunately, many organizations are infected with FES. Most executives are familiar with FES, but have different terms for it. Disconcertingly, many do not think that FES is an important issue or a reason for concern.

Why Is FES a Problem?

When people are involved in simple physical activities—such as digging a trench, carrying logs, or roofing a house—you can motivate them to do good work with minimal incentives. However, motivation becomes more difficult when the activities involve creative thinking and decision-making. In these situations, different types of incentives are required to motivate a project team. Every job has incentives in place to motivate individuals to perform at higher levels. But in many organizations these incentives are structured incorrectly and provide little motivation. This leads to frustration and eventually to FES. Table 7-1 presents motivators and incentives, as expressed by project managers and team members, in the order of their priorities (based on an example of a software project manager).

As you can see from the table, purely financial rewards do *not* rank in the top five incentives for either project managers or team members. Others—"achievement," "recognition," "the work itself"—are more important. And if organizations fail to understand these underlying motivations of their employees,

Table 7-1. Motivations and Incentives. *Source*: McConnell 1996

	Project Managers	General Population
1	Responsibility	Achievement
2	Achievement	Recognition
3	Work itself	Work itself
4	Recognition	Responsibility
5	Possibility for growth	Advancement
6	Interpersonal relationship	Salary
7	Advancement	Possibility for growth
8	Salary	Interpersonal relationship
9	Company policies and administration	Status
10	Job security	Technical supervision opportunities
11	Technical supervision opportunities	Company policies and administration
12	Status	Working conditions
13	Personal life	Personal life
14	Working conditions	Job security

they are ripe to come down with FES. FES is subtle, though, and does not instantly lead to the failure of the company—a fact that often leads executives to believe that inadequate emphasis on incentives is not a problem. Let's examine how FES could affect an organization, using a simple model.

How Does FES Spread?

Most start-ups do not have FES; if they do, they quickly fail. As an organization gets over its growing pains and starts to expand, more people join the organization, more processes are established, and relationships among people and between project teams become more formal and complex. In many cases, FES infection occurs as a company evolves from a start-up to a steady-state company. If executives are not familiar with the creeping effects of FES, or if they don't pay attention to it, an organization can quietly become infected. In many cases, FES infection occurs during an acquisition. If a company with FES acquires an FES-free organization and tries to impose its own corporate culture on the smaller organization, FES very quickly infects the newly acquired entity.

The story is told about a young engineer, fresh out of university, who had just been hired by a design company.

- *On his first day, the manager asked her, "What do you want to do?" "I want to design a beautiful city with nice buildings, wide boulevards, parks, and canals," the engineer replied. "That's great," the manager answered, "but for now you need to design a staircase."*
- *Three years later the manager repeated his question. "I want to design a beautiful building with large apartments and a big lobby with a fountain," the engineer answered. "That's great," the manager answered, "but for now you need to design a staircase."*
- *Three years later the manager again repeated his question. "I want to design a beautiful apartment with big windows and a nice bathroom," the engineer answered. "That's great," the manager answered, "but for now you need to design a staircase."*
- *Three years later the manager again asked the engineer, "What do you want to do?" "I want to design a staircase," the engineer replied.*

Often, when an organization becomes infected with FES, people who like a creative environment move out. Or, as in the case of our young engineer, they become complacent and their career may stall.

Another effect of FES is that people start concentrating on small technical issues, which are the only things over which they can exert some influence. The larger picture is often hidden from them by the management, which typically does not communicate sufficient information about the project with the team. As a result, management's and team members' goals begin to diverge and over time can become completely different. For example, the goal of managers of software companies is to develop an application that is simple and fast. By contrast, an individual programmer in such a company may have a different goal, of wanting to introduce a new programming tool that will improve the product. Unfortunately, the tool is more difficult to use and makes the code so complex that it adversely affects the application's performance. But the programmer persists. Why? He argues that this new, innovative tool is "architecturally sound" or is "scalable," but in fact he simply needs to express himself, and choosing this software tool is the only significant decision he can make.

When top managers do not realize the corporate culture has a problem, they start behaving irrationally. When sales go down, they think they will solve the problem by shaking up the sales team. When this fails, they look at the development process and start to implement additional and often unnecessary steps. For example, if managers believe there is a communication problem within the organization, they often try increasing the number of meetings and duration of meetings. What this really does, though, is distract people from their jobs as they get increasingly bored and irritated if the meetings start to creep into their lunch time or quitting time. When this approach does not work, management starts to look at external factors: market conditions, competition, and other aspects that the organization cannot control directly, so nobody within the company is held responsible.

Failing all else, management starts to reorganize. After one or two reorganizations, nothing improves, and in fact the situation appears to have deteriorated. This is because the reorganization itself is a project, which is just as infected with FES as all the rest of the projects. Then upper management makes decisions regarding the reorganization without consulting the project team members, and very often it becomes just another bureaucratic initiative. Finally, after FES significantly reduces organizational performance, the company is converted to another form in one way or another. Large companies can sell assets or spin off an FES-infected division. Or a company can exist for quite a while as a low-producing entity by surviving on old clients and projects. The tragedy is that the executives who unwittingly worked so hard to spread the infection often get other assignments and never realize that the dying organization is a product of their dysfunctional decision-making process.

Three Common Myths about FES

Myths about FES abound. These are three of the most common ones.

Myth 1: "Our organization is not suitable for an FES-free environment" Some executives say that they are not a "dotcom" or a start-up, they have run their company for many years, and the existing corporate culture works. In reality, all organizations can be infected by FES because corporate culture is a function of interpersonal relationships, not the organization's type, size, or industry. Still, an environment that devalues motivators and incentives is much more common in big companies than in small ones. *Fortune* magazine maintains a list of the best companies to work for (*Fortune* 2018). The magazine has used a number of criteria to create this list, but it pays most attention to corporate culture.

Myth 2: When companies implement organizational processes, the result is often FES Organizational processes such as those used by project management, including decision-making processes, actually have nothing directly to do with the development of FES. In some cases, however, executives use the processes as an excuse to diminish the system of motivators and incentives, which leads to FES.

For example, a company can establish a hierarchical reporting system. There is nothing wrong with such a system in and of itself; all well-organized companies should have one. But if the administrative hierarchy is used as a substitute for team decision-making, and if small decisions require the approval of upper management (which normally has only a remote idea of the individual needs of each team), FES can result.

Myth 3: An FES-free corporate culture leads to anarchy Some managers believe that they will lose control if they allow decision-making to occur at the project team level, or encourage independent work, or build a sense of autonomy for each team member, or even allow mixed roles. They also think, for the same reason, that it is wiser to provide team members with as little information as possible. The experience of most successful organizations illustrates that an FES-free environment does *not* lead to anarchy. Such a company can be well organized, and decisions can be well informed and balanced because everybody takes part in the decision-making process.

In reality, FES can be a primary cause of anarchy because management and project team members do not share the same goals. Management tries to do one thing, development does another thing, and sales has a completely different agenda. Often, upper management does not know about the state of the business because its subordinates are engaged in "creative" reporting. This is a classic case of anarchy.

The Roots of FES

FES is not a natural phenomenon, like the flu. Rather, it is the result of management actions. The questions that always arise are: "What were they thinking? And why did management think that damaging corporate culture would improve the business?"

Can you imagine a world without FES? Companies would be so productive that humanity would already have settled on Mars, eradicated cancer, reversed climate change, and perfected the sky hook. The only drawback would be that Scott Adams wouldn't have any more material for his *Dilbert* cartoons.

The first thing to realize is that management does not deliberately set out to ruin the corporate culture. Rather, the roots of FES lie in the human psychology of judgment and decision-making: management overconfidence, selective perception ("I see what I want to see"), inability to recognize personal limitations and mistakes, and many of the other biases we have discussed in earlier chapters. Appendix B contains an extensive list of these biases. So, while good management practices and training may reduce the negative effect of these biases, unfortunately we cannot completely eradicate FES any more than we can get rid of plagues or unwanted hair, because they are all an integral part of our existence.

Treating FES

Even when top managers realize that their organization is infected with FES, treatment is extremely difficult, and the contagion cannot be removed without major organizational disruptions. Making radical changes to the corporate culture is especially difficult for the simple reason that FES-infected organizations usually do not support *any* type of initiatives, let alone ones that would attempt to completely transform the manner in which the organization conducts its internal processes. In most cases, successful organizational changes occur when new management instigates changes to improve company business. But remember: treatments work only if they fully involve everybody in the organization, not merely the management team.

If management wants to repair the corporate culture, major organizational changes may be required, and very often extensive retraining is also necessary.

On March 27, 1977, two Boeing 747s, Pan Am flight 1736 and KLM flight 4805, were preparing to take off on the only runway of Los Rodeos Airport in Tenerife, one of the Canary Islands in Spain (Aviation Safety Network 2019). KLM Captain Jacob Veldhuyzen van Zanten was known as a first-class pilot and was even the preferred pilot for the airline's publicity shots, such as KLM's magazine ads. As the KLM aircraft lined up for take-off, the Pan Am flight was still taxiing on the same runway. Due to fog, the KLM crew was unable to see the Pan Am 747 taxiing on the runway ahead. As they lined up for take-off, the KLM crew received clearance from the control tower to fly a certain route after take-off. Captain van Zanten apparently mistook this clearance as permission for take-off. The KLM flight engineer quickly expressed his concern about the Pan Am flight's not being clear of the runway. The engineer repeated his concern a few seconds later, but he was overruled by Captain van Zanten and made no further challenges to this decision. Shortly after taking off, KLM 4805 crashed into the Pan Am aircraft, killing 583 people and injuring 61. The Tenerife disaster resulted in the highest number of fatalities of any single accident in aviation history.

According to the subsequent investigation, communication problems and weather conditions were the primary causes of the accident, though another cause for the disaster was identified. Some experts suggested that the KLM captain, van Zanten, may have developed a kind of governance attitude that impaired the decision-making process in the cockpit. The flight engineer apparently hesitated to further challenge him, possibly because van Zanten was not only senior in rank but also one of the most experienced pilots working for the airline.

As a consequence of the Tenerife accident, the airline industry adopted changes in cockpit procedures. The hierarchical relationship among crew members was deemphasized, and more emphasis was placed on decision-making by mutual agreement. This is known as crew resource management (CRM) and is now standard training in all major airlines (McAllister 1997). CRM training originated from a NASA workshop conducted in 1979 that focused on improving air safety. The NASA research found that the primary cause of the majority of aviation accidents was human error, and that the main source of human error is the failure of decision-making in the cockpit. CRM training today encompasses a wide range of knowledge, skills, and attitudes, including communications, situational awareness, problem-solving, decision-making, and teamwork.

Unfortunately, the project management industry still trails aviation, fire safety, and other industries in understanding the importance of decision-making by all team members. Moreover, many consider the project manager, who is in most cases considered to be an administrative manager, the ultimate decision-maker. This is a direct path to FES.

As you remember, training can help to improve our decision-making skills. So, training the project team to work together, to make decisions as a group, and to share rewards together can help to battle FES. If you have a health problem, you consult your doctor. If your organization contracts FES, you need to contact a project management consultant, rework your organization's training, and try to relieve the FES symptoms.

But if you are not an executive and you work in an FES-infected organization, you are in a very unfortunate circumstance. You can do little to treat the condition. Your best option is to raise awareness of the situation with your managers; but if you pursue this route, you might also want to freshen up your resume. At the other extreme, you can keep your head down and hope that management recognizes the situation and starts to do something about it.

Perhaps the most sensible course of action is to concentrate on improving the particular circumstances of your projects and, within your circle of power, focus on making this the best possible environment for you and your team. This strategy can actually help improve your local project environment, even if the rest of the organization remains infected with FES.

The Second Russian Revolution

Sometime around 1988, a few hundred, mostly young, Russian engineers and computer programmers met with industry experts to discuss what could be done to improve software development for personal computers in Russia:

- The first panelist argued that the primary problem was lack of hardware and that the government should undertake the production or importation of more computers.

- The second expert thought that the government should establish R&D organizations specifically for the development of PC software.

- The last expert said that while he agreed with all other panelists, he did not believe that major government investments, establishment of state-run companies, or any other government programs were going to help the industry. The answer, he said, was to create conditions in which private individuals (engineers and programmers) would be able to sit in their basements (actually, apartments in Russia), develop software, and sell it.

For anybody involved in software development, the third suggestion made perfect sense, but what the expert said was absolutely revolutionary—and almost seditious. Remember that it was 1988. Private enterprises in the then–Soviet Union were illegal. Operating one was a criminal offence. If you developed software and sold it over the phone, you went to jail; if you painted a picture and then sold it on the street, you went to jail. (You get the picture?) One might say that the whole country was suffering from FES.

The underlying message was that a solution to the problem was to allow individual initiative and private enterprise, which could not be done without a regime change. When the revolution occurred a few years later, in the forefront of this so-called second Russian Revolution stood engineers, programmers, and anybody else who wanted to make their own decisions and earn something as a direct result of their own risk-taking and initiative.

Please don't get us wrong. We are not advocating revolution, rebellion, guerilla warfare, or other types of insurgency in your organization. We don't want this book to be labeled heretical and burned at a corporate bonfire. But what we *do* want to point out is that any attempt to set up an advanced decision analysis methodology will most likely fail if your organizational culture is infected with FES. Before undertaking any new major processes, the culture of your organization must be fundamentally sound. In many cases, however, project teams can still benefit from improved decision analysis even if FES is present. A good first step is establishing a proper decision-making process within your project team.

- Frustrated Employee Syndrome, or FES, is a disease that infects corporate culture. FES limits decision-making and does not provide sufficient incentives for project contributors.
- Many executives don't realize that their organization is infected with FES because the negative effects of FES can take a long time to manifest themselves.
- In most cases, project managers should act as facilitators in the decision-making process, *not* as the primary decision-makers.
- Even if your organization is infected with FES, there are certain things you can do to improve your working environment. In particular, your project teams can benefit from an improved decision-making process.

PART 2

Decision-Framing

CHAPTER 8

Identifying Problems and Assessing Situations

The decision analysis process involves a number of participants. Among them are decision-makers, decision committees or review boards, subject matter experts, and decision analysts. Assessing a business situation involves collecting and analyzing data relevant to the decision. A variety of tools are available to help identify problems and assess business situations.

Who Are the Players?

Before we start our review of decision-framing, which is the first phase of the decision analysis process, let's discover who the players are. To use an analogy, each type of movie we see has its standard set of characters. For example, spy movies have:

- **Heroes,** who manage projects that are not possible for us ordinary humans (as do most project managers)
- The **villain,** whose first small project is to destroy the galaxy; he may have the means to do it, but is not sure why (as occurs with many project sponsors)
- The **heroes' girlfriends,** who are among the heroes' project stakeholders; however, they may be completely unaware of their stake in the project (as is common with many project stakeholders)
- The **master spy controller,** who provides the hero with incredibly expensive spy technology that the hero uses only once and that therefore never pays for itself

Similarly, project decision analysis has its standard cast of characters:

- **Decision-maker.** The decision-maker is the one who controls the purse strings. It can be the project manager, an administrative manager, or even the company's CEO. The project is completely dependent upon the decisions that this person makes. Unfortunately, it is not always clear who the decision-maker is. Does the project manager have the authority to buy project management software, or will this decision be made at a higher level? It is very important to define who the decision-maker is for a specific decision, especially a strategic one.

- **Decision committee.** A panel, which includes subject-matter experts, coordinates the decision analysis process within the organization. The committee is responsible for coming up with the alternative that will be put in front of the decision-makers. The decision committee can have a variety of names: review board, leadership review board, decision board, and so on. The committee may include decision-makers, project managers, administrative managers, product champions, and subject-matter experts. In many cases, if it is a small team, the decision committee may include the complete team. Why do we need the committee if we already have a decision-maker? If you remember, we learned in chapter 6 that groups make better decisions than individuals.

- **Subject-matter experts.** These experts may or may not be part of the decision committee; however, they provide valuable input into the decision analysis process.

- **Decision analyst.** An expert in decision analysis helps to guide the decision committee and subject-matter experts through the process. Decision analysts help with decision-framing, building a valuation model, performing quantitative analysis, and applying adaptive management. Several individuals can perform the specific tasks of the decision analyst: for example, a professional modeller can build the valuation model, and a decision process facilitator can act as a moderator during meetings.

These sets of distinct roles and responsibilities are required for complex decisions within big organizations. In reality, in most projects these roles are combined, and the majority of team members wear several hats. Still, it is important to involve as many different people as is practical in the decision-making process.

Before the decision committee and subject-matter experts start the analysis, it is vital that you take care of two things:

1. The team should be made aware of any personal interests that the experts may have regarding any particular project alternative, because such interests may cause motivational bias.

2. Decision committee members and subject-matter experts should be motivated to come up with good decisions, using common incentives that are tied to the project's successful completion.

Identifying Problems and Opportunities

The step of identifying problems and opportunities is not as trivial as it may seem. When you begin a new project, it is very important to first identify the real or root causes of potential problems.

Consider the case of the Soviet Union again. For many years Soviet leaders could not grasp why the USSR economy was not performing at the level of Western countries. Communist Party First Secretary Leonid Brezhnev thought that the problem lay in the weak ideological commitment of the people. Another leader, Yuri Andropov, thought that it was poor discipline. Konstantin Chernenko probably had an opinion, but he died so quickly in office that we will never know it. Finally, Mikhail Gorbachev initially thought the problem was the widespread alcoholism in Soviet society; he later came to believe that it was a lack of state control, and finally it became clear to him (and a great number of other people) that the problem lay in the very nature of the socialist system.

We are not bringing this up to point out how decision analysis would have helped the leaders of the USSR to identify their problem. The point we are trying to make is that our cognitive and motivational biases can cause us to have great difficulties in discovering the real causes of problems and then in finding opportunities to resolve them.

Here is another example: you have developed a technology that you believe has great potential, but there is some uncertainty about whether there is any demand for it. Regardless, because you like the technology and want to realize your return on your investment, you want to get it to market as soon as possible. This is called a technology push. Because you are highly motivated to get your technology on the market, you might not analyze whether people actually need it (industry need) or even want it. A common dilemma in new product development is technology push versus industry need. Many projects have failed because of unrealistic identification (or no identification at all) of opportunities.

Alas, there is no magical tool that will help identify a project's problems and opportunities. But it is crucial to be aware of your motivational or cognitive biases, which may leave you unable to identify problems or opportunities. Use the techniques we described in chapter 5 to avoid creativity blocks. Whenever possible, use brainstorming and expert interviewing techniques when groups are involved.

Assessing Business Situations

In this step you need to collect data, identify how relevant it is to your decision, and prioritize which information will have the greatest effect on your decisions. Depending on the particular type of project, the kinds of information related to the business situation can differ. So, you should create a checklist of issues that need to be considered for your particular project.

Potential issues that should be reviewed during the project initiation stage include:

- Resource availability, including material and human resources
- Cost of labor, materials, and supplies
- Competition
- Market situation, including potential market trends
- Expertise available within the organization for the specific project
- Business processes and best practices in the organization that are suitable for the particular project
- Organizational performance and corporate culture suitable for the project
- Legal and regulatory environment
- Site-specific issues related to doing business in a particular region or country
- Customer relationships
- Weather and other environmental factors
- Project funding

The assessment of the relevant business situations is important not only when a project is initialized but also when key project decisions are made during the course of a project.

We do not claim to be experts on the espionage business or the spies who practice it, but, compared with project managers, spies in the movies demonstrate a superior ability to quickly and accurately assess business situations. For example, in the James Bond movie *Dr. No*, when James Bond arrived in Kingston (Jamaica), he first assessed the availability of local resources or people who could assist him in his assignment. He met with a CIA agent, Felix Leiter, and his assistant, called Quarrel. He also collected information about local sites that were related to his assignment. In particular, he measured the radiation levels in several locales. Based on this information, he was able to make a decision regarding the time and place for his final encounter with the villainous Dr. No and what he could expect from it. In fact, assessing a business situation is what James Bond was doing in every movie (figure 8-1).

Some Tools and Techniques

Several tools and techniques can be useful for identifying problems and opportunities as well as for assessing business situations.

Mind maps. It appears that mind-mapping tools can do virtually everything when it comes to decision-framing. The reason is that these tools are designed to record each step of our mental processes and then to present them in a structured way, which is exactly what we want to do during decision-framing.

Figure 8-1. James Bond Assessing a Business Situation. Sean Connery shooting the movie *Diamonds Are Forever* in Amsterdam (Photo by Rob Mieremet)

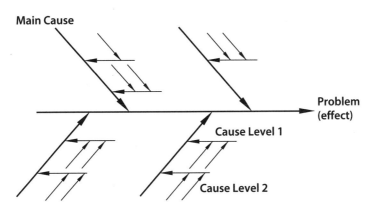

Figure 8-2. Cause-and-Effect Diagram

Flowcharts. Business situations are always changing. Flowcharts are useful to show this process. You can use diamond ("if") blocks to define which steps you would take if, for example, the business environment changed in a certain direction.

Cause-and-effect diagrams. The *PMBOK Guide* recommends using cause-and-effect diagrams for both quality management and risk management. If

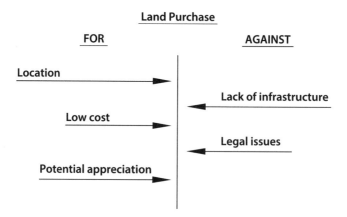

Figure 8-3. Force-Field Diagram

you are trying to identify the root cause of a problem, you may find these diagrams useful. Cause-and-effect diagrams are the brainchild of Kaoru Ishikawa and are sometimes called "fishbone" diagrams (figure 8-2).

Force-field diagrams. These diagrams represent the driving and restraining forces that affect a central question or problem (figure 8-3).

- Participants in the decision-making process are decision-makers, decision committees (also called review boards), one or more teams of experts, and a decision analyst. In smaller projects, these roles can be combined.
- Identifying problems and opportunities is not a trivial process, especially in new product development.
- Assessing business situations involves the collection of information and then the analysis and prioritization of the issues related to the project.
- Mind maps, flowcharts, cause-and-effect diagrams, and force-field diagrams are all useful tools for decision-framing.

CHAPTER 9

Defining Project Objectives

A project can have several objectives and therefore a number of decision-making criteria. To select a viable alternative, decision-makers need to make a number of trade-offs. Aligning objectives is important to be able to achieve project goals. Project objectives and trade-offs can both be determined by defining a hierarchy of fundamental objectives or a network of means objectives.

Different Objectives and Different Criteria for Decision-Making

Sgt. Bilko was a hilarious 1996 movie (starring Steve Martin) and a long-running TV series (starring Phil Silvers). While on active duty in the U.S. Army, Bilko was involved in a number of operational and project-related activities (actually, they were more like escapades), including gambling, organizing of sport competitions, renting out military vehicles, and even planning for a day care center in the military barracks. Clearly, Bilko had different objectives than his employer, the U.S. Army. In the movie, one of the main objectives of the military unit at the fictional Fort Baxter was designing and developing a hover tank, not advancing Bilko's fortunes.

Identification of project objectives can seem to be a trivial process. In many cases, project managers just skip this step because from their point of view everything is quite clear: the project must be completed on time, within budget, and according to requirements. However, project objectives can often conflict with each other, and decisions should be made by carefully balancing all of them.

According to the *PMBOK Guide*, one of the important steps in project management is "establishing clear and achievable objectives." The *Guide* defines project objectives as something toward which work is to be directed, a strategic position to be attained or purpose to be achieved. According to the *Guide*, identifying project objectives belongs to the area of "project integration management," and particularly to the stage for developing [a] preliminary project scope statement.

When making a decision, a project manager needs to use various indicators to determine which alternatives will best achieve the project's objectives.

These indicators are called decision criteria. If we take our example of Sgt. Bilko, we can see that because Bilko and the U.S. Army had different objectives, they also had different criteria for decision-making (table 9-1).

In fact, different project objectives are classic fare for any comedy. If you want to make a successful comedy, here is a simple step-by-step recipe:

1. Come up with a project; the most common comedy projects are engagements, divorces, bank robberies, and alien encounters.

2. Define different project goals for each project stakeholder.

3. Hire Steve Martin as a star.

4. Relax and have your accountant count your millions.

Regrettably, poor project management is never a comedy for those who suffer its consequences; therefore, realigning project objectives has to be a priority for project managers. In a project with multiple objectives, project managers should consider a number of decision criteria. This process is called multi-criteria decision-making. Examples of decision criteria can be:

- Economic indicators, such as net present value (NPV), rate of return (ROR), and project cost

- Project duration indicators, such as total duration, finish time, and duration of particular phase

- Resource usage, including material and work resources

- Project scope indicators, such as number of features implemented

Table 9-1. Different Goals and Decision-Making Criteria for U.S. Army and Sgt. Bilko

	Sgt. Bilko	**U.S. Army**
Objectives	1. Financial performance of Bilko's army unit 2. Entertainment and gambling	1. Improve military preparedness 2. Design and production of a prototype hover tank
Decision-making Criteria	1. Revenue 2. Quality of entertainment and gambling 3. No transfers to a location in Greenland	1. Quality of military training 2. Completion of hover tank project on time and within budget

- Quality indicators, such as number of defects
- Safety indicators, such as number of accidents
- Environmental indicators, such as level of emissions

Unfortunately, not all criteria can be quantified. For example, it is difficult to measure improvements in the work environment or in business communication. Still, these indicators should be considered decision-making criteria, as well.

Aligning Project Objectives

Why do we have different objectives and different criteria for making our choices? There are two principal reasons:

1. The project must satisfy different conditions and constraints, such as being completed within budget, brought in on time, and implemented according to the specifications.

2. Project stakeholders may have different expectations, and therefore they may use different objectives and decision-making criteria.

An example of conflicting objectives is found in the difference between long-term and short-term goals. Should a company complete a software development project as fast as possible? Contrariwise, should it extend the schedule to implement software architecture improvements that will ensure that future changes to the software will be easier to implement?

The *PMBOK Guide* includes a few examples of conflicting objectives. For instance, the vice president of research and development of an electronics manufacturing company wants to use state-of-the-art technology; the vice president of manufacturing wants to concentrate on world-class practices; and the vice president of marketing is focusing on a number of other features. This is not necessarily a bad thing. When different stakeholders hold different objectives, the project can benefit as long as the project manager is capable of balancing them properly.

In many cases, conflicting project objectives should not exist in the first place. Nevertheless, individuals, groups, project teams, and departments manage to come up with conflicting expectations. A classical example of conflicting goals is share price. Senior management's goal to improve and maintain a company's share price does not necessarily require improving the performance of the company's projects.

Personal objectives may differ from organizational ones because each member of a project team may have personal considerations and specific incentives. If a person is trying to make a career in the organization, he or she may be risk-averse and might avoid any project that entails a large amount of risk, such as product improvements. In this case, the less the person is involved in changing the product, the less likely it is that he or she will be blamed if anything goes wrong. Not being associated with a bad project will help you in the promotion process, but it means that the organization will be less likely to take on risky projects and thus to gain the potentially larger benefit that they can produce.

Does this scenario sound familiar? Because of different objectives, personal criteria of success (promotion) may be different from the project's success criteria.

There are many other situations of unaligned objectives. Often, project sponsors and project teams have different goals. Moreover, project objectives, and therefore the decision-making criteria, may change during the course of a project.

Decision Analysis as an Art of Trade-Offs

In many cases we will not be able to satisfy all our objectives at the same time. So, we must be prepared to make trade-offs. With a full understanding of the project objectives and decision-making criteria, project managers will be able to make an informed decision about when to sacrifice (in most cases, only partially) one objective to achieve another.

> The decision analysis process will not resolve a difference in project objectives among project stakeholders. However, the process may expose potentially different expectations and goals.

How can decision analysis help identify objectives and potential trade-offs?

In reality, with most projects you will not need to perform a convoluted quantitative analysis. Instead, we provide you with the following three simple recommendations. Consider this a small mental exercise you may need to go through during the project initialization phase, or anytime you are required to make a critical project decision.

1. Identify project objectives. Include the objectives of the project stakeholders, and consider where and how they differ; based on these objectives, identify your decision-making criteria.

2. Rank these objectives. Determine which objectives are the most important.

3. Identify potential trade-offs. True, trade-offs are very subjective, but decision analysis methodologies offer a framework in which to make these trade-offs logically and consistently.

Decision analysis offers a number of tools that you can use to perform these steps. One of the common methods used to determine project objectives is a project objectives hierarchy.

Project Objectives Hierarchy

As you have already seen, a project can have a number of objectives, and there may be a complex relationship among them. The easiest way to discover these relationships is to create a diagram that includes objectives with their ranking, as well as trade-offs.

In general, there are two types of objectives:

1. **Fundamental objectives** are the goals that need to be accomplished during the course of the project. For example, maximizing the profit of Sgt. Bilko's unit and providing entertainment are the fundamental objectives that Bilko wants to accomplish.

2. **Means objectives** help to achieve fundamental objectives. For example, "organizing golf tournament," "selling Bilko beer," or "renting out military vehicles" will help Bilko achieve his fundamental objectives.

How do you distinguish between means and fundamental objectives? The simplest way is to apply the **WITI** test (Clemen and Reilly 2013) by asking, "**W**hy **I**s **T**hat **I**mportant?" This question is sometimes called the "Why does Sgt. Bilko need to sell magazine subscriptions to his soldiers?" test. The answer is: to maximize profit, which is Bilko's fundamental objective.

Relationships between objectives can be presented in the form of a hierarchy (for fundamental objectives) or a network (for means objectives) (Keeney 1996). Figure 9-1 is a type of diagram that we recommend for analysis of objectives. Let's assume that you are involved in a project to find a spouse. Anybody who has been involved in such a project will realize that if this project is not well managed, the results can be frustrating. Finding the "right spouse" is the fundamental objective. Now, you can ask yourself, "What do I mean by that?" Your answer will probably be that you want to find a person who shares your interests; is reasonably attractive; belongs to a similar cultural,

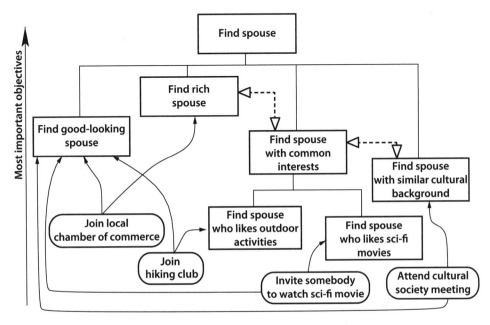

Figure 9-1. Project Objectives Hierarchy

religious, or social group; doesn't have too many bad habits; and is independently wealthy.

Each of these objectives may have other, more specific, objectives. For example, if you are trying to find somebody who shares your interests, your partner may or may not have to like football. Fundamental objectives are shown in the diagram as rectangles.

After you have created this hierarchy, ask yourself this question: "How can I achieve these objectives?" It will help you come up with means objectives. For example, if you want to determine whether a person shares your cultural preferences, you can attend certain events, such as concerts, opera performances, duck hunts, or meetings of wiccans. Means objectives are shown on the diagram as ellipses.

The next step is to rank these objectives. Place the most important fundamental objectives at the top of the diagram. Finally, you may need to determine potential trade-offs. If you are trying to achieve several goals at the same time, you will likely not be able to complete the project at all. In our example of seeking a spouse, you may not want to put much weight on personal wealth if you meet a person with similar interests. (But if you do, don't go making trouble in your FES-infected company.) These types of trade-offs can be depicted using dashed lines on the diagram.

Maximizing the Probability of Meeting Project Objectives

There is always a chance that project objectives may not be achieved. For example, the requirements may be uncertain and change over time. The goal of a project manager is to maximize the probability of meeting project objectives (Keisler and Bordley 2015). This is equivalent to maximizing project customers' expected utility, as described in chapter 4. Solutions can be found using the multiattribute utility function when multiple project objectives need to be satisfied at the same time (Bordley and Kirkwood 2014).

- Most projects will have many different objectives, some of which can conflict with each other.
- Project objectives are associated with decision-making criteria or indicators used to select project alternatives.
- Project stakeholders may have different expectations and, as a result, different project objectives. Some of these conflicting objectives can be aligned as a part of Project Integration Management processes.
- Decision-framing includes (1) identifying project objectives and decision-making criteria, (2) weighting such objectives, and (3) identifying trade-offs.
- The hierarchy of fundamental project objectives and the network of means objectives can be presented using a diagram, which helps analyze relationships between objectives and trade-offs.

CHAPTER 10

Generating Alternatives and Identifying Risks

We can use several techniques to identify risks and generate alternatives: documentation reviews, information-gathering techniques (Delphi, SWOT, and others), assumption analysis, and various diagramming processes. Risk templates can be useful in the risk-identification process. Risk-response planning helps determine the course of action if a risk occurs. Risk registers help monitor and manage risks during the course of a project.

Identifying Risks and Uncertainties

Almost everything in a project is uncertain. There is no certainty that you will still be the project manager in two weeks. Today you *are* a project manager; maybe tomorrow you will win $10 million in a lottery and retire to Palm Beach. (So, don't get too comfortable.) Before you start a project, you need to determine the potential uncertainties, identify the risk events that may affect the project, and generate alternative project scenarios. Various uncertainties can affect a project scheduled, including:

- Duration and cost of activities
- Lags between activities
- Resource allocation to different activities
- Rates for the resources
- Probabilistic risk impacts: uncertain outcomes of events that affect activities, such as an increase of cost by 30% to 45%
- Calendars: for example, certain days can be lost due to weather conditions
- Work breakdown structures: certain tasks will or will not be executed under certain conditions

The *PMBOK Guide* defines risk identification as one of the core processes of project management. According to the *Guide*, "risk identification is an iterative process because new risks may become known as the project progresses though its lifecycle." The *Guide* suggests a number of tools and techniques for risk identification. They can be used for generating alternatives, as well:

- **Documentation review** is a review of relevant project documents associated with current and previous projects. If a plan is inconsistent with its requirements, that can be a source for potential risks.

- **Information-gathering techniques** include brainstorming, the Delphi technique (see chapter 11), interviewing, decision conferencing, and SWOT (strengths, weaknesses, opportunities, and threats) analysis.

- **Assumption analysis** identifies risks by reviewing inconsistencies or inaccuracies in original project assumptions.

- **Diagramming techniques** include flow charts (see chapter 8), cause and-effect diagrams (see figure 8-2), influence diagrams (see figure 12-4), event chain diagrams (see figures 17-4 to 17-9), and mind maps (see figure 6-3).

Generating Alternatives

We often forget to come up with alternatives and then think about them only if we are concerned that our primary plan may not work. This tendency is reflected in the behavior of many of our fictional heroes: Batman, Superman, and Spider-Man rarely analyze different alternatives. They are single-minded about their jobs as they apprehend criminals and villains and bring them to justice. Even James Bond, whom we respect for his logical analysis of situations, rarely considers any alternatives. Perhaps he could convert the villain's hideout into a community center instead of reducing it to a smoldering wreck. Instead of killing the criminal mastermind by strapping him onto a missile and firing it into space, he could ask him to perform community work lecturing teenagers about the dangers of smoking. One famous character who was deeply concerned about alternatives was Hamlet. He had two project alternatives: "To be or not to be, that is the question."

Unfortunately, project managers get too much inspiration from headstrong heroes like Superman instead of the uncertain Hamlet. If you want to select the best available course of action, stop and ask yourself what the alternatives are in as many project situations as possible. This very simple habit should dramatically reduce the burden of poor decisions. At this stage it is important to be creative; but be aware of creativity blocks, which we discussed in chapter 5.

You can develop alternatives in several ways. First, think of all the parameters that cannot be changed. For example, quality and safety should never be jeopardized; however, in reality they are often the first tossed overboard when trade-offs are made. Come up with alternatives related to cost or duration. A good tool for analyzing alternatives for each objective is a strategy table (figure 10-1), in which alternatives for each objective can be connected.

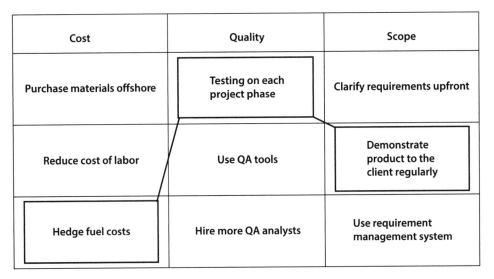

Cost	Quality	Scope
Purchase materials offshore	Testing on each project phase	Clarify requirements upfront
Reduce cost of labor	Use QA tools	Demonstrate product to the client regularly
Hedge fuel costs	Hire more QA analysts	Use requirement management system

Figure 10-1. Strategy Table for Identifying Project Alternatives

To identify problems and opportunities, and to channel your creativity, use sets of filters (see figure 5-2). These filter diagrams are a useful tool for an analysis of problems and opportunities. Here is a list of filters for new technology-driven products for start-up businesses:

- Your idea should not be completely new. Avoid joining the ranks of technology pioneers, for they rarely succeed in business. Instead, try to provide a better solution for existing problems.

- Your idea should be extendable. You should be able to build a number of products and services around this idea.

- Your idea should not be trivial. All trivial ideas either have been implemented or cost a lot of money to produce and market.

- Your idea should have a hidden technological value that would be difficult for somebody else to implement.

Risk Breakdown Structures

Absolutely everything can be classified and categorized. Aliens whom we have not yet encountered have already been classified in science fiction movies—there are little green men and women, and the gray figures with the slim bodies and enormous heads. Our tendency to create various hierarchies and classifications is not an obsession: it actually helps us to understand the nature of a problem. For example, risks can be assigned to different categories, such as external and internal risks, or organizational and technical risks (see appendix C). This type of hierarchy not only is useful for risk identification; it can also be used with quantitative analysis. When we perform an analysis using Event chain methodology, this type of risk breakdown structure is one of the main inputs.

Risk Templates

The *PMBOK Guide* recommends using a checklist analysis as one of your primary risk identification techniques. With it, you create a standard set of risks that can be applied to many projects. When you review the list, you can ask yourself: "Could that occur in my project?" This can mitigate the negative effect of the availability heuristic, where you may remember only those events that occurred recently or are related to a major incident.

The *PMBOK Guide* recommends that you create risk templates from historical data. Unfortunately, there are no universal risk templates that can apply to all industries and all types of projects. Most templates, including the example from the *PMBOK Guide*, are generic and may not be relevant to your specific project. But they *can* be useful as a starting point for creating your own risk templates. Your customized risk templates should be reviewed and updated regularly.

Project management literature includes many examples of different risk lists, which can be used as templates. Kendrick (2015) proposed a more advanced type of template: risk questionnaires. These provide three choices for each risk, and the project manager can select when the risk is likely to manifest itself during the project: (1) at any time, (2) about half the time, or (3) less than half the time. This helps project managers understand qualitatively the chance that a risk can occur.

Appendix C contains three risk templates. Some of the software tools listed in appendix A will help you create new, and maintain existing, risk templates and use them effectively as part of your qualitative and quantitative risk analysis.

Risk-Response Planning

Let's assume that you have identified the risks, performed an analysis, and properly communicated the results to the decision-maker, resulting in the project's being initiated. So, what do you do if a risk actually occurs? Your action depends on your advance risk-response planning. This type of planning is very important because you need to account for your potential future responses at the time you estimate a project's cost and duration.

The *PMBOK Guide* recommends performing risk-response planning *after* quantitative and qualitative risk analysis. We have not yet covered quantitative analysis, but we recommend that you perform your risk-response planning during the modeling phase of the decision analysis process. Is there a contradiction between the *PMBOK Guide* and our book? No, because most quantitative methods, including Event chain methodology and decision-tree analysis, require detailed information about risk impacts as an input. However, based on the results of your analysis, you may need to update your original risk-response plan. It is an iterative process of finding the most effective solution.

The *PMBOK Guide* describes several strategies, depending on whether you are dealing with a threat or an opportunity. We will start with threats. Let's assume that you are responsible for airport security and have received intelligence that a terrorist will attempt to smuggle explosives onto one of your airplanes. What should you do?

1. **Avoid.** Completely eliminate the risk. You can close the airport and cancel all flights—a very reliable, but hugely disruptive, solution. Another way to avoid risks is to clarify the situation. Perhaps it is a false alarm. Many project risks defined in the early stages of a project can be eliminated by clarifying the requirements and obtaining more information.

2. **Transfer.** Move the ownership of the risk to a third party. Your security measures may dissuade the terrorist from hitting your airplanes, but he may target a train, a bus, or an apartment building instead.

3. **Mitigate.** Reduce the probability of the risk or the severity of its impact. In most cases it is hard to eliminate risk completely, and it is not necessary to do so. You can put extra security personnel in place and intensify your screening of passengers and luggage. If you choose this option, you can create a risk mitigation plan. You need to define the activities that will be executed when a risk occurs.

4. **Accept.** Passive acceptance is a "do nothing" strategy. If the probability or impact of a risk is insignificant, you may elect not to address it at all. If you think that intelligence about the terrorist is not credible, you may accept this risk. In an active acceptance strategy, you may create a reserve of resources, such as extra security personnel, to deal with an unknown threat.

Now let's look at this picture from the other side—from the point of view of the terrorist. He is trying to find a strategy that will allow him to smuggle explosives onto a plane to blow it up. To come to a better understanding of a problem, it is important to understand the behavior your adversary. Here is what the terrorist can do to improve his opportunity:

1. **Exploit.** Create conditions where the opportunity will definitely materialize. The terrorist may try to use a creative bomb-making technique (edible bomb parts or explosive socks), which make it undetectable for particular security devices.

2. **Share.** The terrorist may involve a third party to better capture the opportunity. For example, he may solicit the help of airline security personnel.

3. **Enhance.** To increase the probability of an opportunity, the terrorist may try to reduce the chance that he will be detected during screening. He could wear expensive clothing and act in a manner not usually associated with the stereotypical terrorist.

4. **Accept.** The terrorist may elect to do nothing extra to improve his opportunity.

How people shape their particular risk-response strategy depends on the decision-maker's risk attitude (part of what we described in chapter 4 as decision policy): the level of risk the organization or individual is willing to accept. For example, airport security in North America and Israel has very low risk tolerance; airport security in other countries may have a different risk tolerance, and it is reflected in their procedures.

Risk Registers

By now you have created a risk list for your project, but what does it actually look like? In simple cases it can be just a document or spreadsheet with risk names, descriptions, and associated risk responses. Information about probabilities and impacts of risks will be added during the modeling stage of the decision analysis process. (We'll discuss that stage in chapter 13.) This document is called a risk register.

Many organizations maintain long lists of risks that can affect different projects. Information about these risks can be updated by various personnel at different times. In these cases, the risk register is stored on a complex database system (see appendix A). In addition to risk descriptions and responses, each risk may include the following information: category, root cause, trigger, owner, project activity associated with risk, current status, historical information associated with the risk, and dates of approval and revision. If you manufacture spacecraft, for example, and you discover a crack in a critical pipe that will jeopardize safety, you had better record this information in the database. That way, the crack will be noticed, tracked, and eventually fixed by the people responsible for it. The risk register can be updated rigorously, based on qualitative and quantitative risk analysis.

- Brainstorming, interviewing, reviewing documentation, diagramming techniques, and other methods help to identify risks and uncertainties, and to generate alternatives.
- Strategy tables and filter diagrams are easy-to-use techniques for generating alternatives.
- Organizations define risk templates and use them as part of the risk identification process.
- Four risk-response strategies for threats are: avoid, transfer, mitigate, and accept; four risk-response strategies for opportunities are: exploit, share, enhance, and accept.
- The results of risk identification can be recorded in a risk register, which for large organizations and complex projects is a sophisticated database.

PART 3

Modeling the Situation

CHAPTER 11

The Psychology and Politics of Estimating

Estimation errors arise from three sources: political, psychological, and technical (process-related). Internal politics plays a large role in such errors because corporate planners often intentionally make unrealistic estimations to get their projects approved. Optimism bias, planning fallacy, the rule of pi, and other cognitive biases also skew estimates. A number of simple techniques can improve estimations: avoid making wild guesses, do reality checks, collect relevant historical data, and perform independent assessments.

How Do We Make Estimates?

We now come to one of the most important topics in project decision analysis and project management: estimations. How many books have been written on the subject, how many consultants make a good living at it, how many estimation software packages have we bought (and are not using)? Unfathomable numbers. Still, we cannot always deliver accurate project estimates.

In essence, estimates are merely forecasts of the future; unfortunately, we are not very good at forecasting. It is difficult to make forecasts of natural phenomena like the weather; it is even harder to make forecasts of any processes that involve people, who come with certain knowledge, behaviors, and biases. Project management is one of these processes.

Estimating is an extremely important step in modeling and decision analysis. Without proper assessments of project duration, finish time, cost, resources, success rate, and other parameters, it is almost impossible to select the best alternative for carrying out the project.

Why do many activities—in our professional projects or in our personal lives—take much longer then we originally estimated? Let's analyze a simple hypothetical example that shows how estimation is done in a software development project. We'll assume that a programmer is already familiar with the scope of the task but has not yet performed any estimates. Here is a conversation between the programmer and the project manager at the launch meeting.

The project manager asks the programmer, "How long is it going to take to build this component?"

"Oh, abo-o-out . . . five days," the programmer answers.

The project manager asks, "Are you sure?"

"Yes; if everything goes well, it should take about five days."

A few hours later the project manager enters this information into the project schedule. As schedules go, it is a masterpiece, containing more than a hundred different tasks and a dozen milestones. The project manager prints the schedule and sticks it to a wall. She is enjoying her creation the same way artists might enjoy theirs. "We had a big rush at the end of our last project," she thinks. "But this time everything will be great."

Now the project starts. Actually, it does not start on time because three programmers are busy cleaning up some problems from a previous project. Then there is a change in the requirements. By the time they get around to the task discussed by the project manager and the programmer, the project is already at least three days behind schedule. The project schedule may be in tatters, but no one really cares. They all know there is more realism in a *Star Trek* movie than in the Gantt chart hanging on the wall.

Finally, after a delay of three days, the programmer is ready to work on his task. He recalls his original estimate. "I should be able to do it in five days, maybe even faster," he thinks. On Monday he starts to code and realizes that he doesn't have a clue how to start, even though originally everything looked very straightforward. Tuesday, he spends the entire day learning about the new programming tools that he must use. Wednesday starts off with a fire drill, and he spends an hour twiddling his thumbs and worrying in the parking lot. After that, he spends a few hours on the phone answering questions about a previous project. Still he manages to begin coding. Throw in donut day on Friday, which is slow at the best of times, and our programmer has already burned through his original estimate.

The following Monday, the programmer talks to the project manager.

"Everything is almost ready," he asserts. "I had some delays because I had to learn a new tool, but I've solved almost all of the problems," the programmer reports during the meeting. ("Almost," in IT language, means about half the work.) The project manager realizes she's hearing IT talk but prefers to ignore it; she doesn't have a choice. After resolving a few major issues and working on some other minor issues that were discovered the previous week, the programmer finally completes the task on Friday, a week longer than the original estimate. Fortunately, the task is not on the critical path. Unfortunately, other tasks that *are* on the critical path have suffered the same fate.

Software projects don't necessarily fail completely or get canceled. Often, releases are delayed or released with are euphemistically called "quality and usability issues." In the software world, this means that it will work, but not completely as planned. If it were a car, it might not have headlights and would occasionally shift into reverse when you turn on the windshield wipers. Customers may complain, but in most cases the software will not be used extensively anyway. It becomes "shelfware."

This is the end of our saga, which started with a poor estimate and the creation an of unrealistic project schedule and ended ignominiously. Now we'll try to understand how these mistakes were made. The root of the problem lies in human psychology, which we will try to analyze first.

How Do We Think When We Make Estimates?

Let's go back to the original conversation between the programmer and the project manager. How long does it take to say, "Oh, I think abo-o-out . . . five days"? Try to do it. It shouldn't take longer than four seconds, even if you pause before the sentence. Remember, we assume the programmer already understands the scope of the task. He uses this time to make an estimate. Here is his mental process: he recalls the scope of the task. He tries to recall similar projects, mostly with comparable scope or similar development tools. He checks how relevant these projects are to the current task. That gives him an approximate answer: around four or five days. The programmer does this analysis almost instantaneously. It is not really an analysis; it is an intuitive response based on his memory input.

The programmer spends the rest of these four seconds trying to come up with an acceptable estimate. If it's too low, he won't be able to complete his job on time. Too high, and the project manager will be unhappy (she is not an idiot and has her own silent estimate). This is a good example of a motivational bias, where the programmer has a personal interest in expressing this judgment.

When the project manager asks, "Are you sure?" the programmer doesn't repeat his analysis; he is just trying to determine whether his answer has satisfied the manager. Moreover, as you might have noticed, he did not have the time or information to understand any potential pitfalls, which he implicitly acknowledges with the phrase "if everything goes well."

It is truly amazing how much thinking can be done in only four seconds. It is even more amazing that estimates done this way may be absolutely correct. This type of estimation works well when the person has participated in similar activities many times and has an excellent memory of those experiences. However, in research and development projects or almost all new projects, this is often impossible.

Impact of Politics on Estimation

Why do people generally make poor estimates? There are at least three reasons:

1. Political and organizational pressure.

2. Psychological issues.

3. Technical issues, including problems related to the implementation of the project management process.

Bent Flyvbjerg and his colleagues reviewed a significant number of large transportation projects (Flyvbjerg et al. 2002). They found that project planners often intentionally underestimate costs and overestimate benefits to get their projects approved. Flyvbjerg found that costs are underestimated in nine out of ten transportation infrastructure projects (table 11-1). He studied data for the last 70 years and found that cost underestimation has not decreased over time, even with new project management tools and techniques.

So, how *do* project planners underestimate? One of the ways to "cook" a forecast is to deliberately reduce the probability of risk occurrence. When Eurotunnel, a private company that owns the tunnel under the English Channel, went public in 1987, investors were told that risks of cost escalations would be relatively small, just 10%. The actual risks were significantly greater, and the real cost was two times higher than the forecast.

The British politician Benjamin Disraeli famously said, "There are three kinds of lies: lies, damned lies, and statistics." He was noting an interesting phenomenon about probabilistic analysis. By deliberately using inaccurate probabilities for certain events, it is possible for a project manager or planner to improperly influence a decision, which may have disastrous consequences for the organization or stakeholders. In addition, it is difficult to catch these activities: they never said the event could not happen—they just knew that the chance of its occurrence was very small.

Impact of Psychology on Estimation and Rule of Pi

Organizational politics definitely plays an important role in estimation. But what about cognitive psychology?

An interesting phenomenon in the world of estimation is the rule of pi, which states that the actual duration (cost) of an activity will be about pi (3.1415 . . .) longer or bigger than the original estimate, even if the estimator was aware of this rule. Regardless of how we do our estimates,

> Rule of pi: The actual duration (cost) of an activity will be about pi (3.1415 . . .) bigger than the original estimate, even if the estimator was aware of this rule.

Table 11-1. Inaccuracy of Transportation Project Cost Estimates (Adapted from Flyvbjerg et al. 2002)

Project Type	Number of Cases	Average Cost Escalation
Rail	58	44.7%
Fixed-link (bridges and tunnels)	33	33.8%
Roads	167	20.4%
All projects	258	27.6%

we always underestimate, even if we are aware of the tendency to underestimate. Sound strange? Well, not if you think about it. Why are we repeatedly late and running out of time and money? We try to fit too many activities into the project and hope against all hope that we will be successful. This wishful thinking is often the cause of the problem.

You might ask why it is called the "rule of pi." In fact, it is an arbitrary number, and the reference is a bit tongue in cheek, but it emphasizes the fact that mistakes in estimates can be very significant. Also, this rule was invented by programmers, who like to remind everybody that they know math.

The rule of pi is related to known psychological issues, such as the planning fallacy (Buehler et al. 1994) and the optimism bias (Kahneman and Lovallo 2003). How do these issues pertain to estimation? According to one explanation, people often fail to account for risks or other factors that they perceive as lying outside the specific scope of a project. They also may discount multiple and improbable high-impact risks because each one has a glancingly small probability of occurring. For example, our programmer did not take into account four potential events: answering questions regarding a previous project, learning about the new programming tools, participating in a fire drill, and enjoying donut Friday.

This problem is the result of limitations of our mental capacity, and in many cases it may be impossible to account for such events without special tools, such as data-mining and risk-management software.

The optimism bias is widely acknowledged by project management practitioners. For example, some organizations perform an adjustment for optimism bias through the performance of a risk analysis to come up with accurate estimates. It is good idea to perform this type of adjustment. However, here is an interesting paradox of the rule of pi: adjustments for the rule of pi often cannot be done. In other words, even if a project manager has adjusted duration and cost estimates for a forecast, it will still take longer, roughly 3.1415 times longer, to complete the project. This sounds almost too fantastic to be true, and most likely mathematically incorrect, for it can lead to an infinite project duration and cost ($3.1415 \times 3.1415 \times 3.1415 \ldots$). However, the problem is that project managers do not adjust duration and cost significantly enough to keep these parameters within expectations, as a result of confirmation bias and other mental traps. And if they do, they are subject to another bias: student syndrome.

Student Syndrome

In his book *Critical Chain* (2002), Eliyahu Goldratt described "student syndrome." It refers to a student's way of waiting until the last minute to cram for an exam, which leads to the wasting of any contingency buffers built into the estimates of the task duration. A good example is how we saw that our programmer fully concentrated on the job only when the deadline was looming. Therefore, setting really distant deadlines may not help, because most of the work will be done just before the deadline anyway.

By the way, our own project to write this book took us much longer than we originally estimated—because of the rule of pi. How could this happen if we knew about these

> Many people will only start to fully apply themselves to a task in the wake of a deadline.

rules, as well as many other mental pitfalls? The answer is that knowledge of an illusion does not spare us from being a subject of the illusion. If you were a professional magician with many industry awards and citations, you would still enjoy somebody else's magic show. Moreover, according to another bias called the bias blind spot, people tend not to see their own cognitive biases (Pronin et al. 2002).

Other Cognitive Biases in Estimating

When people perform estimates, they often apply heuristics or simplification techniques that help them to reduce the burden of processing complex information, which we discussed in general in chapter 2.

One simplification technique is the anchoring heuristic. Again, let's return to our original example of estimation. The programmer instantly comes up with the number of five days. This number might be wrong, but further estimates will likely remain close to his original estimate. For example, the programmer might then reestimate the duration of an activity at between four and six days.

The availability heuristic can also affect our estimates. To see how, let's do a very simple psychological exercise:

1. Take three seconds to try to recall all the projects or large activities you were involved in during the last year.

2. Now repeat step 1, but take 15 seconds.

3. Repeat steps 1 and 2, taking up to three minutes for each step, and write down the results.

You will find it difficult to remember more than a few previous activities unless you spend some time thinking about it. Even then, you will probably have a clearer memory of your most recent projects. It is also easier to recall your most successful or largest projects. If the programmer calculates the likelihood of the task's taking five days based on the projects he remembers, and if he remembers only his successful activities, he will underestimate the duration. To illustrate this phenomenon, table 11-2 shows the set of his previous activities relevant to the current task of developing a computer program to display a bar chart.

Since at the time of estimation the programmer clearly remembers only two out of the five activities, he deems it very probable that the activity will be completed in five days. In reality, it could take much longer.

Table 11-2. Example of Previous Activities Related to the Current Task

Date	Activity	Clearly Remembers	Duration
Q1, 2017	Pie chart	No	10 days
Q2, 2017	Interactive bar chart	No	12 days
Q1, 2018	Multiple line chart	Somewhat	7 days
Q2, 2018	Small bar chart	Yes	3 days
Q4, 2018	Bar chart	Yes	5 days

Further Explanations of Problems with Estimation

A number of other issues will lead to forecasting errors. Among them:

- There is no established project estimation process
- Inaccurate data is used, or historical data may not be complete
- The forecasting techniques and tools are inefficient
- There is no ability to track actual project performance, which can be used to refine estimates
- The project planners are inexperienced

The *PMBOK Guide* points out that performing a project estimate is part of two knowledge areas:

1. Project time management, including activity duration estimation, activity resource estimation, and the schedule development processes

2. Project cost management, including cost-estimating and cost-budgeting processes.

Organizations that have established project management processes that forecast both time and cost usually produce more consistent and accurate estimates.

Where Does the Problem Lie—in Psychology or Politics?

The balance between the optimism bias and pressure of politics was the subject of an interesting debate involving the Nobel laureate Daniel Kahneman, along with Dan Lovallo and Bent Flyvbjerg, conducted in the *Harvard Business Review*. Kahneman and Lovallo (2003) believe that the optimism bias is to blame for inaccurate estimates. For his part, Flyvbjerg (2003, 2006) acknowledges the existence of the optimism bias and believes that in fact it plays a major role when political pressure is insignificant. However, when political and organizational pressures are significant, he believes that the problem with incorrect estimates is mostly related to deliberate deception by project planners. He argues that wrong estimates are so widespread and have continued for so many years that it is highly unlikely that human psychology plays a major role.

It is hard to make a clear distinction between cognitive biases (such as mental mistakes in processing information) and motivational biases (intentional lies) in forecasting and estimating. For example, in large capital projects throughout the construction industry, politics and organizational pressures play major roles in causing incorrect estimates. In other industries and in smaller projects, political pressure is not as significant. For example, in research and development projects, including IT projects, mental mistakes and psychological biases play a critical role in causing poor estimates. The two main reasons for this are:

1. Only James Bond, in movies such as *Dr. No* and *Moonraker*, can dress up as a member of a project team for the purpose of completely destroying the project. As far as we know, all other project managers and planners want projects to succeed. As a result, they will have some expectations about the project. As soon as people have expectations, they will demonstrate selective perception: "What I see is what I want to see." Planners or project managers sometimes cease to review data as soon as they find something that supports their estimate. They can also discard evidence that contradicts their estimates. This is called a selective search of evidence. Similarly, there is a confirmation bias, or a tendency to assign more weight to evidence that confirms an estimate and to ignore evidence that could refute their hypothesis.

2. Planning of large projects is performed by many people, and each of them expresses different biases. Different project stakeholders have different preferences and different risk profiles. Because of this, it is hard to judge how the balance between cognitive and motivational bias can affect a particular project. It is even more difficult to extrapolate conclusions on a group of projects.

Why is understanding the balance between optimism bias and politics so important? Depending upon what the cause of the errors is in estimation, various solutions could be suggested to resolve the problem. If wrong estimations are caused by optimism bias, then the ultimate solution is a systematic analysis of projects. To avoid motivational biases, project managers should analyze similar projects and use actual data from completed projects to make estimations for new ones. In reality, project managers often use a "hybrid" approach for their estimations: using historical data and decision analysis methods.

Many Mental Errors and One Wrong Estimate

When people make estimates, they can make many mental mistakes at the same time. In the movie *The Father of the Bride,* George Banks (played by Steve Martin) was trying to organize his daughter's wedding. Because it was a complex project, he and his family hired professional event planners, who can be viewed for our purposes as a project management office. If your CEO is not completely convinced of the importance of a project management office, tell the CEO to watch that movie. When George got the price tag from the event organizers, there was the typical comic moment where he had to reconcile his (affordable) expectations with the projected bill of the event planners. In fact, he was so far off that he had a nervous breakdown and ended up in jail, much to the embarrassment of himself and his family. But the real issue we want to investigate is why his estimate was so different from the realistic cost.

First, daughters do not get married very often, so George had few historical data of his own to draw upon. He had to make up his own estimation process, during which he made the following mental errors:

1. He wanted to spend as little as possible and therefore was motivated to come up with an unrealistically cheap estimate. He ignored all evidence that would have suggested the true cost of the wedding (expensive cake, large number of guests, a relative whose two airline tickets from Europe must be paid) when he did his rough estimate.

2. He used a reference point (the cost of a house) to come up with the estimate. It was completely irrelevant to a wedding and therefore was nonsensical for this particular estimate (though good for the movie). This is a classic example of anchoring.

3. Finally, he was overconfident. The wedding was a one-day event that would take place in his house, so he thought the amount of money required would be manageable.

What should George Banks have done to avoid a nervous breakdown?

1. Ask some other people how much the wedding would cost and use their number as a reference point.

2. Make a rough estimate by summing up all known expenses without ignoring any items.

3. Make necessary contingency plans by continually asking, "What else could happen?"

Figure 11-1. Risks and Uncertainties of Budgeting

Weddings will always be more expensive than we plan because: (a) the number of guests will be twice the original estimate; (b) food will cost at least three times more, even if you serve hamburgers instead of tenderloin; and (c) you will be charged for many things that you did not imagine (figure 11-1). If in the future you are planning a wedding, make accurate estimates and hire a professional project manager.

Simple Remedies

So, how can we integrate information about risks and uncertainties into our estimates?

NEVER MAKE A WILD GUESS

Estimates are possible even when based on partial information; however, we often try to make estimates with very little information, or none at all. We can call this type of estimate a "wild guess." (If you dislike the word "wild," just call it an "intelligent guess.") For example, how much would it cost to develop one medication to treat all forms of cancer? There is no reliable information to support an answer. Still, we will try to answer the question, either because we don't want to look incompetent or because we are being pushed by management or our colleagues to do so. The manager's position is quite understandable; he or she does not want to end up with question marks on the project schedule.

Unfortunately, as soon as we deliver our estimate, everybody instantly forgets that it is a wild guess and, because of the anchoring heuristic, this estimate becomes the anchor for all future discussions. Could you imagine this newspaper headline: "Project manager of PharmaCo Inc. estimates that a universal cancer drug will cost only $5 billion"? Inevitably, people will use this number as a starting point in any future analysis or discussions.

What should we do if we are asked to make an estimate without any information? The only solution is to try to get as much relevant information as possible. If previous relevant data is not available, we can take a small task and see what happens. How long will it take and what level of resources did it require? For example, you can make a prototype or an evaluation tool. Unfortunately, management often wants to forego this strategy and asks for an estimate immediately. This is where the big problems begin.

COLLECT RELEVANT HISTORICAL DATA

Most project managers know how important it is to collect and analyze data from previous projects, but very few actually do it. If we had a full data set on relevant activities, our estimates would be far more accurate. In some industries this data is available through various software applications, forms, and methodologies. If you are lucky, you work for an organization that routinely collects and analyzes historical data as part of its project and portfolio management processes.

But what if you don't have any such tools? The simple solution is to keep your old project schedules handy, so that you can easily access and review them when you are trying to make estimates.

Here is a simple way to analyze your information:

1. Look at previous project schedules or try to recall similar activities.

2. Write down activities and their relevance to the current one (table 11-3).

3. Use this table to assess the duration of the current activity.

Table 11-3. Analysis of Relevant Activities

	Activity	Duration	Relevance
1	Development of user interface (UI) for customer support software	20 days	Relevant
2	Website development	32 days	Not very relevant
3	Charts in business analysis software	10 days	Almost the same
4	UI improvements for selected client	5 days	Relevant

Collection and analysis of relevant historical data will help to mitigate the negative effect of both motivational and cognitive biases, and will specifically help you address the availability heuristic.

PERFORM REALITY CHECKS AND BENCHMARKING

Reality checks are a simple way to improve the accuracy of your estimates. Their objective is to compare your estimates with known project results. Below is an example of cost estimation for movie production.

As you probably realize, movie production has significant uncertainties in project cost and duration:

- Movie set collapses
- Producer has a bad day
- Actress goes to rehab
- Director decides to change the plot and kill (or resurrect) the protagonist

Cost estimation with many uncertainties can be extremely challenging. The movie studio may have planned other movies of similar budget and projected revenue, thus needs to determine whether the new budget is roughly in line with previously released movies (figure 11-2).

Benchmarking is more advanced than simple reality checks. Benchmarking helps to compare business processes and their performance indicators with other similar processes. In project management, benchmarking assists you in comparing the cost and duration of various projects together with other indi-

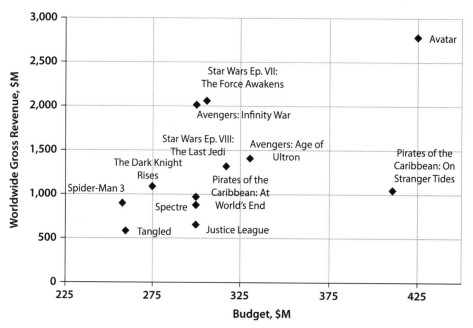

Figure 11-2. Gross Revenue of Most Expansive Movies vs. Budget

cators, such as scope, deliverables, net present value, and resource usage. In theory, you can benchmark everything:

- Oil well drilling
- Missile production
- Brain surgeries
- Cake baking

Moreover, everything can be measured. However, it is important to determine if a measurement provides value in view of the resources expended to gather it.

Many benchmarking exercises require detailed analysis of business and technological processes. You can use specialized software tools to perform benchmarking. Estimates for project or activity cost and duration are only a few of the results that benchmarking easily produces. Primarily, the results of benchmarking are recommendations for process improvements.

CONDUCT AN INDEPENDENT ASSESSMENT

For some projects, especially those with huge budgets, independent assessment is a firm requirement. But getting independent estimates by different members of the same team or by different teams can be a double-edged sword. On the one hand, they offer an additional look at the estimated parameters. On the other hand, psychologists know that assessments made by separate individuals may be different and difficult to reconcile. Sometimes an independent assessment is as biased as the original estimate.

For example, the cost of NASA's space missions is often independently assessed by separate NASA divisions. Most important, after the independent assessment, an analysis is usually performed to discover the causes of the difference.

Sometimes an independent assessment may not be practical, because it might be difficult to find independent experts familiar with the particular project. Nevertheless, any discussions regarding the results of estimates by team members or independent experts have proven to be effective in helping to incorporate more information into the estimates.

- Poor estimates can cause a wrong strategic decision and eventually derail a project.
- Motivational and cognitive biases will significantly affect your estimates.
- Political and organizational pressures are several critical sources of estimation error, especially in large capital projects.
- Simple remedies will help mitigate the negative impact of heuristics and biases. You should never make an assessment without reliable data. Try to improve your assessments using comprehensive historical data, and always perform both reality checks and independent assessments.

CHAPTER 12

Project Valuation Models

Quantitative project decision analysis can be performed using a project valuation model, which in most cases consists of a project schedule or an economic model. A number of techniques for schedule network analysis are used in project management, including the critical path method, critical chain methods, Event chain methodology, and resource leveling. Influence diagrams can also be used to create a project valuation model. Modeling based on the agile approach to project management does not require determining all project details up front, because it focuses on short project iterations with tangible deliverables.

Model of the Project

Who do you think are the best project managers? One could argue that they are those who use valuation models to help them understand the process without actually experiencing the process. A project manager can even learn how to model a project from the criminals in popular action movies, who always seem to have amazing abilities for precise project planning and execution. Unfortunately, for these characters, in most movies they also have problems with project closing, so the loot ends up on a bus overhanging a cliff. In spite of this, you really believe that they deserve some reward for the slick execution of the project (figure 12-1).

A great example is the 1960 version of *Ocean's Eleven,* with Frank Sinatra, and its 2001 remake with George Clooney, Julia Roberts, Brad Pitt, Matt Damon, and Andy Garcia. In the 2001 version, Danny Ocean is an experienced "project manager." Less than 24 hours after his release from a New Jersey penitentiary, he has already initialized a new project: the most elaborate casino heist in history. First, he assembles a project team of the best professionals money can rent. Then he arranges financing. But, most important, he creates a detailed model of the robbery—an intricately choreographed plan, with every action detailed down to the second. The team analyzes all possible obstacles and carefully models the behavior of their counterparts, the casino security team. If real project managers were able to manage their projects as precisely as Danny Ocean, that would create a revolution in most industries. Perhaps the issue lies in motivation: Danny Ocean and his colleagues stand to make $150 million if they manage to pull off their heist (that, or a lengthy stay in the pen).

Figure 12-1. Robbing a Bank Involves Complex Modeling

Whether you're a criminal or a project manager, it helps to predict what could happen during a project and what would be the best choices, given the results of this analysis. For example, climatologists create weather models to predict climate change, aircraft engineers build models of new planes to research aerodynamics, and bank robbers draw up plans to rob a casino.

In all these cases, project management models contain inputs, outputs, and calculation algorithms. The inputs include:

- Project activities and their relationships, including estimates of start and finish times, costs, resources, and other parameters
- Risks, with their probabilities, outcomes, and other properties
- Financial information associated with the project, including risks and uncertainties related to financial projections
- Inputs related to quality, safety, and environment

A model's outputs could include:

- Project schedules, including estimates of project duration and cost
- Project budgets
- Quality and safety-planning evaluations

What kinds of models are we talking about? We'll discuss two: the schedule model and the economic model.

SCHEDULE MODEL

A schedule model is defined in the *PMBOK Guide* as "a model used in conjunction with manual methods and project management software to perform schedule network analysis and generate the project schedule . . . ." Schedule network analysis employs a schedule model, together with various analytical techniques, such as critical path, critical chain, and resource-leveling, so to calculate the project schedule. We will learn how this schedule model can be used to come up with certain decisions in part 4 of this book, which focuses on quantitative analysis.

ECONOMIC MODEL

When criminal masterminds are planning a heist, they are concerned about more than timing and scheduling. They also make decisions based on certain financial considerations. How much would it cost to buy a machine gun? What is the chance that they could rob a bank without one? How much money is required to bribe the bank's security officer to obtain insider information about the vault code? And, most important, how is the gang going to share the loot among themselves? In fact, the criminal mastermind is concerned about the complete project life cycle. The project schedule may also include costs associated with activities and resources. But in many cases, a special model is required for decision-making based on monetary criteria.

Economic models can include an analysis of project performance derived from incremental project cash flows. The foundation of financial analysis is discounted cash flow analysis, which assesses the value of an investment based on predicted cash flows at a discounted value to account for the reduced value of money over time. The economic model should be quite complete and include many details: various sources of revenue and cost, as well as inflation rates, tax rates, and royalties, among other parameters. These models can be created with general-purpose spreadsheet tools or with specialized financial software.

Economic models are used in the decision-making process. Choices can be based on the analysis of outcome indicators and of value measures. Two value measures used for discounted cash flow analysis are *net present value* (NPV), which is the present value of a series of future net cash flows, and *rate of return* (ROR), which is a measure of the profitability of an investment.

ALTERNATIVE MODELS

In addition to schedule and economic models, you can create many types of models for the same project. You can analyze technical and business benefits, performance, safety, quality, and environmental issues, and many others, as well. In this book we concentrate mostly on schedule models; however, project decision analysis processes, including quantitative analysis methods, can be similar for other types of models.

If a model contains information related to risks and uncertainties, it is called a probabilistic approach. Otherwise, it is considered a deterministic approach. In this chapter we will discuss modeling techniques for both approaches. Sometimes you will need to create different models for different project alternatives by using common value measures. But in most cases, single probabilistic models should handle most of the possible uncertainties.

The Critical Path Method

Although it was invented way back in the 1950s by the DuPont Company and Remington Rand Univac, the critical path method (CPM) remains one of most popular planning tools, despite all its limitations. It employs the deterministic approach.

The steps in the critical path method are:

- Calculate the start and finish times of each activity chronologically through a network diagram or Gantt chart (from left to right). These are the earliest start and finish times.

- Calculate the start and finish times of each activity the same way, but this time from right to left. These are the latest start and finish times.

- The difference between the latest and earliest times represents "free float" or "slack," the amount of time the activity can be delayed without delaying any other immediately following activity.

- Activities with zero free float lie on the critical path.

Let's say a bank robbery project manager creates a schedule that includes the four activities shown in the Gantt chart in figure 12-2. In this case, the activity "secure escape route" has three minutes' slack: the robbers cannot leave the bank without taking money. Taking money from the vault takes longer than securing the escape route. As a result, the critical path includes, first, "break into the bank," second, "take money from the vault, and third, "leave the bank." To reduce project time, this critical path and in particular the activity "take money from the vault" need to be optimized. Maybe the robber needs to consider a better blowtorch or the use of explosives. (Although, if you remember from chapter 3,

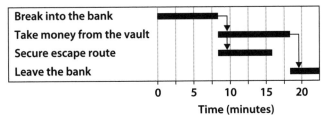

Figure 12-2. Gantt Chart for Bank Robbery Project

Gopher's explosives were rejected as a strategy for getting Bear out of Rabbit's doorway. They might be helpful here!)

But here is the problem. Let's assume that something happens while the robber secures the escape route. A security guard could notice something, or the rear door might be locked and cannot be opened. This is a scenario that you see in the movies all the time. Because of such risk events, the activity "secure escape route" will become critical. However, the robber spent all his efforts on optimizing the "take money from the vault" activity that was on the critical path and probably spent no time planning for any risk events that might occur during the "secure escape route" activity.

A problem with the critical path method, then, is that it does not take resource allocation into account. The activity "secure escape route" may require more resources than breaking into the vault, and as result it might deserve greater planning and attention. Due to that shortcoming in the critical path method, the robbery attempt may be in jeopardy.

The critical path method sounds very simple, but keep in mind that in reality a number of contingencies can significantly complicate the calculations. Among these contingencies are:

1. Activities may have different logical relationships between them. In addition to finish-start relationships (when previous activity finishes, new activity starts), they can be start-start, finish-finish, and start-finish relationships. Moreover, there can be a time delay between activities.

2. Nonworking time that occurs during the course of the project must be accounted for. Also, different resources may have different calendars.

3. In most cases, project schedules include summary tasks and subtasks. If a summary task is the predecessor or successor of other tasks, this can significantly complicate the algorithm.

4. Schedules may include time constraints. For example, an activity must start or finish on a certain date. This can lead to scheduling conflicts.

Fortunately, many project-scheduling software tools are available to help you perform the critical path analysis.

The critical path method by itself is a deterministic approach. Probabilistic analysis can be implemented in conjunction with the critical path method. The *PMBOK Guide* mentions a number of other deterministic techniques to use in schedule network analysis. One of them is the what-if scenario analysis, which is the analysis of project schedules under a multitude of conditions and situations.

The *PMBOK Guide* also describes resource leveling, another schedule network analysis technique that can be implemented at the top of the critical path method. Resource leveling helps you come up with a project schedule when resources are limited.

The Critical Chain Method

The critical chain method, another schedule network analysis technique, derives from Eliyahu Goldratt's theory of constraints. In his book *The Goal* (Goldratt 2014), he applied the theory to manufacturing processes. The idea was to improve manufacturing processes by identifying and removing bottlenecks. In 1997 he wrote *Critical Chain*, in which he applied the theory of constraints to project scheduling (Goldratt 2002). The critical chain method is included in the *PMBOK Guide* as a schedule network analysis technique.

The critical chain method focuses on managing constrained resources and buffer activities. It applies both deterministic and probabilistic approaches, because it combines deterministic project schedules with buffers designed to deal with uncertainties.

The three key steps in the critical chain method are:

1. Create a project schedule and calculate the critical path in the same manner as performed for the critical path method. This project schedule is deterministic. Goldratt suggested using a median (50% confidence) estimate of duration for the activities.

2. Enter resource availability. You may need to adjust the project schedule to exploit constrained resources. As a result, the critical path can be altered. Using this method, you can then identify the critical chain, which is a resource-constrained critical path.

To deal with uncertainties, you may need to add buffers to the end of the project and also add a "feeding" activity chain, which merges into the critical path. These feeding buffers, which are nonwork schedule activities, will protect activities from the slippage of preceding activities. Slippage may occur because of uncertainties and the student syndrome, but buffers are supposed to absorb the uncertainties of future events.

Several software tools (see appendix A) are specifically designed to implement the critical chain method in project management. The critical chain method has become increasingly popular in some organizations.

Event Chain Methodology

Event chain methodology is another probabilistic technique used to perform schedule network analysis. We will discuss the methodology in detail in part 4, because it is a quantitative analysis method, but here is a short introduction (Virine and Trumper 2013, 2017).

Event chain methodology is based on the notion that regardless of how well we develop a project schedule, something may happen that will dramatically affect it. Identifying and managing these events or "event chains" (when one event causes another event) is the focus of Event chain methodology. Why do we focus on events, rather than a continuous process for a changing project environment? We do so because when continuous problematic events come up within a project, it is possible to detect and fix them early.

> Event chain methodology combines uncertainty modeling and the schedule network analysis technique, which is focused on identifying and managing events and event chains that affect the project schedule.

Another function of Event chain methodology is mitigation of the negative effects of cognitive and motivational biases. As we have seen, in many cases we intentionally or unintentionally create project schedules that are not possible to implement.

In Event chain methodology, you first need to create a schedule model, using a best-case estimate of duration, which in most instances will be optimistic. Why optimistic estimates? As a result of a number of cognitive and motivational factors—including the planning fallacy or optimism bias, overconfidence, and the rule of pi—we tend to create optimistic estimates even when we are trying not to. Since it is impossible to prevent project managers from defining an over-optimistic schedule, we have to accept it and work with it.

Next, define a list of events and event chains with their probabilities and impacts on tasks or resources. In this process we need to identify events separately (separate time, meeting, experts) from the schedule model in order to avoid confirmation bias, where our expectations about the project (cost, duration, and so on) affect event identification. You can visualize these events using event chain diagrams. Then you perform a quantitative analysis to generate a new schedule that takes these risk events into account. You can repeat the analysis regularly during the course of a project to provide up-to-date forecasts of project duration or cost.

If you are using a critical chain project management process, you may apply Event chain methodology to determine the size of a buffer. The buffer duration is the difference between project duration with risks and uncertainties and the original optimistic project schedule.

Although Event chain methodology is a relatively new approach, it is used in many organizations, including large corporations and government agencies. You can find a list of software tools that implement Event chain methodology in appendix A.

Modeling with Influence Diagrams

Influence diagrams are a useful graphic tool to help you model problems. The concept of influence diagrams originated at Stanford University and the Strategic Decision Group in Menlo Park (Howard and Matheson 1984/2005; Shachter 1986). In chapter 11 ("Project Risk Management") of the *PMBOK Guide*, influence diagrams are recommended as one of the diagramming techniques for information gathering.

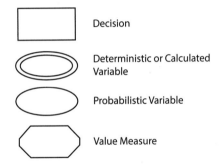

Figure 12-3. Different Types of Nodes

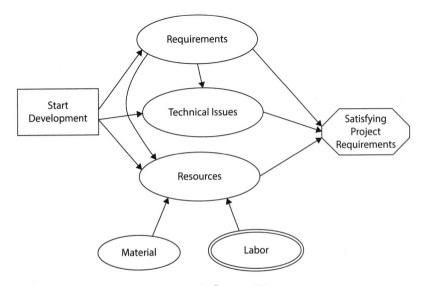

Figure 12-4. Influence Diagram

Elements of decision problems are represented by different types of nodes (figure 12-3). An example of an influence diagram is shown in figure 12-4. It represents a decision about the design and development of a new product that has to be made at the project launch. Construction of an influence diagram starts with defining a value measure. In this example, it is the project's net present value. The decision to launch the project is affected by three uncertain variables: availability of resources, requirements, and abilities to solve technical issues.

Remember that influence diagrams do not have feedback loops: variable-predecessors cannot rely on variable-successors. Sometimes influence diagrams can be very complex. In these cases, it is important to break the diagram into a number of smaller diagrams.

An influence diagram can be converted to a decision tree, which is another representation of the decision problem. We will discuss decision trees in chapter 15.

In many cases, it is easier to create valuation models using influence dia-grams than to create them in spreadsheets or other software. In appendix A, you will find information on software that will generate project models using influence diagrams.

The Agile Approach and Project Decision Analysis

In February 2001, a group of 17 software gurus met at a Utah resort to talk, ski, relax, and eat. Out of that meeting came what they called the "Manifesto for Agile Software Development" (Manifesto 2006). It defined high-level guidelines for software development processes. Here are few ideas from that document:

- Customer satisfaction is increased by rapid, continuous delivery of useful software.
- Changing requirements are welcomed, even late in development.
- Working software should be released frequently, within periods rang-ing from a couple of weeks to a couple of months.
- Business-people and software developers must work together every day throughout a project.
- Team motivation and creative environments are important to deliver good projects, and individuals should be trusted to get the job done. To quote from the manifesto: "The best architectures, requirements, and designs emerge from self-organizing teams."
- "The most efficient and effective method of conveying information to and within a development team is face-to-face conversation."
- "Working software is the primary measure of progress."
- "Continuous attention to technical excellence and good design en-hances agility."
- "Simplicity—the art of maximizing the amount of work not done—is essential."

Few successful business ideas are absolutely new. An idea becomes successful when the right individual is able to express and popularize it in such way that the idea becomes appealing to many people. Surprisingly, if you think about it, we use the agile approach all the time in our lives. We humans cannot define right at the start every single step that we will have to take to accomplish our goals. Therefore, we tend to solve problems iteratively, based on the results of our previ-ous activities. This is partially related to our bounded rationality, which we dis-cussed in chapter 2. That is, we are not capable of comprehending all of life's complexities, so we apply simplified mental models to our problems. As a result, we develop specific methods to implement our general plans as we progress.

The agile approach is actually a family of different methods, the develop-ment of which started in the mid-1990s as a response to "heavyweight" methodologies that focused on micro-management of projects. Essentially, these "waterfall" methods, which required defining all requirements up front, contradicted the ways in which engineers were actually performing their work. Waterfall methods are sequential project management processes in which project development is seen as flowing steadily downward like a waterfall through the various phases such as requirements analysis, design, and implementation.

Agile has become increasingly popular for research and development projects, not only in the area of software development but also in other industries. The agile approach is not a panacea and cannot be completely implemented in many situations. It is hard to rob a bank iteratively. And criminal masterminds may not allow members of the gang to express the full extent of their creativity, because creativity during a robbery can bring unexpected results. However, often, in projects where an agile approach would be appropriate, it lies unused. At first glance, the idea of not defining all the requirements and designs up front and trying to develop a product iteratively may appear counterintuitive. How can we produce something without knowing exactly what the end result is supposed to be? Do self-organizing teams equal team anarchy? These are valid questions, yet the measured results of projects managed on agile principles confirm the benefits of the approach (Highsmith 2009).

How do decision analysis and agile project management relate to each other? An effective decision analysis process shares the same foundations as agile project management:

- Creative environments free of frustrated employee syndrome (FES) are a component of effective agile management and a necessary condition for effective decision analysis.

- Identifying and managing risks is one of the cornerstones of agile processes and a fundamental element of the decision analysis process.

- Adaptive management and review of decisions made (phase 4 of the decision analysis process) is also an important step in the agile approach.

- Decision analysis processes include a mechanism for improving decisions in an environment where requirements are always changing. Decision analysis includes a notion of target-oriented decision-making, which we discussed in chapter 3. Similar to agile project management, target-oriented decision-making is a process that increases the probability of meeting changing project requirements.

The agile approach is a highly rational concept in project management, because it helps to mitigate several common biases and mental traps that may arise in waterfall approaches. For example, the sunk-cost effect that may occur in waterfall approaches prevents us from giving up on an activity that is failing or not meeting its objectives despite many resources having already been spent on it. Another psychological bias, also related to the waterfall approach, is the illusion of control: project managers believe that they are in control of situations when in reality they are *not*.

- Models are a key element of decision-making. A model helps to evaluate various project alternatives and identify the best course of action.
- The critical path method is a common technique for schedule network analysis. However, it has major limitations related to managing uncertainties and dealing with constrained resources.
- The critical chain method generates resource-constrained project schedules and helps to manage project uncertainties, by using buffers.
- Event chain methodology helps to mitigate cognitive and motivational biases in project planning. As a result, it can supply more realistic project schedules.
- Creative environments within project teams, effective risk management, and adaptive management are the principal foundations of the agile approach to project management.

CHAPTER 13

Estimating Probabilities

Estimating probabilities in project management can be done either subjectively or by using a relative frequency approach based on historical data. Subjective assessment of probabilities can be affected by a number of cognitive biases, such as wishful thinking and overestimation of the probabilities of compound events. A number of methods can be used to make judgments about probabilities. Qualitative risk analysis helps prioritize risks, based on their probability and impact.

Approaches to Estimating Probabilities

Wrong estimations of probabilities can lead to major project problems, including failure. During the decision-framing phase (the first phase of the decision analysis process), you identified possible risks and uncertainties. Now you have to define the probabilities that these risks will occur. The probabilities of project risks become part of the project modeling (the second phase of decision analysis) that will be used in the subsequent quantitative analysis (the third phase).

The two approaches to estimating probabilities are:

1. The **relative frequency approach,** where probability equals the number of occurrences of a specific outcome (or event) divided by the total number of possible outcomes. This calculation can be based on either historical data or measurements of actual project performance. For example, if nine of the last 10 plays of a particular director were canceled after the first performance, it is easy to calculate that the director's probability of success equals 10%, one out of every 10 shows.

2. The **subjective approach,** which represents an expert's degree of belief that a particular outcome will occur. For example, will a new Broadway show be successful? It is hard to tell and depends on many factors. Ultimately, it is a subjective judgment of a decision-maker who is willing to bet on the success of the play.

Many people believe that subjective judgments about probabilities are inaccurate. Wharton professor Philip Tetlock showed that in general, experts' predictions are only slightly better than chance (Tetlock and Gardner 2015). However, people can deliver quite accurate assessments if certain techniques and tools for elicitation of judgment are used and if the negative effects of cognitive and motivational biases are mitigated.

Subjective Estimation of Probabilities

One of the funniest, but most instructive, stories about a failed project is the movie and later musical *The Producers*. In it, Leo Bloom and Max Bialystock decide to produce a play, called *Springtime for Hitler,* that would be in such bad taste that it would turn off the public and quickly fail, allowing them to pocket their investors' money. Not only is the subject matter distasteful, but to make sure their trick works, they hire the worst possible director and the worst cast and engage in some additional skullduggery to undermine the play. In spite of all their efforts, the first performance is a huge success, the scheme is uncovered, and Leo and Max end up in jail. In short, they didn't do a very good job of estimating probabilities.

The problem was that Leo and Max fell victim to the same psychological bias that has laid low many project managers before them. They were overconfident, which led them to overestimate the probability of their project failure (failure in this "anti-project" being the show's success). As a result, they had no contingency plans. In fact, they spent almost all their money before the first performance.

The insurance industry, for one, uses advanced risk-analysis methods and techniques (Simons 2006) to evaluate its exposure to large payouts. Yet recently it has also had to rely on the subjective estimations of experts in predicting what the weather will be in the future. Insurance companies world wide are trying to adapt to a new reality: climate change. The industry agrees that there has been a recent shift in weather patterns. As shown in figure 13-1, insurance losses averaged over a few years constantly grew and significantly fluctuate year over year (Statista 2018). The success of an insurance company depends on its correct assessment of the probability of certain events, be they automobile accidents, house fires, hurricanes, or even an injury to a high-priced (and highly insured) athlete. So, how does the company estimate the probability of weather disasters?

The insurance industry uses complex mathematical catastrophe models to analyze historical weather data, particularly information about the paths and intensities of future hurricanes. Companies try to calculate the potential damage that could be inflicted on different buildings, depending on the buildings' location, age, and structure. Until recently, the models worked quite well. But the recent surge in weather activity means that insurance companies cannot rely solely on historical data. In response, they have turned to expert judgment. Today, insurance companies commission the services of leading climatologists to come up with these

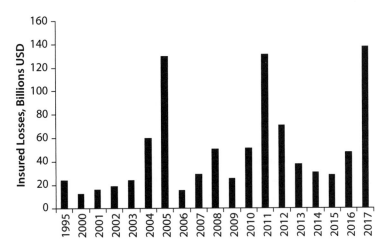

Figure 13-1. Insured losses caused by natural disasters worldwide from 1995 to 2017 (in billion U.S. dollars)

judgments. What do they foresee? Apparently, the weather will not get any better over the next few years, meaning that insurance payout fluctuation will increase.

Most uncertainties in project management are related to our lack of knowledge about the future. For these uncertainties, historical data and actual project measurements may be insufficient to come up with probabilities. For example, what is the chance that someday a hurricane will hit New York City? Or, what is the chance that a requirement will change as you are creating a brand-new type of product? In these cases, we have to use a subjective assessment of probabilities, either alone or in combination with the relative frequency approach.

How We Subjectively Assess Probability and Risk

Many people seem concerned about the avian flu and other exotic infections that have yet to kill anyone in the United States. At the same time, the Centers for Disease Control estimates that the more common influenza strains have resulted in between 9.3 million and 49.0 million illnesses, between 140,000 and 960,000 hospitalizations, and between 12,000 and 79,000 deaths annually since 2010 (CDC 2018). After the attacks on September 11, 2001, many people refused to fly and chose instead to drive whenever possible. As a result, from October 2001 to December 2001 a thousand more traffic fatalities occurred than in the same period the year before. This is an example of how we tend to misjudge risks and make wrong assessments of probabilities due to the inherent cognitive and motivational biases that we discussed in chapter 2. (See appendix B for a list of heuristics and biases related to peoples's assessment of probabilities.) For example, because of biases related to the availability heuristic (people's having ready access through the media to vivid images of airline crashes), many folks believe that flying is far riskier than driving a car. In truth, at most a few hundred people are killed in commercial airline crashes each a year in the United States, compared to some 44,000 in motor vehicle accidents.

Factors that can significantly affect our estimation of risk include:

- **Wishful thinking:** This occurs when we overestimate the probabilities of opportunities and underestimate the probabilities of risks.
- **Overestimating the probability of compound events:** If the probability of a defect in a component is 20% and the device uses three redundant components, the probability of the defective device will be $(0.2 \times 0.2 \times 0.2) = 0.008\%$. People tend to think this number is much higher.
- **Ignoring base-rate frequencies** (probabilities of prior events): Here is a question for you. Historically, the probability that a particular component will be defective is 1%. The component is tested before installation. The test successfully identifies defective components 80% of the time. Your test indicates that a particular component is defective. What is the probability that other components are also defective? The correct answer is close to 4%. However, most people would think that answer is a little bit lower than 80%. Actual calculation can be done using the Bayesian theorem (Plous 1993).

Psychologists and neuroscientists have discovered that we (and other animals) have developed a special mechanism to deal with risks (Ledoux 2015). In the event of danger, groups of neurons located above the brain stem pump stress hormones into the bloodstream. This happens in a fraction of a second. The result is that we experience emotions—in particular, fear—in cases of danger. Because of this primal mechanism, in cases of risk, people tend to rely on intuitive (emotional) responses rather than on analysis. While this effect is felt most acutely in those cases where we face imminent peril, it also can affect us in the face of the more abstract, less life-threatening risks that we encounter during the course of a project.

Getting back to our play example, after the successful performance of *Springtime for Hitler*, its playwright, Franz Liebkind, pointed a gun at Leo Bloom and Max Bialystock and threatened to kill them for bastardizing his drama. Under threat of imminent death, Leo and Max's limbic systems kicked in, and while pleading for their lives they suggested that Franz kill the actresses instead. This is an example of how our emotions can cause poor judgment. Later, when the situation had calmed down somewhat and the first suggestion was rejected, they suggested that blowing up the theater would be a more appropriate act of revenge for Franz. Still, their choices were quite irrational and emotion driven: the possibility of being caught and spending a lengthy period in prison would increase dramatically if Franz were to take them up on either suggestion. (In case you are wondering, this is not a recommendation to blow up your office or perform other rash acts in the case of a project failure.)

Scientists believe that the mechanism behind our reaction to imminent risks was hardwired into our brains in prehistoric times, when "primitive" people were more concerned about judging the dangers posed by predators and other dangers than making complex multicriteria decisions. Today, project managers face a relatively small chance of being eaten by a predator, but they *will* still react emotionally to information related to their projects: whether deadlines are missed or not missed, whether the product works well or does not work at all, and so on. Together with heuristics and biases, emotional responses to risks and uncertainties affect our perception of risk and, in turn, our estimation of probabilities. Moreover, emotions can also affect our overall risk preferences or risk attitudes (Hillson and Murray-Webster 2007). Emotion is one of the important factors that contribute to the shape of the utility function, as shown in figure 4-3 in chapter 4.

Emotions affect not only our ability to assess risks and opportunities. Many small businesses close their doors because their owners emotionally cannot cope with losses, even though they technically have the financial resources to continue doing business. They overestimate short-term opportunities (the short-term probability of success) and underestimate long-term opportunities.

Methods of Eliciting Subjective Judgments in Project Management

Psychologists and decision scientists have developed a number of methods that can help elicit subjective judgments about probabilities. A project manager can benefit by calling in specialists to help. But before you start asking your experts about probabilities, you need to have the following:

1. A clearly defined problem, which was developed during the decision-framing phase of the decision analysis process.

2. Either an identified list of risks or a risk breakdown structure for the project.

3. A project model (for example, a project schedule).

4. A clearly defined set of questions you will ask the experts, to elicit their judgment concerning probabilities.

In addition, your experts should be prepared in the manner discussed in chapter 8. This will ensure that the project team is aware of any personal interests the experts may have regarding particular issues.

But how do you frame questions to elicit an accurate assessment from an expert? You can use a number of methods:

1. Ask for a specific assessment of an event's probability. Pose a direct question: "What is the probability that the project will be canceled due to budgetary problems?" In many cases, experts will be reluctant to answer this question if they feel they may not have sufficient information.

2. Ask the experts two opposing questions: (a) "What is the probability that the project will be canceled?" and (b) "What is the probability the project will be completed?" The sum of these two assessments should be 100%. In other words, say 40% for the first question, 60% for the second. This method is called a coherence check, and it helps experts to adjust their judgment.

3. Use a probability wheel, a diagram that looks like a pie chart (figure 13-2). Each area of the pie chart is associated with the probability of a certain outcome. Imagine that you spin the wheel as it is done on the *Wheel of Fortune* TV game show. The larger the area, the greater the chance that the wheel will stop on this area. The experts can adjust these areas until they are in agreement with the specific probabilities. Basically, the probability wheel helps in visualizing the probabilities and performing a coherence check. This is like preferring an analog car speedometer to a digital speedometer; the former is a better instrument for visualizing speed.

Different methods for estimating probabilities will often deliver different results for the same project. What should you do in these cases? While decision science does not give a definite answer to this question, one way to reconcile answers from several experts is to invite another expert. You may also arrange a discussion between experts. Our preferred method to deal with this problem is to further break down the problem. Break compound events into simple events and review them separately. For example, instead of asking a single question about the probability that the project will be canceled due to budgetary problems, you may ask two questions:

1. What it is the chance that a budgetary problem will occur?

2. What is the chance that the budgetary problem will lead to a project cancelation?

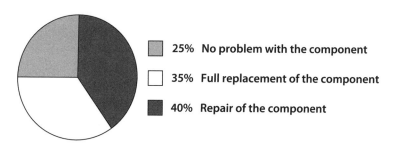

25% No problem with the component

35% Full replacement of the component

40% Repair of the component

Figure 13-2. Probability Wheel

Uncertainties in duration and cost of activities, as well as other uncertainties in project parameters, can be defined by using continuous probabilities or statistical distributions. Uncertainties should be quantified in the modeling phase of the project. We will cover the assessment of continuous probabilities in chapter 16.

What If a Decision Is Sensitive to Probability?

Maj. Ernest Y. Wong and Lt. Col. Rod Roederer of the US Military Academy (2006) used decision theory to review the US government's decision to attack Iraq in 2003. They hypothetically assumed that the decision to attack that country was based on only one criterion: the existence of a stockpile of weapons of mass destruction (referred to as WMD). Using the analytic methods we have discussed, they demonstrated that the outcome of the decision to attack Iraq was highly sensitive to the range of uncertainty surrounding the assessments of whether Iraq actually had WMD at the time.

If probability is greater than a certain breakeven number (say, 75%), the decision may be correct, and vice versa. However, if the probability is expressed as a range (from 60% to 90%), and if the breakeven point is within this range, it is very hard to tell what course of actions should be taken. Often, estimation of probabilities will affect the decision dramatically. If probability is assessed subjectively, inaccuracy can be even greater. The solution in this case should be to try to improve the quality of probability estimates: so, ask more experts to express their options, have additional discussions, try to obtain more data, and use more advanced techniques to elicit judgment. If the decision to attack Iraq had hinged on the assessments regarding its possession of WMD, the decision makers should have made every effort to minimize the uncertainties associated with the assessments.

Qualitative Risk Analysis

When we determine the probability of events, we can use it as part of a qualitative risk analysis. The *PMBOK Guide* defines qualitative risk analysis as "a process of prioritizing risks for subsequent further analysis or action by assessing and combining their probabilities and impact." The idea is to prioritize risks based on probability, impact on project objectives, time frame, when the risk may occur, and risk tolerance.

One of most exciting recent space missions, the New Horizon, is supposed to explore Pluto and a region of the outer solar system called the Kuiper Belt. The New Horizon was launched on January 19, 2006, and it reached the planet in July 2015 (figure 13-3). The spacecraft contained 24 pounds of plutonium, intended for use as power generation. NASA estimated that there was a 1 in 1.4 million to 1 in 18 million chance that an extremely unlikely launch area accident could release up to 2% of the plutonium.

Figure 13-3. The Atlas V Rocket with New Horizon Liftoff from Cape Canaveral, September 24, 2005 (Credit: NASA/Kim Shiflett, 2006)

Karl Grossman, however, did not agree with NASA's interpretation of the risk. "If it's 2 percent or it's 6 percent or if it's 20 percent or if it's 100 percent, when you are talking about plutonium, you are talking about the most radioactive substance known" (Grossman 1997). Fortunately, the New Horizon was launched successfully without incident; however, the controversy over using nuclear energy for space missions continues.

The issue here is that it is not sufficient to simply determine the probability of risks. We must also quantify the impact of those risks. The combination of probability and impact will give us an input necessary to make a decision. Quantitative and qualitative risk analysis can be used to analyze the combined probability and impact of the risk. Interpretation of the results depends on personal or organizational preferences—risk attitude and risk tolerance, both part of the decision policy we discussed in chapter 4. Apparently, Karl Grossman has much lower risk tolerance than NASA itself.

In many projects, especially smaller ones, a quantitative risk analysis is not required to determine which risks are most important. It is enough to know their probability of occurrence and impact on project objectives, such as time, cost, scope, and so on. Negative impacts are considered threats; positive impacts are opportunities. When you assess both probabilities and impacts, you may use a probability and impact matrix to prioritize the risks (figure 13-4). Black areas represent high risks that have first priority for mitigation or avoidance. White areas represent low risks. Organizations define the classifications of high and low risks based on risk preferences: the more risk-averse an organization is, the more black areas the matrix will have.

In *The Producers*, Leo and Max properly estimated the impact for the "show success" risk, but underestimated its probability. Moreover, as with most criminals, they were risk-takers. If they had constructed a probability and impact matrix, their high-risk area would have been quite small. The risk "show success" probably would have found itself in the gray or even the white area, instead of the black area. If they had correctly judged the importance of the risk, they probably would have been more prepared for the eventuality that the show might succeed, rather than completely ignoring it, which led to their downfall.

Here is another consideration: Gene Gigerenzer (Gigerenzer 2015) promotes the concept of statistical thinking. The problem, he asserts, is the illusion of certainty. We believe in certain information related to risks—for example, medical tests. However, in reality these test results are uncertain predictors of eventual health problems. To solve this problem, statistical analysis must be performed and the results of analysis must be properly framed, defined, and communicated.

Modern quantitative analysis techniques—for example, Event chain methodology—can automatically prioritize risks by using sensitivity analysis, which is a relatively easy process as long as you have both a project schedule and a risk breakdown structure. However, the probability and impact matrix remains a useful tool, especially in situations where you want to prioritize risks, such as quality, reliability, and safety, that are not directly related to the project schedule.

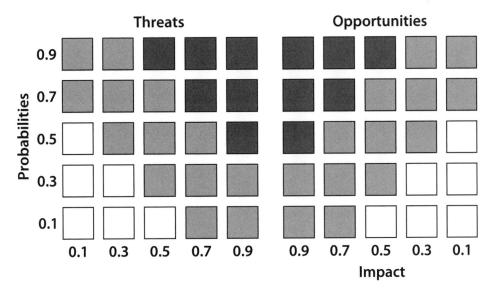

Figure 13-4. Probability and Impact Matrix

As we discussed in chapter 10, a risk register contains all the information about risks, such as name, description, category, cause, responses, owner, current status, and so on. When we know the probability and impact of a risk, we can save it in the risk register, as well.

- Subjective assessments are often the only way to work out probabilities.
- The relative frequency approach can be applied if reliable historical data or actual project performance measurements are available.
- When assessing risk, we often rely on intuitive thinking. When we do, emotions can significantly affect our perception of risk.
- The quality of subjective assessments can increase if effective techniques to elicit judgment are applied.
- Qualitative risk analysis helps to prioritize risks based on their probability and impact. Results of qualitative risk analysis can be used for further analysis.

PART 4

Quantitative Analysis

CHAPTER 14

Choosing What Is Most Important
Sensitivity Analysis and Correlations

To establish project priorities, it is important to identify which activities will have the greatest effect on a project and also to understand how those activities correlate. Our judgment about correlation and causation is affected by a number of biases, such as illusory and invisible correlations and covariation assessment. Sensitivity analysis helps us discover correlations within a project.

What Are Correlations? Why Do We Need to Analyze Them?

Let's assume that you were extremely lucky and found a map of treasures hidden on a remote island, similar to the map from Robert Louis Stevenson's classic novel *Treasure Island* (figure 14-1). You arrive at the site ready to dig. However, as you can probably guess, such maps can be highly cryptic: treasures can be in different locations. You can start from different places with different probabilities of finding treasure. The good news is that you have a few friends along with you so you can work on several sites at the same time. But remember that in addition to digging, you need to perform other related activities: deliver supplies, find local water and food sources, build a shelter, and so on. This causes other issues—such as where to store these additional resources? Which tasks are critical to achieving your final goal of finding the treasure and surviving? The answer is not trivial, because you have many uncertainties in your project schedule.

One of the problems that project managers and teams face is that human beings are not built to think about different things simultaneously. Project teams cannot deal with all the tasks and all the problems at the same time. Tasks that have the greatest impact on the project schedule and project deliverables obviously require the most attention. But activities that require the most attention often carry the greatest risk and may require significant

Figure 14-1. Stevenson's Map of Treasure Island (Credit: Robert Louis Stevenson)

mitigation efforts; we must identify them before the project starts. Essentially, we need to be able to analyze first the correlations between the main project parameters (duration, cost, finish time, and others) and then each task's parameters.

It is important to understand how correlations between different activities affect the project. You know, for example, that your supplier may be very busy. If your activity is delayed because the components did not arrive on time, other activities that use components from the same supplier can also be delayed. Similarly, there can be synergies between different projects. These correlations will significantly affect the course of each project.

So, when you plan your project, you should determine which project management activities and procedures would be most effective for that particular project. For example, for some teams a 10-minute meeting every morning to coordinate activities is very useful, but in others it can be an utter waste of time. In other words, you need to find a correlation between project management activities and project results. To do this, you need to:

1. Identify which activities have the greatest effect on the project so that you can set up your priorities.

2. Understand how various projects and activities within the project are correlated with each other, and analyze the effect of these correlations on the project.

3. Identify particular project management processes and procedures that address the effects of these correlations so that they can be adopted by your team or organization.

Sources of Correlations in Projects

How are different tasks in a project correlated? Schuyler (2016) describes three sources:

- **Common drivers.** Different project parameters may share a common influence. For example, changes in project scope will affect many tasks. If an issue arises with a resource, all tasks in which this resource is employed will be affected.

- **Common constraints.** If different project activities are competing for the same resources, these activities will be correlated. For example, if you have only one developer trained on a particular tool that is needed to complete several tasks, all of these tasks will be correlated to some degree.

- **Common causes.** The results of one activity will lead to changes in another activity. For example, a delay in a particular activity will cause several tasks that are linked to that activity to be delayed, as well.

Psychology of Correlation and Causation

Project managers usually believe that setting up priorities is a trivial task—one that they can accomplish quickly and without tools. But if it is so easy, why do so many projects start without any prioritization when failing to perform it results in missed deadlines, poor quality, and huge cost overruns? The answer lies, as it does in so many things, in human nature.

Here's an example. After several major delays in your recent projects, you decide to analyze how your subcontractor has affected project deadlines. As part of this investigation, you create table 14-1.

A quick glance at this table may lead you to believe that your subcontractor is a major source of your problems; the largest number of failures (eight) occurred when the subcontractor was involved in the project. But you may be misled by the higher numbers in the first row (with subcontractor) than the second row (without subcontractor). In reality the project success ratio (four failures versus one success) is the same, regardless of whether the subcontractor was involved or not. In psychology, this phenomenon is referred to as covariation

Table 14-1. Example of Covariation Assessment

	Project Deadline Missed	Project on Schedule
Subcontractor involved in project	8 times	2 time
Subcontractor not involved in project	4 times	1 time

Source: Adapted from Plous 1993.

assessment, or the analysis of whether two parameters are related to each other. If we use only a small data set, as in this example, it is easy to draw misleading conclusions. To understand the correlation between two parameters, you need to consider all the available information.

Another interesting observation is that people typically pay more attention to events that have negative effects than those that have positive effects, even though events with positive effects may yield as much information. For example, we pay more attention to events that caused a delay than to events that caused the project to be on time. A clear understanding of these positive events (opportunities) may be important for the planning of future projects (Nisbett and Ross 1980).

Sometimes a small number of samples can skew our judgment about correlations. This situation is very common in project management because the total number of projects performed by the same organization is usually limited. In addition, the personnel involved tend to forget what happened in previous projects; the farther back in the past they occurred, the more likely they will be overlooked, even if they are more relevant to the current project. For example, if you had problems with a supplier twice in the past three projects, this does not mean that you need to switch to another supplier. The information you have may not be enough to analyze this correlation. First, you need to understand the underlying reason for the problems. It might lie with the supplier, or perhaps your organization's procurement system has been tardy in sending out its purchase orders, causing late delivery of supplies.

Sometimes people tend to find correlations where they do not exist. Psychologists refer to this phenomenon as *illusory correlations* (Chapman and Chapman 1971). For example, match these two events: a programmer is always late for work, and sales of the software she is working on are not doing well. Is there any correlation between the two? Most likely not. However, if the manager focuses a lot of attention on team discipline and sales numbers, he will expect the two numbers to be related and will perceive that the slow sales are due to the programmer's inattentiveness.

The opposite phenomenon is *invisible correlations*—ones that go unnoticed because people do not expect them. For example, team members have been complaining to senior management about a certain project manager's lack of "people skills." The effect of this lack of people skills is unclear; some of the projects managed by this individual have problems, but some do not. In addition, the project manager in question has worked in the organization for a long time and is viewed by senior management as a valuable contributor to the business.

Is there a relationship between the manager's perceived inability to work with people and problems with projects? Perhaps, but because not all of the project manager's projects have problems and since the project manager has a high status in the organization, this correlation may become invisible. Because senior management has not expected to find a correlation between the project manager's people skills and poor results, it has not found it. Unfortunately, invisible correlations often go on to cause even larger problems. In this case, the effects of the project manager's poor people skills are cumulative and, over time, the project team's effectiveness may diminish as members leave for other teams or go to other organizations in search of a less stressful environment.

If a correlation is found between two variables, that does not mean that one variable has caused another one. In other words, correlation does *not* equal causation. Remember, a common cause is only one possible source of correlation. Every day, we are bombarded with all sorts of dubious claims of causation. The media constantly announce research findings that show the health benefit of various types of foods: "eat this and you will live 20% longer," or "fail to include this in your diet and expect to die 20% sooner" (which, by the way, is often the same product). Although for some groups of products these claims may be true, in many cases other factors, which can have a positive or a negative effect on our health, are not taken into account. For example, research into the health benefits of red wine may not include an analysis of situations when people do not drink wine because they are already sick.

Similar situations occur in project management. We may think our project succeeded because we created and managed a risk list. But the correlation between a project's success and the presence of a risk list is not enough to make a judgment that the risk list caused the positive result.

The "causation" illusion is often used by people who are trying to sell you something. Salespeople want you to believe that their technology or services are actually the cause of successful projects. On their resumes, project management consultants might claim that 23 projects they worked on, with an overall budget of $3 billon, succeeded because of their involvement. That may be true, but these projects may have succeeded without the consultants. It is difficult to prove or disprove such a connection. As you can see, many biases are related to correlations and causation. Is there any way we can overcome these mental pitfalls?

How to Improve Your Judgment

From what you have just read thus far in this chapter, it must be obvious that gaining a proper understanding of correlations is far from easy. People have great difficulty judging project correlations. Let's suppose you have just implemented a new software tool and you must decide whether it is important to provide formal training for your team or you can count on them to learn it themselves as they go. Basically, you want to determine the correlation between training and project success rates. Training could delay the project by a few weeks, but without training the project may fail completely. So, it is important to take the time to research this issue.

Jennifer Crocker has proposed a six-step process for performing this analysis (Crocker 1982):

1. **Decide what information is relevant.** At this stage you need to discover which data should be used for the analysis. Do you have enough data within the organization? What will happen with the project if training is not provided? Do the people who will provide the training have the requisite experience and education?

2. **Get samples or observations (randomly, if possible) that are related to your problem.** This is the data-collection step. You need to collect as much data as you can from all previous training sessions and then see how it affected project results. At this stage you fill your table with data.

3. **Interpret and classify these observations.** Should data be placed in separate categories: long and short training, training for recent grads, training for experienced engineers? What counts as a project success? Are there categories of project success? At this stage you design a table similar to table 14-1.

4. **Estimate frequencies** of how often a positive correlation occurred or did not occur. At this stage, you fill out the table.

5. **Integrate your estimates to come up with a measure that can be used to make a judgment.** For example, you can come up with some rough averages. With training there is a 60% chance that the project will be on budget. Without training there is a 30% chance that it will be on budget.

6. **Use the integrated estimate** to make a judgment.

As you can see, this is a complex mental process that cannot be done intuitively. Unfortunately, wrong judgments related to correlation and causation are extremely common, even with plenty of training. Because this is such a complex process, can anyone perform this type of analysis? The answer is definitely "yes," but only if the following conditions are met:

- Reliable data is available.
- The problem is serious enough to justify spending scarce resources on the analysis. If you performed an advanced analysis on everything, you would never start a project. The project would paradoxically end up being the analysis of how to do the project.

Fortunately, there are a number of tools that you can use to improve your judgment.

Sensitivity Analysis

The sensitivity analysis technique determines how sensitive the results of your analysis are to uncertainties in input variables. If you have a valuation model related to your project, you can determine which parameters in the model have the most potential to affect your project. Simply change one parameter, for example a task duration, while keeping all the other parameters the same, and see how this change affects your results. Those input parameters that cause the largest fluctuations in the results will be most important.

> Sensitivity analysis determines how sensitive the results of the analysis are to uncertainties in input variables.

For example, you have a model that calculates revenue based on unit price, cost of fuel, and cost of labor. For these three parameters, you have three estimates: low, base, and high. To start, calculate your revenue using the base values of all the parameters. In this trial, revenue equals $400,000. Then recalculate the revenue multiple times by changing one parameter—for example, unit price—and keep the other parameters constant. When we use the low unit price, revenue is $200,000; with the high unit price, revenue is $640,000.

These results can be displayed on a diagram (see figure 14-2). The ranges of revenue are displayed as a bar associated with each parameter. Parameters are sorted in such a way that parameters with a higher range of revenue will be displayed on top. This diagram looks like a tornado and is therefore called a tornado diagram.

The same results can be presented in another format, such as that in figure 14-3. Logically, because it can resemble a spider web, it is called a spider diagram. One problem with tornado diagrams is that it is difficult to visualize how an increase in one parameter affects another. Spider diagrams address this issue. If you calculate results with a low, a high, and an additional intermediate estimate, it is possible to grasp the nonlinear relationship between inputs and outputs. In our example, the relationship between the cost of fuel and

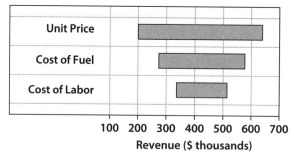

Figure 14-2. Tornado Diagram

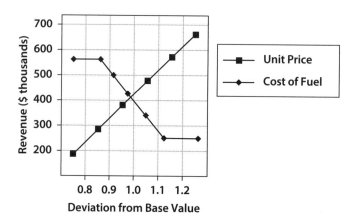

Figure 14-3. Spider Diagram

revenue is nonlinear, because an increase in fuel costs above a certain level does not lead to further reduction in revenue.

Using sensitivity analysis, it is possible to determine which parameters are the most important. They are the upper bars of a tornado diagram as well as the line with the steepest slope on a spider diagram.

This type of sensitivity analysis is widely used in economic evaluations, where a quantitative economic model of the project has been created. Because these models can be very complex, tornado and spider diagrams have proven to be very useful tools.

Please note one key fact about this type of sensitivity analysis: as with any quantitative analysis, the results of sensitivity analysis are "only as good as the model." If the model does not take into account an important parameter, you will not be able to see it in a tornado or a spider diagram.

How do you develop low, base, and high estimates for input variables? Why, for example, did you select low and high cost estimates as 80% and 120% of the base value? In theory, these estimates should come from an analysis of the underlying nature of the parameter. But in reality, people usually do not bother to learn about the nature of the variable, or the data is simply not available. To get their low and high estimates, they just multiply their base estimate by 0.8 and 1.2, respectively. This is a classic case of anchoring, which almost always leads to misleading results.

Sensitivity analysis is one of the quantitative risk analysis techniques recommended in chapter 11 of the *PMBOK Guide*.

Quantitative Analysis of Correlations

Suppose that you spent a great deal of time and effort collecting data on how the average experience of team members is related to their hourly pay rate, the cost of materials, and the total cost of the project. These results can be presented in a scatter diagram (see three types in figure 14-4).

Each point on these diagrams represents an actual data sample. Here is what we discover:

1. In most cases you have to pay more (a higher hourly rate) for more experienced team members. There is a positive correlation between the two variables.

2. Cost of materials has no correlation with team member experience.

3. Overall project costs may be reduced with more experienced team members. This is a negative correlation. By the way, this is also a classic example of an invisible correlation in project management. Managers know that experienced workers will cost more, but they don't want to admit that a more experienced team will most likely lower overall project costs because they tend to focus on a short-term goal (reduced monthly payroll) rather than long-term results.

It is possible to use a number, referred to as the correlation coefficient, to define these correlations. The coefficient for a strong positive correlation (higher

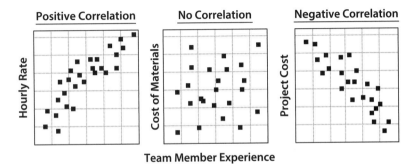

Figure 14-4. Scatter Diagrams Showing Different Types of Correlation

values of one parameter are always associated with higher values of another parameter) is 1. The coefficient for strong negative correlation is −1. If there is no correlation, the coefficient is 0. Many statistical formulas can be used to calculate the correlation coefficient, among which is the Spearman rank order. You can find the actual formula for these correlations in statistics textbooks. It should be noted that these formulas enable you to calculate correlation coefficients for various types of data, such as experience and cost in our example. Experience would be defined in years and cost in dollars.

Once you know how to calculate correlations between two different sets of data, you can answer the two main questions: What is most important, and How are different project variables related to each other?

Crucial Tasks

Tasks that can have the most effect on your project parameters (duration, cost, success rates, and so on) are obviously called crucial tasks. They rep-

> Uncertainties associated with crucial tasks should be analyzed first.

resent a positive correlation between the task parameters and project parameters. Because crucial tasks are so important, uncertainties associated with them should be analyzed first.

To explain the correlation between crucial tasks and project duration, we use the spring analogy (figure 14-5). Let's assume that each task within a Gantt chart is one spring within a big system of springs. When we start moving springs back and forth, we find that some of them significantly affect the movement of the full spring system, while others do not. The amount of movement depends on how the springs are connected to each other (links between tasks) and how flexible they are (the types of risks and uncertainties assigned to them).

Here are a few questions commonly asked about crucial tasks:

Question: How do you determine crucial tasks?
Answer: Crucial tasks are by-products of Monte Carlo simulations (which we will discuss at some length in chapter 16). A Monte Carlo simulation produces an array of project durations, cost, success rates, and other parameters. You will also have an array of task durations, costs, and other parameters as a result of sampling. If you input these arrays into a correlation coefficient formula, it will return a correlation coefficient. Those tasks with the highest coefficients are the crucial tasks. (If you are *really* ambitious, you can do the input manually, but it is better to use one of the many applications on the market that can do it for you.)

Question: What is the relationship between crucial tasks and critical tasks?
Answer: Critical tasks lie on the critical path. Crucial tasks do not necessarily lie on the critical path. They are called crucial to distinguish them from tasks that have been identified using the critical path method.

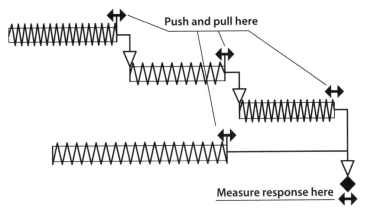

Figure 14-5. Spring Analogy for Crucial Tasks

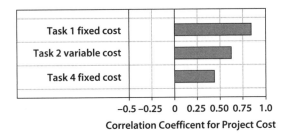

Figure 14-6. Sensitivity Chart

Question: Can a task be crucial based on cost sensitivity and not crucial based on duration?

Answer: Yes. This is a fairly common phenomenon that depends on the combination of two factors: uncertainties in cost and duration associated with the task, and the task's position in the project schedule.

The results of your analysis can also be shown using a sensitivity chart (figure 14-6). Input parameters are sorted in such a way that variables with higher correlation coefficients will be shown on the top of the chart (similar to a tornado diagram). In our example, uncertainties in the fixed costs of task 1 could have the greatest effect on the project's success. Therefore, task 1 should be the first candidate for analysis and risk mitigation.

Correlations between Tasks

Now we have analyzed correlations between project inputs and outputs or the main project parameters. This allowed us to determine which parameters are the most important to the project. But we also need to analyze how correlations between different task parameters can affect the project schedule.

We have discussed how to calculate the correlation coefficient between two data arrays. We can also perform an opposite operation where we predefine correlation coefficients (from −1 to 1) for certain variables and then perform a Monte Carlo simulation. The mathematics of the analysis is quite complex, but again, leave it to the software. The result of this analysis will illustrate what might happen to a project if a correlation exists between certain task parameters. For example, say we have two activities that involve the same subcontractor. If one activity is delayed because of the subcontractor, there is a 90% chance that another activity will be delayed, as well. When you run the Monte Carlo simulation, assign a correlation coefficient of 0.9 for the duration of these tasks, to calculate the effect of this correlation.

We strongly recommend that you employ correlation tools when you use Monte Carlo simulations to analyze projects. Without this analysis, it is impossible to tell how correlations could affect the project schedule.

- You must identify and address the important issues first. Many projects have problems because project managers are unable to identify the most important issues.
- Different project parameters can be correlated with each other. These correlations can significantly affect a project schedule. Sources of these correlations are common drivers, common constraints, and common causes.
- Sensitivity analysis is a quantitative method that helps identify which project input parameters are the most important.
- You can make a more accurate probabilistic analysis of your project schedule if you define correlations between different input variables.

CHAPTER 15

Decision Trees and the Value of New Information

A decision tree is a graph that represents a decision problem. It can be easily generated from a project schedule. Decision trees are used to calculate the expected value or expected utility of an alternative and, as a result, they allow you to make a rational choice. Value-of-information analysis is a process that helps determine the price someone should pay to determine the actual value of an uncertainty.

What Is a Decision Tree?

Burglars usually lack good judgment, let alone any expertise in decision analysis. Case in point: Harry and Marv, the two would-be burglars in the movie *Home Alone* (1990). Based on how they selected their targets, it would be safe to say that neither has a degree in decision analysis from Stanford or Duke (see figure 15-1). What kind of decision process would lead them to choose to rob a home in the Chicago suburbs when it was occupied—granted, by a young boy—if they could break into an unoccupied home nearby? It may be that they constructed a simple decision tree (figure 15-2) to help them select which home they should consider for their burglary project. (In chapter 4, if you recall, we briefly mentioned decision trees when we discussed the concept of the expected value of projects.)

Perhaps Harry and Marv used this process to develop their decision tree:

1. They identified the decision they wanted to make: choose which home they would break into.

2. They identified the criteria for the selection: Harry and Marv wanted the home to be as "loaded" as possible.

Let's assume that three houses (1, 2, and 3 in figure 15-2) in the neighborhood met their criteria. Due to some prior "casing" of the homes, Harry and Marv knew approximately how much loot they could steal from each: House 1 = $20,000, House 2 = $10,000, and House 3 = $8,000.

Figure 15-1. Applying Decision Analysis to Make a Better Choice

3. Using this information, Harry and Marv started to construct a decision tree. First, they drew a decision node (rectangle) associated with their strategic decision—which home they would rob. From this node, they drew three branches, one for each alternative.

4. Then the two would-be robbers brainstormed to come up with the risks and uncertainties associated with each of the three homes. As it turned out, they did not anticipate any risks or uncertainties that were unique to either home 2 or home 3: the tasks were to pick the lock, locate the valuables, and grab the loot. Nice and easy work! However, they discovered that in home 1, which contained a larger amount of valuables, there was a possibility that a little boy was inside—definitely an uncertainty. So, Harry and Marv drew a circle representing an *uncertainty or chance node* on the decision tree. They estimated the chance that a boy was inside at 80%.

5. Even if the house were inhabited, they could still rob it. Harry and Marv believed that if the boy were present, he would be too frightened to stop them. So, they drew another circle with two branches representing the chances that the boy would be either scared or not scared.

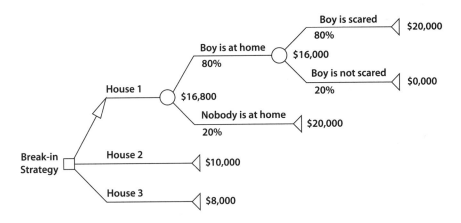

Figure 15-2. Analysis of Break-In Strategy Using a Decision Tree

6. They closed each branch with a triangular *end node*. Harry and Marv attached a value to each end node. If the boy was home and not scared, the value would be zero, for it would be difficult to get anything out of the home without the boy's raising an alarm. For the other end nodes—"boy is home and scared," "boy is not home," "house 2," and "house 3"—the values would be the estimated amount of loot in the home.

7. Now that they had set up their decision tree, it was time to calculate. They started calculating values from right to left. For each uncertainty node, Harry and Marv needed to calculate an *expected value*. The expected value for the "boy is at home" branch equals: (boy is scared) + (boy is not scared). Mathematically, it looks like this: ($20,000 × 0.8) + ($0,000 × 0.2) = $16,000. As we calculate to the left, we can see that the expected value for house 1 equals: (boy is home) + (boy is not home), or $16,000 × 0.8 + $20,000 × 0.2 = $16,800.

8. Using expected value as their criterion, the decision for Harry and Marv is now easy to see. House 1 has the highest expected value, even when taking into account the uncertainty associated with the possibility of the boy's being in the house.

Here are a few further thoughts regarding the quality of Harry and Marv's decision tree:

- Sometimes a number of decisions that rely on each another can be made up front. In this case, decision nodes are not confined to the beginning (on the left) of the tree, but they can be placed throughout the decision tree wherever a decision must be made. For example, Harry and Marv might have wanted to see the effect that scaring the boy out of the house would have on the expected value.

- You can incorporate risk profiles by applying a utility function to the decision tree analysis (discussed in chapter 4). Apparently, Harry and Marv, like most criminals, are risk-takers, and this risk profile could affect their choices.

- In most situations, the value associated with the end node can be calculated by using a valuation model. For example, Harry and Marv's valuation model could include a number of parameters: house type, habitation status, and so on. It would be possible to set these parameters, and the valuation model would return a value for each node.

- As we mentioned in chapter 12, influence diagrams can be used to construct a decision tree representing the same problem.

Why Project Managers Avoid Decision Trees (and Why They Shouldn't)

It is not only burglars who use decision trees; many honest people use them, as well. Trial lawyers (we'll call them honest for the sake of our argument) routinely use decision trees when they try to determine their strategies—to sue or not to sue (with apologies to Shakespeare). If they sue, should they accept an out-of-court settlement or go to trial? If they go to trial, what is the chance that they will win? If they win, what is the chance that the other side will appeal? This analysis depends on the potential payout at each step and can make for a very complex decision tree.

Honest people can make other choices with a decision tree: Which product that they are developing has the greatest chance of success, given unknown market uncertainties? What movie should the studio produce, given the wide range of ideas and scripts on which they have options? Which mineral deposits should a company explore and develop first? Many companies use decision trees to make their strategic decisions. How can organizations use them for project management?

The *PMBOK Guide* recommends using decision trees as one of your quantitative risk tools for analyzing different project alternatives. Chapter 11 of the *Guide* includes an example of a simple decision tree, plus explanations for calculating a project's expected value. Although a great deal of information about decision trees is available, the actual use of this tool in project management remains limited. We think there are a number of reasons:

- If a project is relatively small, most project managers believe that they can make a choice intuitively and don't need to use a sophisticated analysis tools like a decision tree. In these cases, project managers have made an assumption that is not necessarily true—that the size of a project and the number of potential choices in it are positively related. In reality, a small project may have many alternatives that require a sophisticated analysis.

- If a project is large and complex, like the construction of a highway, project managers prefer to delegate the decision analysis to a business analyst in the strategic planning department, or to hire a consultant.

It is important to remember that as soon as you have to make a decision that depends upon other decisions, it is *not* trivial, and that a purely intuitive solution may lead to mistakes. In these cases, decision trees will help you to make the right decision.

Here is another observation related to the use of decision trees in organizations: as with all quantitative methods in project decision analysis, decision trees rely on the valuation model of the project. In most cases, project managers do not create a valuation model specifically for a decision tree analysis; they already have too many other issues to worry about. But if they already have this model, which in many cases is the project schedule, it is easy to convert the model into a decision tree using available software tools (see appendix A). With this in mind, project managers should not have any reasons—excuses, maybe—*not* to use decision tree analysis for small and medium-sized projects, since the process provides a great deal of value for a little additional effort. Let's see how this conversion works.

Converting Project Schedules into Decision Trees

Let's assume that your project schedule includes several alternatives (figure 15-3). If one project scenario depends on another scenario, the number of potential alternatives can be substantial. It is always easier to use one project schedule for multiple alternatives than to create separate schedules. Value measures for a project schedule can be cost or duration.

Here is how the conversion from a project schedule to a decision tree works:

First, create a project schedule that contains alternative scenarios. These can be represented by different parallel paths through the schedule. Different paths of a project schedule are the result of branching when a predecessor activity has more than one successor activity.

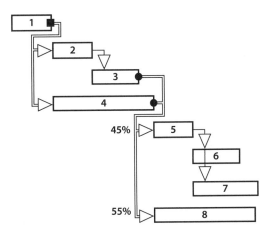

Figure 15-3. Project Schedule to Be Converted to a Decision Tree

There are two types of paths:

1. Some activities are performed in parallel. (In our *Home Alone* scenario, Harry is looking for cash in the bedroom, while Marv is collecting electronics from the family room.)

2. Different scenarios apply. (Either both Harry and Marv start with family room, or they go to separate bedrooms.)

To distinguish between these two types of paths, they need to be visualized differently on a Gantt chart. We recommend using double lines and horizontal arrows for alternative paths versus single lines, and also vertical arrows for parallel activities. In our example, a double line connects task 1 with task 2 and task 4. This represents that tasks 2 and 4, with all their successors, are alternative scenarios.

Activities can have alternative successors, for two reasons:

1. A decision must be made. The solid square at the end of the predecessor indicates that a decision is being made (see task 1 in figure 15-3).

2. The activity has uncertainties associated with it. The solid circle at the end of an activity indicates that there is an uncertainty (see tasks 3 and 4) and the need to specify a probability associated with each branch (in our example, we have assigned probabilities of 45% and 55% for the branches after tasks 3 and 4).

After you have entered all the information to construct a decision tree, perform separate network calculations (a forward path in the critical path method) for each alternative. The end nodes of the decision tree represent the cost or duration of each alternative; branches represent tasks or group of tasks.

In practice, of course, project schedules can be large and complex. To prevent the decision tree from becoming too large and unmanageable, a schedule consolidation algorithm can be applied. With this algorithm, the cost and duration of all activities between the decision and uncertainties nodes are calculated separately and represented as one branch of the tree.

Figure 15-4 shows the results of converting a schedule to a decision tree. Even if you don't go as far as converting your schedule to a decision tree, this approach can be beneficial since it enables you to visualize decisions and uncertainties on any Gantt chart. This provides a useful tool for discussing various project scenarios and the probabilities that they will occur.

The Value of Perfect Information

Here is an anecdotal story that we came across:

At a chemical plant, a huge reactor had broken down, and nobody knew the exact reason for the failure. To understand what went wrong, management had

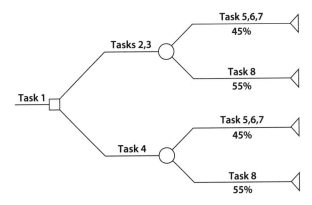

Figure 15-4. Results of a Schedule-to-Decision Tree Conversion

two choices: disassemble a major section of the reactor, or examine many little sections of the reactor one at a time. In either scenario, it would cost millions of dollars, because of the lengthy downtime. So, before starting the investigation, the project management team invited a guru (translation: a consultant), hoping that he could pinpoint the cause of the breakdown faster.

The guru walked around the reactor a couple of times and soon became interested in a particular section of it. He pulled out a small hammer, tapped lightly on the reactor, and listened intently. After a few more minutes of tapping and listening, the guru turned around and said, "Cut a small opening here and replace the pipe." A supervisor quickly put some workers on the task, although he was skeptical and thought the whole process a bit odd. (But remember the first rule: never question a guru!) Much to the astonishment of the supervisor and the rest of the management team, this almost miraculous fix had the reactor up and running at full capacity the very same day. The plant manager was extremely happy. "What is this going to cost me?" he asked the guru. "One million dollars," the guru replied.

The manager protested: "One million dollars for hitting the reactor with small hammer?" "No, hitting the reactor only costs you one dollar. The other $999,999 is for saving you at least triple the amount that you would have spent if you had gone ahead with your original plans," answered the guru.

The guru had calculated the value of the information he provided, which was the amount of money that was saved through his investigation. His concept of the value of information is extremely important in project management, especially when answering questions such as these:

- Should you spend the time and money to create a prototype of a new device?

- Should you perform additional testing of a software or hardware component to ensure its reliability?

- Should you buy new software to perform a more detailed analysis?

- Should you hire a consultant to solve a complex problem?

Here is how the value of information is calculated. Harry and Marv want to break into a house, but do not know exactly how much money is inside. It can be a "loaded home" worth $20,000 (80% probability) or worth nothing (20% probability). For the other houses, Harry and Marv already know with 100% certainty that they would take $10,000 from house 2.

Recognizing the uncertainty around the target home, Harry and Marv decided to get additional information. If you saw *Home Alone* (spoiler alert!), you will remember that Harry visited the homes before Christmas, dressed as a police officer. But before he did this, they needed to estimate whether it made sense to get this information. First, Harry needed to procure a police uniform; in addition, visiting the homes impersonating a police officer could increase the chance that they would be discovered. So, Harry and Marv constructed the decision tree shown in figure 15-5. They had three alternatives:

1. Break into house 1. Expected value will be $0,000 × 0.2 + $20,000 × 0.8 = $16,000.

2. Break into house 2. They know for sure that they can get $10,000.

3. Get additional information about house 1.

If Harry goes to house 1 and acquires the additional information, he may find that the probabilities are 80% "loaded" and 20% nothing. If the first house has nothing, it would be wise to break into the second house instead and get a

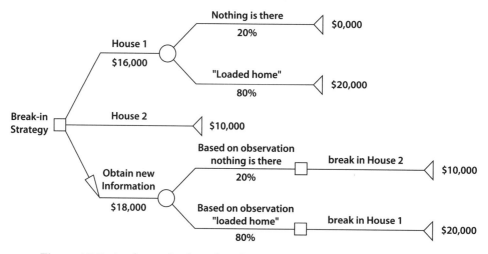

Figure 15-5. Analysis of Value of Perfect Information for Break-In Strategy

certain $10,000. If the first house is loaded, they should rob that house. This logic is represented by the third branch, "Obtain new information." The expected value of this alternative is $10,000 × 0.2 + $20,000 × 0.8 = $18,000, or $2,000 more than the first alternative ($16,000). As a result, the expected value of information is $18,000—$16,000 = $2,000. Now Harry can use this number to decide whether the risks of procuring (buying or stealing) a police uniform and visiting the houses is worth the additional $2,000 in potential benefit.

The Value of Imperfect Information

This value-of-information analysis has one significant stipulation: Harry and Marv assume that the information Harry received is perfect. In other words, the burglars assume that Harry's observations are absolutely reliable. In reality, his assessments will not be absolutely accurate. There will be some things he could not see, and others that he will have difficulty evaluating. In other words, there is a probability that Harry's assessment is inaccurate.

> The value of new imperfect information can be analyzed using the Bayes theorem, which is a formula that revises probabilities based on new information.

Decision theory offers methods to incorporate imperfect information into the analysis and calculate an expected value for it. If the probability of event A is conditional on event B, it is generally different from the probability of event B when it is conditional on event A. The Bayes theorem, which we discussed in chapter 1, actually defines this relationship. The Bayes theorem is a formula that revises probabilities, based on new information.

You should be skeptical if an expert or consultant tells you that the Bayes theorem is a straightforward concept. The formula itself is really quite simple; however, the explanation and actual application of the formula have been known to cause some confusion. Therefore, we have not included the formula in this book. You may find the actual formula in most of the books on decision analysis mentioned in the Future Reading section. If you want to calculate the value of imperfect information for your project, you can find software tools that will do this for you in appendix A.

- Decision trees are tools that help to analyze and select various project alternatives.
- Decision trees can be easily generated by using a project schedule. You can create diagrams representing the project schedule to visualize alternative scenarios, along with their probabilities.
- The value of information determines whether additional information, such as tests, prototypes, and more detailed modeling techniques, can save more than was spent on acquiring that information.

CHAPTER 16

What Is Project Risk?
Monte Carlo Method

One of the fundamental questions of project management is "What will the duration and cost of the project be, given the multiple risks and uncertainties?" Monte Carlo analysis can help to answer these and other questions. This form of analysis is a straightforward approach for dealing with complex sets of project uncertainties. However, Monte Carlo analyses have a number of limitations that are related to how we identify and interpret uncertainties.

How Much Will It Really Cost?

East Side Access is a project under construction in New York, which will extend the Long Island Rail Road (LIRR) from its Main Line in Queens (figure 16-1) into a new station under Grand Central Terminal on Manhattan's East Side. The new station and tunnels are scheduled to start service in December 2022. It is an enormous and expensive project. For example, the new terminal will contain eight tracks and four platforms. The two-level station will be 100 feet below street level and the original cost estimate of $3.5 billion had grown to $11.1 billion by April 2018. In fact, East Side Access is one of the world's most expensive underground rail-construction projects. With a length of only 3.5 miles, East Side Access has earned the dubious honor of being the most expensive subway track per mile on Earth.

The cost overruns have surged, for numerous reasons. The New York Times found that for years public officials in New York City have stood by a small group of politically connected labor unions, while the associated construction companies and consulting firms have amassed huge profits (Rosental 2017). For example, the original budget showed that some 900 workers were being paid to dig caverns for the platforms. But the project accountants could only identify about 700 jobs that needed to be done. Officials could find no reason for the other 200 people to be onsite getting a paycheck. As a result, in New York, underground construction employs approximately four times the number of workers as in similar projects in Asia or Europe. Another reason for cost overruns is that contractors in New York add between 15% and 25% contingency because of how hard it can be to work

Figure 16-1. Starting Point for the Four Tunnels of East Side Access in Queens
(Photo by Metropolitan Transportation Authority/Patrick Cashin)

with the bureaucracy of the transit authority, the owner of the project. Normal contingency factors in the industry are about 10%. The lack of the completion is also a major problem, leading to cost overruns.

When cost overruns and delays of these proportions occur, two questions need to be asked:

1. Why did it happen?

2. What do we do next?

Nothing is certain in our world, of course, and this especially includes project durations, finish times, costs, and other parameters. Therefore, it was never possible at the beginning to say that the East Side Access construction would cost exactly $11.1 billion. Remember that originally it was estimated to be three times less. What we *could* say was that there was a chance that the project would end up costing $12 billion, given all issues related to this project. By knowing the actual range of possible final costs, it would be possible to focus on mitigating factors that lead to cost overrun.

> The chance that the project will be completed on time and within budget is one of the most important indicators for decision-making.

If we say that there is a 90% chance that the project will cost $12 billion or less, we imply that we are very confident that the project will be completed within that budget. If the chance is 20%, we are saying that we do not have a lot of confidence in the estimate and that we need to either review the project scope and resources, or accept potential cost overruns. By quantifying the chance for each project scenario, you can review various project alternatives and choose the one that has the highest chance of successful completion.

So, we need to find the answers to two very important questions, which will help us make our decision:

1. How much would the project cost and how long would it take, given all the risks and uncertainties associated with it?

2. What is the chance that the project will be completed on time and within budget?

If we know the risks and uncertainties associated with activities within a project, we can perform calculations to find an answer to these questions. The simplest way to calculate the effect of risks and uncertainties is to create many schedules of the same project with combinations of input parameters: risks, different estimates of an activity's cost and duration, resources, and so on. We can then analyze all these scenarios together to find the answer to these questions. This method is called *scenario analysis*, a simple and straightforward approach that you can use without any sophisticated tools. It works very well for simple projects or for a particular phase of a project. The *PMBOK Guide* recommends "what-if" scenario analysis as one of the preferred methods for using schedule network analysis technique.

The problem with this approach is that accurately representing the combinations of risks and uncertainties that will crop up in most projects will produce an unmanageably large number of scenarios. Each project has a large number of tasks and resources, and each task and resource can have different risks and uncertainties. To further complicate the analysis, these risks can occur at different times, and we need to find the cumulative impact of these risks on the project. A number of quantitative methods can help overcome this problem.

PERT

Often, major technological advances are by-products of military research. Between 1956 and 1958, for example, the consulting firm Booz Allen Hamilton assisted the US Navy's Special Project Office with the development of the Polaris Fleet Ballistic Missile program. This project was one of the largest and riskiest research and development efforts the US military had ever undertaken. Managers wanted estimates of the probabilities of meeting important milestones, such as test launching a missile on a particular date. A by-product of this project was the Program Evaluation and Review Technique, or PERT. Developed 50 years ago, PERT is still well-known today, although applications are limited. Here is how it works:

The expected duration (t) of the activity, or mean, is calculated using the following formula:

$$t = \frac{(\text{optimistic duration} + \text{most likely duration} \times 4 + \text{pessimistic duration})}{6}$$

This formula enables managers to use expected durations to create project schedules. But why not just create an optimistic or pessimistic schedule using these durations? Let's look at a simple example that will help to explain why PERT uses expected durations instead of optimistic or pessimistic durations separately.

You are engaged in a construction project that requires the installation of 10 prefabricated columns. The installation of one column takes between two and four hours, and the columns are installed one after another. If there is a problem with the installation of one column, it does not mean that there will be a problem with the other columns. If one column can take four hours, is it rational to determine that the pessimistic duration for installing all the columns will be 4 hours × 10 columns = 40 hours? Not really. This would be an extremely pessimistic duration, which could happen only if installation of all columns experienced the same problem, which is highly unlikely.

This example illustrates one of the biases associated with the anchoring and adjustment heuristics. People tend to significantly overestimate or underestimate the probability of conjunctive events, where two conditions must exist. The four-hour duration in this example is an anchor that can lead to an incorrect judgment.

As we can see, if we use optimistic (or pessimistic) task durations to create optimistic (or pessimistic) schedules, frequently we will get misleading results. Therefore, the development of PERT, by using the expected-duration approach, was a major step toward the incorporation of uncertainties in project management.

More important, PERT also included simple formulas and methods to calculate the probability of meeting specific milestones and therefore was easy for project managers and teams to use without any arduous training.

Despite all the elegance of PERT, it has a number of problems:

- PERT gives accurate results only if there is a single dominant path through a precedence network. When a single path is not dominant, classic PERT usually provides overly optimistic results.

- According to PERT, uncertainties associated with tasks are independent of each other, which is not true in many cases.

- When we are trying to estimate the most optimistic, the most pessimistic, and the most likely duration of a task, we will be affected by the anchoring heuristic. The most likely duration will become an unwanted anchor, which will skew our ability to accurately estimate task or project durations (see chapter 13).

To address these and other challenges, additional analytical approaches have been developed. But before we can discuss them, we need to give a quick overview of some basic concepts that are used with these methods.

Statistical Distributions

Many people have difficulty when reading maps. Maps are an abstraction of the real world, and these individuals are unable to mesh the abstract (map) with the concrete (the actual landscape) and then place themselves in it. A similar situation can occur with statistical distributions. Many project managers are familiar with the concept of statistical distributions, perhaps from having taken a basic course on probability and statistics, yet they are unable to tell anyone (including themselves) how it actually works or its practical application. If you find yourself in this group, here is a quick primer.

Let's assume that you are trying to analyze the duration of the activity "install kitchen sink." Depending on the type of sink, configuration of pipes, and other factors, it can take varying lengths of time. If you've already installed 20 sinks and recorded the duration each time, you can develop a record of the task durations, such as that in table 16-1.

You can actually represent this information as a chart, with duration on the horizontal axis and frequency on the vertical axis. The chart, called a *frequency histogram*, can also display the probability for certain durations (see figure 16-2).

A *statistical distribution* is an arrangement of values showing their frequency of occurrence. You may redraw this chart in another format. For each point of the chart, you can add up all frequencies (probabilities) associated with all points on the left of the selected point. This is how we calculate cumulative probability, and the chart is called a *cumulative probability plot*. These manipulations allow us to determine the probability associated with a certain value.

Table 16-1. Activity Duration on Different Trials

Duration of the activity "install kitchen sink"	Occurrences	Probability: Number of occurrences divided by total number of installations (20)
Between 0 and 0.5 hour	2	$2 \div 20 = 0.1$ (10%)
Between 0.5 and 1 hour	10	50%
Between 1 hour and 1.5 hours	5	25%
Between 1.5 and 2 hours	3	15%

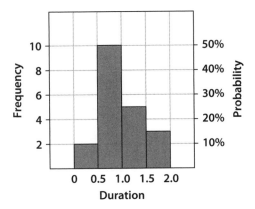

Figure 16-2. Frequency Histogram

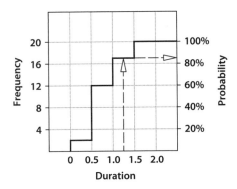

Figure 16-3. Cumulative Probability Plot

For example, what is the probability that the duration will be 1.2 hours? Look at figure 16-3. To find the probability, locate the duration 1.2 hours on the horizontal axis and draw a line up to the solid line. Then draw a straight line to the right to find the probability, which in this example equals 85%. Unfortunately, cumulative probability plots can be confusing. They do not help us understand the interval for the parameter in question (in this case, task duration). It is only useful if we draw lines and get a probability, as shown in figure 16-3.

If you have an empirical data set, you can create an irregular or spiked distribution curve, and you may then want to make this distribution smoother by using one of the continuous distributions. Continuous distributions are defined by different mathematical formulas. A continuous distribution is usually a better reflection of the nature of the real-life data, because it has a continuum of possible outcomes. While there is a large list of different continuous distributions, only a few of them are used in project management (figure 16-4).

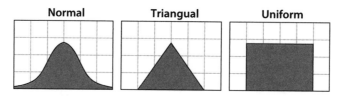

Figure 16-4. Different Continuous Statistical Distributions

Among them are:

- **Uniform.** There is an equal probability that the parameter will be within a certain range.

- **Triangular.** The parameter is estimated using minimum, maximum, and most likely estimates. Minimum and maximum are not optimistic and pessimistic estimates; they are extremes.

- **Normal.** This is a symmetrical distribution that occurs very often in business and in nature. But be aware that this distribution is unbounded, which means that it spreads to infinity from both ends; in project management analysis, it needs to be used with some type of cutoff to remove the infinities.

- **Lognormal.** This is a positively skewed (non-symmetrical) distribution, meaning that it has a longer tail to the right.

- **Beta.** This is a bounded distribution, which uses a mathematical formula that includes two coefficients. By changing these coefficients, beta distribution can take a variety of shapes; it can be symmetrical or non-symmetrical. The PERT formula was derived using a beta distribution.

In addition to distributions that are defined by recognizable mathematical formulas, most software tools will allow you to create your own custom distributions. All that is required is data, which in this case is the frequency of occurrence for a certain value. For example, you can enter the distribution shown on figure 16-2 and use it for further analysis. Moreover, if you have empirical data, you can find known statistical distributions that can fit to this data. Numerous software tools will help you to choose the best fit among different types of distributions for your data.

When most people think about statistical distributions, the first thing that comes to mind is an image of a chart. But remember that statistical distributions are really only an arrangement of values, and many parameters can be used to analyze the distribution. The most important parameters are:

- **Mean**—a mathematical average, calculated as the sum of variable values for all the trials divided by the number of trials.

- **Standard Deviation**—a measure of how widely dispersed the values are in a distribution. The greater the standard deviation, the more uncertainty is associated with the parameter.

- **Percentile**—a value on a scale of 0 to 100 that indicates the percentage of a distribution that is equal to or below this value. A value in the 95th percentile (sometimes defined as P95) is a value equal to or better than 95% of all other values in the distribution.

The Monte Carlo Technique

Now that we have provided a little background on statistical distributions, we can explain how you can use Monte Carlo techniques to analyze a project schedule containing uncertainties. Monte Carlo methods were originally practiced under more generic names, such as "statistical sampling." Actually, the name "Monte Carlo," which was popularized by early pioneers in the field such as Stanislaw Marcin Ulam, Enrico Fermi, John von Neumann, and Nicholas Metropolis, is a reference to the famous casino in Monaco. The technique's use of randomness and the repetitive nature of the process are analogous to the activities conducted at a casino. Ulam reveals in his autobiography, *Adventures of a Mathematician*, that the method was named in honor of his uncle, who was a gambler (Ulam 2002).

Here is how the Monte Carlo technique works. Let's assume that you have performed a calculation. (The type of calculation does not matter. For example, it could be an economic model defined in the spreadsheet.) In this example we are performing schedule network analysis using the critical path method. Each project schedule has a number of uncertain (probabilistic) parameters: task duration, task cost, start and finish times of a task, rates associated with resources, and others. Our goal is to come up with a statistical distribution for project cost and duration, which we develop by running simulations.

Here are the steps of the simulation process:

1. Retrieve the values of the parameter from the statistical distribution. This process is called sampling. Basically, you roll a die and return a random number. You will use this number in a mathematical formula associated with the distribution. The formula will return a value. It is at this point that the magic of Monte Carlo occurs. If you roll a die many times, values associated with the hump or spike of the distribution will come up more often than the values associated with the "low-lying areas" (or tails) of the distribution.

2. Use these values in the calculation engine that you are using to run your model, which in this case is the project schedule. In other words, your project schedule will be calculated using a critical path method based on task duration, cost, and the other parameters you retrieved from the statistical distribution in the previous step.

3. Save the results of the analysis (project duration, cost, and other parameters). Repeat the process hundreds of times, each time using a

new set of values from the statistical distribution. Each separate run is called a trial. After you have calculated and saved the results of hundreds of trials, you will now have a distribution of project parameters, which you can represent on a chart similar to charts shown in figures 16-2 and 16-3.

Luckily, you don't have to perform all these calculations manually; there are many software tools specifically designed for this task (see appendix A). Your job is to define the distributions for input parameters and analyze the results.

Here is a more concrete example. Assume that you have a project with three tasks (figure 16-5). The duration of the first task is defined by a normal distribution (with a mean of four days), the duration of the second task is defined by a uniform distribution (between three and seven days), and the duration of the third task is deterministic (always four days).

For this example, we will run only 20 trials. We use a sampling to get the duration distributions for tasks 1 and 2. Take a look at table 16-2. For task 1, we know that durations between three and five days occur more frequently than other durations because that is where the peak of the distribution curve, or the hump, appears. For task 2, because it has a uniform distribution, all durations are equally distributed between three and seven days. For each trial, we add up all the task durations to get the project duration. Results are displayed in a histogram. As you can see, the histogram for the project duration also has a hump due to task 1's normal distribution.

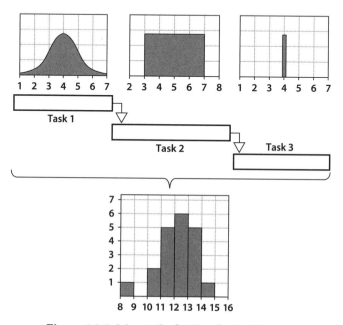

Figure 16-5. Monte Carlo Simulation Process

Using the data from the 20 trials, we can now calculate all the probabilistic project parameters, including the mean (in this example it is 12.185 days), standard deviation, and different percentiles.

Which Distribution Should Be Used?

The distribution you choose for your project schedule can be based on an analysis of the historical data related to this parameter. For example, if the task occurred regularly each time, you can measure the duration of the task, which can then be used to define the distribution.

Unfortunately, historical data simply doesn't exist for many projects. In chapter 13 we learned how to elicit expert judgment related to probabilities of events. Now let's see how expert judgment can help us define statistical distributions. The probability method (Goodwin 2014) helps to mitigate the negative effects of anchoring, including insufficient adjustment:

1. Ask an expert to establish a range of values for the parameter.

2. Ask an expert to imagine a situation that could lead to values' lying outside the range, and then revise the range if necessary.

3. Divide the range into four to seven intervals, and for each interval ask the expert to assess whether he or she can increase or decrease that value. For example, an expert estimated that the duration range is between five and ten days. Ask the expert, "What is the chance that the duration is less than six days?" Then ask, "What is the chance that the

Table 16-2. Monte Carlo Simulation Results

Trial	Task 1	Task 2	Task 3	Project	Trial	Task 1	Task 2	Task 3	Project
1	1.2	3.5	4.0	8.7	11	4.8	3.1	4.0	11.9
2	4.0	2.8	4.0	10.8	12	4.2	4.9	4.0	13.1
3	2.5	4.0	4.0	10.5	13	3.9	5.5	4.0	13.4
4	3.0	6.0	4.0	13.0	14	2.3	5.1	4.0	11.4
5	3.5	4.4	4.0	11.9	15	5.8	3.1	4.0	12.9
6	4.2	3.9	4.0	12.1	16	3.4	3.9	4.0	11.3
7	3.8	6.2	4.0	14.0	17	4.6	3.7	4.0	12.3
8	4.4	4.4	4.0	12.8	18	3.7	4.8	4.0	12.5
9	2.1	5.9	4.0	12.0	19	3.9	3.5	4.0	11.4
10	4.1	5.8	4.0	13.9	20	4.3	5.5	4.0	13.8

duration is less than seven days?" And so on. By the end, you will have elicited a cumulative probability distribution. You can draw the distribution, connect the points by hand, and fit the statistical distribution.

4. Perform a reality check. First, ask your expert to come up with cumulative probabilities using different intervals—for example, 1.5 days instead of 1 day. Then you can compare the results with the previous assessment and make the necessary corrections. You can also ask the expert to define where he or she thinks the peak of the distribution should be, then you can compare that with the results found in step 3.

Another method of eliciting judgment for continuous distributions is the method of relative heights. Using the previous example, you can ask the expert how many times the duration will be between five and six days, between six and seven days, and so on. Then you can draw a frequency histogram, similar to the chart shown in figure 16-2.

Unfortunately, if your project schedule contains more than a few dozen tasks, it could take quite a while to come up with statistical distributions for all uncertainties. The good news is that with most project schedules, if you know the range of the data, the particular shape of the distribution may not be critical for the analysis.

If you choose a triangular distribution for a particular task duration instead of lognormal, this will not completely skew your analysis as long as your range is accurate. Risks and uncertainties that you have not accounted for will cause you more problems than will an inaccurate distribution shape.

How Many Trials Are Required?

One of the first questions many people ask about the Monte Carlo process is how many trials are needed to perform a meaningful analysis. The answer depends upon the nature of the uncertainties associated with the project schedule. In some cases, you may want to incorporate very rare events ending with dramatic outcomes into the project schedule. Let's say that there is 1 chance in 1,000 that a natural disaster will strike in your area. While this event can be modeled using a discrete distribution, you will need to run at least 1,000 trials to see how the event could affect your project schedule. Apart from these special cases, it is our experience that you can perform a meaningful analysis on most project schedules, including very large schedules with over a thousand activities, by calculating only a couple of hundred trials.

Fortunately, most software applications used in this field have a feature called convergence monitoring. After each trial, the software will calculate statistical parameters (mean, standard deviation, and possibly others) of a selected project variable, for example, project cost or duration. The software will calculate the relative difference between these statistical parameters on two consecutive trials, and if this difference stays within a specified variance over a number of consecutive trials, the software will deem that the results have converged and will halt the Monte Carlo process. For example, if the relative difference between project standard deviations is less than 0.5% on more than 25 consecutive trials, the process abruptly ends.

Analysis of Monte Carlo Results

What is the chance that a project will be completed on time and come in within budget? Monte Carlo helps us answer this important question.

Technically, we need to record the number of trials in which the project was on time and within budget, and then divide this by the total number of trials. For example, if you ran 100 trials and in 65 of them the project was on time, the chance would be 65%. The best way to analyze this is to use a statistical distribution associated with the project duration. Fortunately, the software tools you are using will likely have an interactive histogram for the statistical distribution. With these interactive tools, you can select a date and you will see the chance that the project will be completed before or on a particular date.

SENSITIVITY AND CORRELATIONS

Using Monte Carlo, you can identify a specific task's uncertainties that will have the greatest effect on the project schedule. For example, if a task is very risky, it can significantly affect the project duration. In addition, you can identify correlations between tasks and then monitor how they affect the project schedule. We discussed how to define and analyze sensitivities and correlations in chapter 14.

CRITICAL INDICES

If we analyze a deterministic project schedule, we can identify a critical path. However, when we use Monte Carlo, the critical path can be different in each trial. In such a case we can determine the percentage of time a task is on the critical path during the trials. For example, as a result of the analysis, we find that task A will be on the critical path 60% of the time; task B, 30% of the time; and task C, 45% of the time. In this example, task A would be the most critical task, therefore it needs to be examined further. These are called critical indices and are valuable in identifying critical tasks that have both risks and uncertainties.

PROBABILISTIC CALENDARS

If a storm comes up on the coast near you, you cannot continue a seaport improvement project while the storm rages. Using Monte Carlo analysis, though, you can define the chance that a certain calendar with either working or nonworking days will be used. For example, a storm calendar could be used 5% of the time to take into account the effect of poor weather conditions.

DEADLINES

If a task reaches a certain deadline and is unfinished, one of the results can be that the task or project will be canceled. But we do not know whether the project will reach the deadline or what the chance is that the deadline will be missed. Monte Carlo will help you answer this question, because it is easy to count the number of trials in which the deadline is missed.

CONDITIONAL BRANCHING

Let's assume that your project schedule includes two different branches representing two different alternatives. Conditional branching allows the project to branch from one task to another under certain conditions. For example, the task duration is six days +/– two days (figure 16-6). If the task is completed within six days, one project scenario will be selected, but if it is completed after six days, the other alternative will be selected. These types of conditions can be based not only on duration but also on finish time, cost, and other parameters.

PROBABILISTIC BRANCHING

You can also use probabilistic branching, which allows the project to branch from one task to another task or group of tasks as part of the simulation process. For example, there is a 50% chance that one branch will be selected and a 50% chance that another branch will be selected.

CHANCE OF TASK EXISTENCE

If you use both probabilistic *and* conditional branching, some alternatives will be executed in one trial but not in another. Therefore, you can count how many times the task was executed. This is the chance that the task will be executed or is not canceled during project execution.

Is Monte Carlo the Ultimate Solution?

The development of PERT and Monte Carlo represented major steps forward in project decision analysis. By understanding the historical trends for the costs of fuel, labor, and raw materials, and by accurately forecasting these costs into

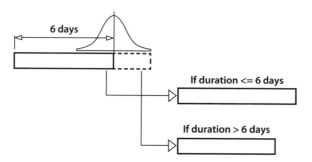

Figure 16-6. Conditional Branching

> In essence, Monte Carlo allows a manager to model a huge number of combinations of project scenarios as part of one straightforward process.

the future, we can realistically predict the cost of projects. Based on these forecasts, we can make decisions for complex portfolios such as the subway construction projects in New York City that we discussed at the beginning of this chapter. PERT and Monte Carlo methods both help us determine what may happen to a project when we take into account the cumulative effect of many risks and uncertainties.

For a number of reasons, Monte Carlo has not yet become part of the standard tool set used by project managers. Many project managers are unfamiliar or at least uncomfortable with the process, even though it is covered in the *PMBOK Guide*. It may be that Monte Carlo and PERT have not been more widely adopted because project managers understand that inaccurate data will lead to inaccurate results (the "garbage in/garbage out" principle). Monte Carlo by itself will not solve the fundamental issues related to defining uncertainties:

1. Terry Williams (Williams 2004) noted that project managers don't sit and wait when a project slips. They perform certain recovery actions, which in most cases are not taken into account by Monte Carlo. In this respect, Monte Carlo may give overly pessimistic results. At the same time, as we already know, we are all subject to the overconfidence bias, which leads to overly optimistic project schedules. Unfortunately, the combination of optimistic and pessimistic results does not equal accurate results. Instead, you will get inadequate results.

2. Defining distributions is not a trivial process. Distributions are abstract concepts that many of us find difficult to work with. To define distributions accurately, we have to perform a few mental steps that can be easily overlooked. Whether we are performing estimates of project parameters or developing distributions, we are affected by our own cognitive and motivational biases.

As with everything else, Monte Carlo is not a panacea, but it is an excellent tool for the following situations:

- You have either reliable historical data or data that you can use to create a reliable probabilistic forecast. For example, you can predict the cost of raw materials within a certain range.

- You have tools to track actual data for each phase of the project and can perform Monte Carlo analysis at each phase to update your schedule.

- You have a group of experts who understand the project, have experience in similar projects, and are trained to avoid cognitive and motivational biases when they define uncertainties and provide estimates.

If your project does not meet at least *one* of these criteria, Monte Carlo analysis may not help to improve your decision-making. Numerous projects do not meet these criteria, particularly research and development projects. Fortunately, you can employ a schedule network analysis technique, called Event chain methodology, which can help to address the shortcomings of both Monte Carlo and PERT. We discuss Event chain methodology in the next chapter.

- Project managers make decisions based on the answer to a fundamental question: "What will the duration and cost of the project be, given its multiple risks and uncertainties?"
- PERT is an easy-to-use analytical method, but it has a number of major limitations.
- Monte Carlo analysis is a straightforward approach to deal with project uncertainties. It can be used effectively if accurate historical data is available, project tracking is performed, and trained project-specific experts are involved.

CHAPTER 17

"A Series of Unfortunate Events"
Or, Event Chain Methodology

Often, in hindsight, projects can seem like best-selling author Lemony Snicket's series of unfortunate events. It is the unexpected effect of a series of events that often derails even the most well-managed projects. Event chain methodology is a schedule network analysis technique that focuses on identifying, modeling, and managing the events that can affect a project schedule. Event chain methodology helps determine project duration, cost, and other parameters while taking into account these events and event chains. It also identifies critical risks and crucial tasks, performs resource leveling, and resolves other complex project scheduling problems.

How Events Can Affect a Project

The Tesla Model 3 is a midsize, all-electric, four-door car manufactured by Tesla Motors (figure 17-1). After unveiling its Model 3 in 2016, Tesla received more than 325,000 reservations for the car. With so much hype around this car, its manufacturing processes were closely followed by electric car enthusiasts. In July 2017, Tesla announced that its goal was to produce 1,500 units in the third quarter of 2017, increasing to 5,000 per week by the end of December 2017. However, due to multiple production difficulties, these numbers were achieved only by the summer of 2018. Tesla experienced what CEO Elon Musk called "manufacturing hell" (Lambert 2018).

As with any new, complex engineering project, establishing the manufacturing process of Tesla's Model 3 had a "series of unfortunate events." Here are only a few of them:

- *An attempt to automate many assemble operations failed. Tesla realized the problem and replaced some robots with humans.*

Figure 17-1. Tesla Model 3 (Photo by Smnt)

- *Tesla lacked enough space for Model 3 production at each factory in Fremont, California, and had to assemble some cars under a giant tent.*

- *Tesla Model 3 relies on batteries produced at what the company calls Gigafactory 1, which itself is an extremely complex engineering project. Because Gigafactory 1 and Model 3 are part of the same supply chain, any issues on Gigafactory 1 could cause delays with the Model 3 assembly.*

- *In May 2018,* Consumer Reports' *Model 3 testing found "big flaws—such as long stopping distances in our emergency braking test and difficult-to-use controls," which caused it to not recommend the car. Tesla responded a few days later (over a weekend), then released an over-the-air (OTA) software update to fix the problem.* Consumer Reports *was impressed and changed its rating to a recommended model.*

Normally, when you create a new project, you spend a lot of time and effort creating a well-balanced schedule and trying to take into account every possible scenario and risk. Unfortunately, as soon as you start implementing your plan, something occurs that instantly makes your schedule obsolete. This "something" is an unpredictable event. As a result, you have to either revise your schedule significantly or create a new one. So, you choose one of these actions, and then another unpredictable event occurs. This can happen again and again, leading you to believe that scheduling is not only a futile exercise but also an entirely

> Event chain methodology helps predict the course of the project by analyzing relationships between different project events.

unnecessary one, for it seems to have no bearing on the actual course of the project. This scenario can be common in projects that have multiple risks and uncertainties, and it is especially true in research and development projects. What should we do in these cases? Completely give up scheduling and risk management, and concentrate only on high-level project planning? Or is there still a way to provide realistic estimates for project schedules that have multiple uncertainties?

Event chain methodology is an attempt to solve this conundrum (Virine and Trumper 2013, 2017). It is a method of modeling uncertainties for various time-related business and technological processes, including project management. At the same time, it is an effective schedule network analysis technique, which helps to build project schedules.

But don't worry. Event chain methodology does not require you to learn a whole new suite of analytical theories and tools, for it is based on existing analysis methodologies, including Monte Carlo analysis.

Basic Principles of Event Chain Methodology

Event chain methodology involves six basic principles. We illustrate these principles using Event Chain Diagram notations, where arrows represent risks assigned to the activity on the Gantt chart.

PRINCIPLE 1: MOMENT OF RISK AND STATE OF AN ACTIVITY

An activity in most real-life processes is not a continuous and uniform process. Activities are affected by external events that transform them from one state to another. The notion of "state" means that an activity will be performed differently as a response to the event. This process of changing the state of an activity is called excitation. In quantum mechanics, the notion of excitation is used to describe elevation in energy level above an arbitrary baseline energy state. In Event chain methodology, excitation indicates that something has changed the manner in which an activity is performed. For example, an activity may require different resources, take a longer time, or must be performed under different conditions. As a result, this may alter the activity's cost and duration.

The original or planned state of the activity is called a ground state. Other states, associated with different events, are called excited states (figure 17-2).

The events have a number of properties. Among them are:

- **Probability of occurrence.**
- **Outcome.** For example: cancel task, increase/reduce duration/cost, move resource to different start point, change probability of a risk, start activity, execute mitigation plan.
- **Impact of the event.** For example: it causes an increase in duration of 10%.

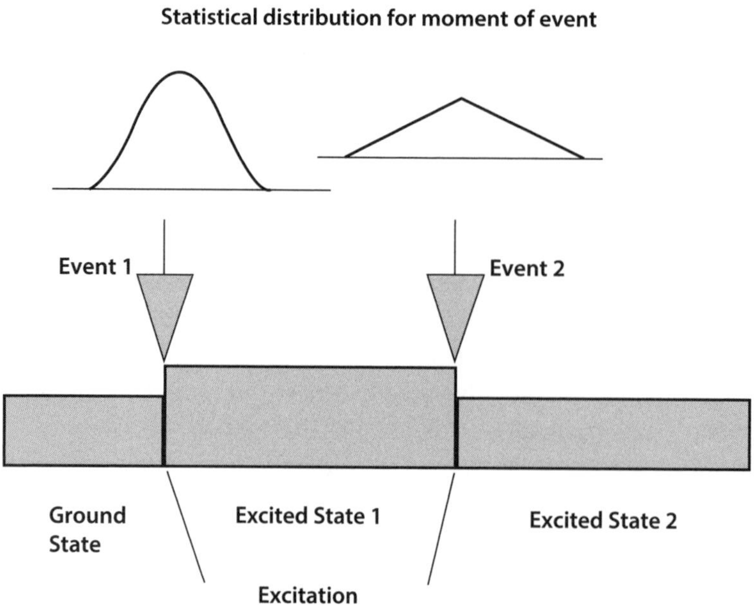

Statistical distribution for moment of event

Figure 17-2. Moment of a Single Event

- **Event assignment.** Events can affect tasks, resources, lags, the calendar, and other project parameters.

One of the most important properties of an event is the actual moment when it occurs during the course of an activity, called the moment of event. In most cases, the moment when the event occurs is probabilistic and can be defined by using a statistical distribution.

The most likely moment of occurrence for a risk event is somewhere in the middle of an activity. The moment of event is important for two main reasons:

1. Often, the impact of the event depends on when it occurs. The moment of the event can affect whether an activity will be restarted or canceled.

2. The probabilistic moment of an event is significant when you are adjusting the duration or cost of an activity in an attempt to track actual performance.

Events can have both negative (threat) and positive (opportunity) effects on a project. For example, there is a chance that a component can be delivered more quickly than was originally planned.

Similarly, resources, lags, and calendars may have different grounded and excited states. For example, the event "Bad weather condition" can transform a calendar from a ground state (5 working days per weeks) to an excited state: non-working days for the next 10 days.

Each state of activity, in particular, may subscribe to certain events. This means that an event can affect the activity only if the activity is subscribed to this event. For example, an assembly activity has started outdoors. The ground state the activity is subscribed to is the external event of "Bad weather." If "Bad weather" actually occurs, the assembly should move indoors. This constitutes an excited state of the activity. This new excited state (indoor assembling) will not be subscribed to the "Bad weather": if this event occurs, it will not affect the activity.

PRINCIPLE 2: EVENT CHAINS

Some events can trigger other events or transform an activity to another state. In this case, the series of risk events together forms event chains (figure 17-3). These event chains can significantly affect the course of a project by creating a ripple effect throughout the project.

Here is an example of an event chain's ripple effect:

1. A change in the requirements of a project causes the delay of activity A.

2. To accelerate the activity, the project manager diverts resources from activity B.

3. Diversion of resources causes deadlines to be missed on activity B.

4. Cumulatively, this reaction leads to the failure of the whole project.

Event chains can be defined in several different ways. For example, a single event can be defined as "a change in the probability of a particular risk." In this case, one event triggers another event. For example, a drop in hydraulic pressure in an airplane's landing gear pump during one activity (cruising) will increase the probability that the landing gear will not open during the next activity

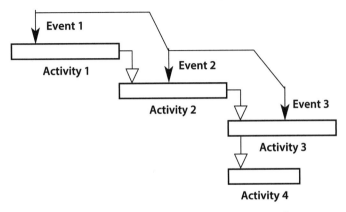

Figure 17-3. Connected Events Forming a Chain

(landing). Another way to define event chains is to use an event "start another task" or "execute mitigation plan."

PRINCIPLE 3: EVENT CHAIN DIAGRAMS

Event chain diagrams are visualizations that show the relationships between events and tasks and suggest how the events affect each other. The chains are presented as arrows associated with certain tasks on the Gantt chart. Here are a few important rules about how to create and interpret diagram:

- Event chains diagrams present events as arrows on the Gantt charts.
- Arrows pointing down are threats. Arrows pointing up are opportunities (figure 17-4).
- Issues are shown as an arrow within a circle. Color of issue arrows is red (or dark in this book's illustrations).
- Closed or transferred risks are shown using dashed lines. Color of arrow is white (or light). Closed issue is shown in the circle with dashed border line (figure 17-5).
- Excited states are represented by elevating the associated section of the bar on the Gantt chart.
- Colors represent the calculated impact of the risk. Higher impacts are red or a darker shade. Low impacts are green or a lighter shade. The size of the arrow represents probability.
- Event chains are shown as lines connecting arrows depicting events (figure 17-6).
- Correlation coefficients between two events are shown on the line connecting the arrow.
- Event chains may trigger another activity. In this case, event chain lines are connected with the beginning of the activity using an optional arrow (figure 17-7).

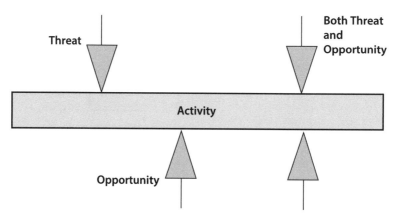

Figure 17-4. Threats and Opportunities

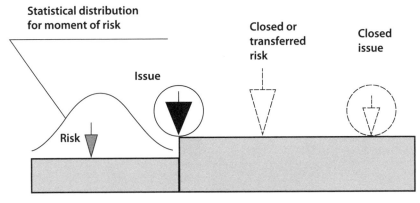

Figure 17-5. Risks, Issues, Transferred Risk

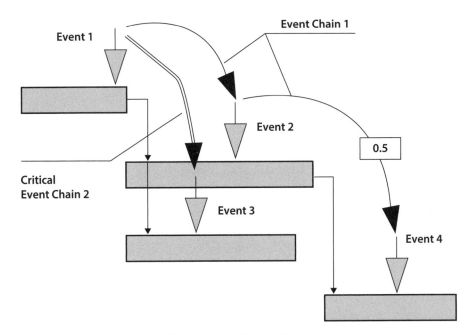

Figure 17-6. Event Chains

- Event chains may trigger a group of activities. In this case, this group of activities will be surrounded by the box or frame and the event chain line will be connected to the corner of the box or first activity within a frame.

By using event chain diagrams to visualize events and event chains, the modeling and analysis of risks and uncertainties can be significantly simplified.

PRINCIPLE 4: ANALYSIS USING MONTE CARLO SIMULATIONS

Once events and event chains are defined, you can perform Monte Carlo simulations to quantify the cumulative impact of the events. Probabilities and

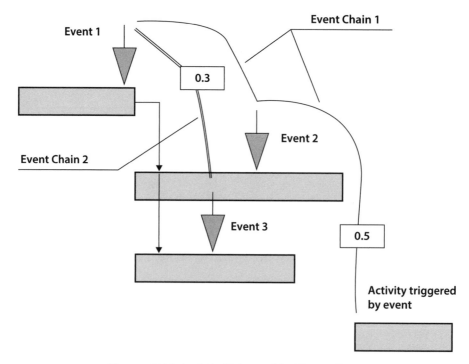

Figure 17-7. Activity Triggered by Event Chain

impacts of events are used as input data for a Monte Carlo simulation of the project schedule. In most real-life projects, even if you have defined all the possible risks you can think of, some uncertainties or fluctuations will always crop up in duration and cost. To take these fluctuations into account, you can define distributions related to task duration, start time, cost, and other parameters, in addition to the list of events. Just remember that these statistical distributions cannot be related to the events that you have identified. If they are, you will cause a double-count of the project's risk.

PRINCIPLE 5: CRITICAL EVENT CHAINS

Single events or event chains that have the most potential to affect a project are the critical events or critical event chains. By identifying critical events or critical event chains, we can mitigate their negative effects. These critical event chains can be identified through sensitivity analysis and by analyzing the correlations between the main project parameters, such as duration and cost, and event chains. Critical events or critical event chains can be visualized using an Event chain diagram (see double line for Event Chain 2 on figure 17-6).

PRINCIPLE 6: PROJECT CONTROL WITH EVENT AND EVENT CHAINS

Monitoring an activity's progress ensures that updated information is used to perform the analysis. During the course of the project, the probability and time of the events can be recalculated, based on actual data. The main reason for doing performance tracking is to forecast an activity's duration and cost if the activity is only partially completed and if certain events are assigned to the activity. Event chain methodology automatically reduces the risk probability and impact, based on the percent of work completed. Advanced analysis can be performed by using a Bayesian approach. It is possible to monitor the chance that a project will meet a specific deadline. This chance is constantly updated as a result of the Monte Carlo analysis. Critical events and event chains can be different at the various phases of the project.

Monitoring the progress of activities ensures that updated information is used to perform the analysis. While this is true for all types of analysis, it is a critical principle of Event chain methodology. During the course of the project, by using actual performance data you can recalculate the probability of occurrence and moment of events. You can then repeat your quantitative analysis and generate a new project schedule with updated costs and durations.

But what should you do if the activity is only partially completed and certain events are assigned to the activity? If the event has already occurred, will it occur again? Or if nothing has happened, will it happen?

You can use a number of techniques to solve this problem. The simple heuristic approach to this problem is to base your analysis on an examination of the distribution of the moment of event, which is one of the event parameters. More sophisticated methods are based on application of the Bayes theorem.

Event Chain Methodology Phenomena

A number of phenomena are commonly associated with Event chain methodology.

REPEATED ACTIVITIES

Sometimes events can cause the restart of an activity that has already been completed. This is a very common scenario for a project; sometimes a previous activity must be repeated, based on the results of a succeeding activity (figure 17-8).

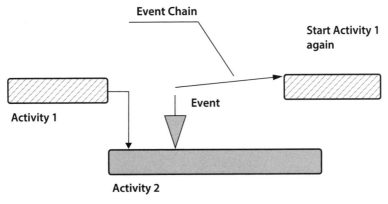

Figure 17-8. Repeated Activity

Modeling of these scenarios using Event chain methodology is quite simple. The original project schedule does not need to be updated because all that is required is to define the event and assign it to an activity that points to the previous activity. Still, a limit to the number of times an activity can be repeated needs to be defined.

EVENT CHAINS AND RISK RESPONSE

Risk-response efforts are considered to be events, which are executed if an activity is in an excited state. Risk-response events may attempt to transform an activity from an excited state to the ground state.

If an event or event chain occurs during the course of a project, it may require risk-response efforts. In some cases, risk-response plans can be created. Risk-response plans are an activity or group of activities (small schedule) that augment the project schedule if a certain event occurs. Risk-response plans can be defined as a part of the original project schedule and to be executed only under certain conditions. However, in these cases, the project schedule may become very convoluted due to multiple conditional branches, which significantly complicates the analysis. Event chain methodology offers a solution: assign the risk-response plan to an event or an event chain. These small schedules are executed when an event or event chain occurs.

Each response plan has an entry point and exit points, as shown in figure 17-9. As a result, the original project schedule and the project schedule with simula-

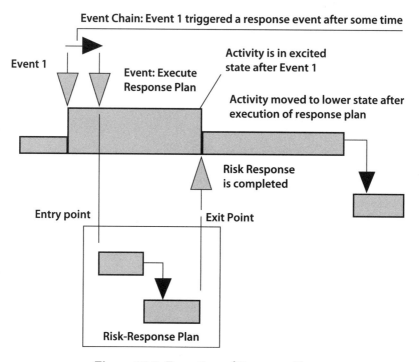

Figure 17-9. Execution of Response Plan

tion results (listing risks and uncertainties) are different. The same risk-response plan can be used for different events.

In the case of risk-response planning, we have an event chain with three events:

1. Original Event, which triggers a response.

2. Event "Execute Response Plan," which executes a group of activities.

3. Event "Risk Response Is Completed." This is can be depicted as an opportunity because it moves activities to a lower excited state.

DELAYS IN EVENT CHAINS

Events can cause other events to occur either immediately or with a delay. The delay can be deterministic, but in most cases it is probabilistic. If the time of the original event and the delay are known, it is possible to determine both the time the new event will happen and, in some cases, the activity that will be associated with it. For example, original event "Relocation of the business" can cause event "Missing data" sometime after the original event.

RESOURCE ALLOCATION BASED ON EVENTS

One potential event is the reassignment of a resource from one activity to another. For example, if completing an activity within a fixed period requires more resources, this will trigger an event to reallocate the resource from another activity. Redeployment of resources can also occur when activity duration reaches a certain deadline or the cost exceeds a certain value.

Events can be used to model different situations with personnel resources, e.g., temporary leave, illness, and vacations. In some cases, this can create an event chain: due to an illness, a resource from another activity is reallocated to accomplish a specific task.

How to Use Event Chain Methodology

Now that we have convinced you of the benefits of Event chain methodology (or even if you are not completely persuaded), you are probably wondering how you might put it to practical use. Here is our recommended workflow:

1. Define a detailed project schedule with resources and costs assigned to the activities—nothing extravagant, just a regular work breakdown structure. This is your base scenario schedule. It is sometimes called "focused work on activities." In reality, because of cognitive and motivational biases, it is an optimistic project schedule.

2. Define a detailed risk breakdown structure and assign risks to each activity and resource. Each risk should include a probability of occurrence, impact, and moment of risk.

3. Define the activities associated with mitigation efforts, and then assign costs and resources to them.

4. Perform a quantitative risk analysis using Monte Carlo. While it is possible to do this for the entire project schedule, we suggest that you perform the initial analysis on each phase of the project separately. This will help identify the chance that each phase will be completed on time and within budget. As a result, you should be able to identify contingencies and reserves.

5. Analyze the results. You can use other analytical techniques, which come with classic Monte Carlo—probabilistic and conditional branching, deadlines, crucial tasks, and so on. What is specific to Event chain methodology is its ability to identify critical events and event chains.

6. Perform reality checks by comparing the results of your analysis with independent expert reviews and historical experience. Identify the potential impact of the critical risks as calculated through the analysis and ask whether it is realistic. If the results are unrealistic and do not pass your reality check, redefine your risks and perform the quantitative analysis again.

7. Monitor the course of the project on a regular basis; perform repeated quantitative risk analysis; reassess the risks, including the probability of risk occurrence based on actual data; and identify new project costs and duration.

Example of Event Chain Methodology

Using event chance methodology, it is possible to solve many interesting problems. Let's say that you are designing a device and considering additional testing and evaluation. For starters, you have two choices:

1. Spend additional time on testing, evaluation, and prototyping to reduce the chance of a major failure in the future.

2. Skip extra testing and accept a higher chance of failure.

What would *you* do? It is very hard to say without analysis. You need to analyze all possible events that may lead to a failure, assign probabilities to them for both scenarios, and perform the analysis using Event chain methodology. Very often, the scenario that originally appeared to have the shortest duration could have the longest.

In the movie *Armageddon*, with Bruce Willis and Ben Affleck, oil drillers are hired to rocket out on two space shuttles to a gigantic asteroid and blow it up before it slams into Earth (figure 17-10). Their plan is to drill a hole into the

Figure 17-10. How Long Will It Take to Drill a Hole in the Asteroid?

asteroid and plant a nuclear bomb in it. How long will it take for them to complete the drilling, and what is the chance that the drilling will be completed before it is too late? Everything depends on what could happen during their trip to the asteroid and during the drilling itself. Let's follow our workflow and try to find the answers to our questions.

1. Let's assume that we have only one activity: drilling. We estimate that it will take 20 hours if everything goes as planned. If the drilling cannot be completed in a more extended 30 hours, a calamity will be imminent. Even with one activity, it is difficult to estimate what will happen if there are multiple risk events with different probabilities, impacts, and times.

2. We need to organize a brainstorming meeting among experienced asteroid drillers (a very select group, as you can imagine). Everybody who has drilled at least one hole in an asteroid will identify the major risks, listed in table 17-1.

3. Now we can perform a Monte Carlo simulation. An event chain diagram and the results of the Monte Carlo simulation are shown in figure 17-11. The actual duration of the drilling can be somewhere

between 20 hours and 43.6 hours. The mean duration is 23.5 hours. The chance that the drilling will be completed in 30 hours (essentially, a chance of Earth's survival) is 86%, a pretty hopeful result.

Event Chain Methodology and Mitigation of Psychological Biases

The main advantage of using Event chain methodology is that it can greatly lessen the negative impact of psychological biases related to estimation of project uncertainties.

1. The task duration, start and finish times, cost, and other project input parameters are influenced by motivational factors, such as total project duration, to a much greater extent than events and event chains. This occurs because events cannot be easily translated into duration, finish time, and cost. For example, your management has imposed an unrealistic deadline, and you are pressured to fit your project schedule into a very short window with limited resources. The first thing you do is reduce durations of tasks even if there is no logical basis for doing it. With Event chain methodology, you can use an optimistic schedule and then apply the risk breakdown structure that you created separately. It will allow you to assess how the project's risks and uncertainties affect your original estimates.

2. Event chain methodology relies on the estimation of duration based on focused work on an activity and does not necessarily require low, base, and high estimates or statistical distributions; therefore, it minimizes the negative effect of anchoring.

3. The probability of events can be easily calculated based on historical data, which can mitigate the effect of the availability heuristic. You can use a relative frequency approach. To calculate the probability, take the number of times an event actually occurred in previous projects and divide it by the total number of situations in which the

Table 17-1. Risks Associated with Drilling into an Asteroid

	Risk	Probability	Impact
1	Problem with landing on the asteroid or delay with finding a drilling site	20% 40%	Delay of 4 hours Delay of 2 hours
2	Problem with drilling in unknown geological conditions	25%	Restart drilling

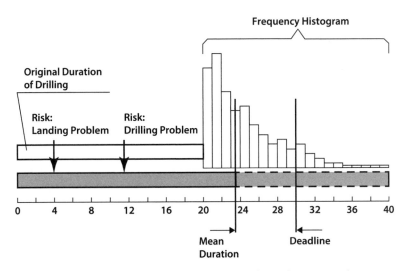

Figure 17-11. Project: Drilling a Hole in the Asteroid

event could have occurred. In a classic Monte Carlo simulation, the statistical distribution of input parameters can also be obtained from the historical data; however, the procedure is more complicated.

4. Compound events can be quite complex, but you can easily break them down into smaller events. Information about these small events can be supported by reliable historical data, which mitigates the effect of biases in the estimation of probability and risk.

Work Breakdown Structure + Risk Breakdown Structure + Analysis = Event Chain Methodology

The elegance of Event chain methodology is that it includes a well-defined mathematical model of uncertain projects that is available in many software applications. We project managers define project schedules and risk lists or risk breakdown structures as part of our standard project management process. So, why don't we use this data to analyze our projects and get to the central question of project risk management? In other words, if an event occurs, how will it affect project duration and cost?

After all this explanation, the question still remains: Does Event chain methodology lead to better project management? We can answer with a qualified "yes." The methodology *does* provide us with a much simpler means of modeling project uncertainties. It also allows us to mitigate psychological biases related to estimation, and as a result it provides superior forecasts and project tracking. With Event chain methodology, if you properly define your project risks and uncertainties, your project schedule will be much more robust—and ultimately you will make better project decisions.

- Events can drastically affect project schedules. Events cause other events and create event chains. Identification of these chains is as important as creating the schedule itself.
- Event chain methodology is a method of modeling uncertainties in project management. Basically, it helps you model and analyze both project schedules and risk lists (the risk breakdown structure) together.
- Event chain methodology helps you identify critical risks and use them to perform reality checks.
- Event chain diagrams can be used to visualize events and event chains.
- Event chain methodology can help mitigate the negative effects of the psychological biases and heuristics associated with project estimations and analysis of uncertainties.

CHAPTER 18

The Art of Decision Analysis Reporting

The results of a decision analysis can be ignored or misinterpreted if they are not reported properly. Interpretations of decision analysis results are invariably affected by cognitive as well as motivational biases. Decision-makers may have difficulties interpreting results related to probability and risk, especially in the case of rare events with catastrophic outcomes. A number of diagramming tools can help in visualizing the results of project decision analysis and can minimize the chance that the results will be misinterpreted.

How to Communicate the Results of Decision Analysis

A young engineer fresh out of college was hired by a large oil company. One of his first tasks was to perform an economic evaluation of an oil reserve. With his classes in probability theory and statistics still fresh in his mind, he performed the full range of decision analysis calculations, including a full sensitivity analysis, a Monte Carlo simulation, several decision trees, and other methods we have described. After weeks of intense work, the young engineer reported his results to his manager. Wanting to impress on his first major assignment, he created a magnificent computer presentation with dozens of slides full of frequency histograms, cumulative probability charts, and other very scientific-looking pictures. After the presentation, the manager was silent for a minute. Then she said, "This is very nice. But what should we do? Should we drill—or not drill?"

(A similar situation is said to have happened in the First World War when a military commander had just received new tanks, which he had never seen before. After three days of training, he had only one question: "How do we harness a horse to this thing?")

At this point the young engineer answered: "Based on my probabilistic assessment and given the uncertainties in cost, production, and prices, there is a 67% chance that NPV will be less than $2 million." From the manager's perspective, the main *question—to drill or not to drill—had not been answered. The engineer had just wasted her time. The feedback the young engineer received after the presentation was to focus on old, proven deterministic techniques and not to bother with any "useless initiatives" that produced probabilistic fluff.*

This situation, where the decision-maker and the decision analyst are different individuals, happens frequently. Here are two common scenarios:

1. You are a project manager and you hire a consultant or ask a member of your project team to perform an analysis. You need to make a decision based on the analyst's report.

2. You yourself are the analyst or consultant and you want to communicate the results of the analysis to the project manager.

Decision analysis reporting is different from regular business communication in a number of ways. Some important issues need to be accounted for when communicating the results of decision analysis:

- As we have discussed, people usually have difficulties making judgments when uncertainties, risks, and probabilities are involved.

- In many cases, decision analysis methods and tools are highly complex. Many project managers are unfamiliar with decision analysis theory and practice, therefore they have difficulties interpreting the results of quantitative analysis.

- Project managers and analysts may bring conflicting motivational and cognitive biases to these discussions. In the next section we will provide a few tips on how to communicate the results of project decision analysis, which should help reduce the opportunity for making a biased decision.

Motivational Biases in Reporting Decision Analysis Results
Let's consider the following scenario.

A senior engineer of a construction company suggested a new design for a large underground structure that was part of the project he was involved in. According to his estimates, the new design would require less material, be quicker to construct, and reduce vibrations of the nearby buildings during construction. A technical committee was assigned to review the two designs—the original and the one proposed by the senior engineer. The committee requested a comprehensive analysis of both alternatives. The engineer wanted his design to be approved, so he furiously lobbied his case.

Before the review meeting, he talked separately with most of the members of the committee to explain the benefits of his solution. He had his subordinates perform a technical analysis of the two solutions, particularly the calculation of the amount of materials and duration of construction. He recommended reducing the probability of events that could cause a delay in the new design and increase the probability of delays in the original design.

He managed to invite to the approval meeting people who were particularly concerned about vibration of nearby buildings. Experts in vibration gave vivid (remember our discussion about the availability heuristic) descriptions of what could occur if the issue were ignored. This approach ensured that the committee would view the issue as critical.

It is very hard to mitigate the effect of motivational factors when you are interpreting an analytical report. The solution is to establish the decision analysis process in the organization, which will reduce the influence of motivational factors on decisions.

The engineer had carefully followed what he thought was a successful plan for anybody looking to get a project, plan, or other agenda approved, but it was not a good decision analysis. You can probably guess which design was approved by the committee, but was it the right choice? The answer is, nobody knows. The committee was given a report that had been effectively "gamed" by the engineer to achieve his own purposes. It is quite possible that the engineer's design was better, but as a result of his lobbying, the committee members became biased against the original design and could not properly review the risks and uncertainties in the project.

Both analysts and decision-makers may have motivational biases. In other words, they may have a personal stake in the results of this analysis. Remember, analysts are supposed to be neutral, otherwise they become just lobbyists.

In our example the construction company had used a decision analysis process, but the process failed in this instance. However, it didn't fail because it selected the wrong alternative. It failed because the selection was biased because of the engineer's efforts. More disturbing, despite the committee members' knowing that the engineer had a personal stake in the new design and that the analysis had been performed by his subordinates, none of the committee members raised this issue.

These types of scenarios are not uncommon; in fact, they may be the norm in many organizations. In many cases, the decision-maker may favor the alternative even before the analytical report is presented. Even worse, the decision-maker can be the analyst's line manager, who has the power to override or hide the analyst's findings.

Are there any methods to reduce or mitigate the effects of these motivations and biases? Unfortunately, by the time you get to the reporting stage, these matters become difficult. But here are some suggestions:

- If you are a decision-maker, try to understand *all* the potential motivational biases involved in preparing a report. In business, it is frequently impractical to request another report or remove someone who may be unduly influencing the decision-making process. However, you can request clarification, additional analysis, and other information. If possible, invite outside moderators and experts to review or audit the report. Remember, defining probabilities is fraught with opportunities for error, so perform reality checks for all probabilities defined in the report.

- If you are an analyst, even if you have not been improperly influenced by somebody, you may have your own biases regarding this project. Try to make sure that your personal preferences are not reflected in the report and to ensure that you include a section describing the methods used to assess the project's uncertainties and probabilities.

This common sense advice is easy to offer but difficult to put into action. A lot depends on the corporate culture and especially on your ability to voice opinions and openly challenge superiors. If the organization has an established decision analysis process, motivational biases should play a much smaller role in decision-making.

Put It into Perspective

The weather forecast for tomorrow calls for a 30% chance of rain. Does this mean clear skies ahead and you can leave the umbrella at home, or should you carry it just in case? A similar situation exists in project management. You have received a report that forecasts an 86% chance that your project's cost will be below $100,000. What does this mean? Should you budget for $100,000? More? Less? Is this good news or bad? If the report has simply said that the cost of the project is $115,000, that total is absolutely clear (whether it is accurate is another matter). But if the results are expressed as probabilities, ranges, or distributions, they are more difficult to interpret.

Regarding your umbrella, how are you going to determine your course of action? You try to remember what happened the last time the forecast called for a 30% chance of rain. Did it pour or was it just a small shower (figure 18-1)? If it was just a shower, the umbrella won't be needed. However, if you are risk-averse, you may take the umbrella and wear a rain jacket just in case. For different people, chance or probability has different implications, depending upon their subjective experiences.

To overcome a subjective reaction to probabilistic forecasts, we recommend that you provide clear comparisons between the alternatives, preferably using historical data to strengthen your presentation. If you have two alternatives—one that generates $115,000 in revenue and a second that generates $150,000 in revenue but is significantly riskier—what is the best method to show this?

You can use several methods to visualize the results of decision analysis. One way to report probabilistic information in a meaningful fashion is to present

Figure 18-1. What Is the Probability of Rain?

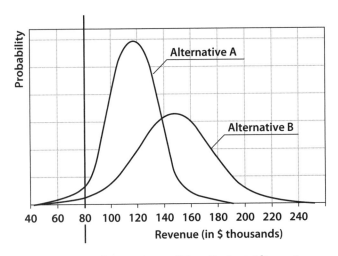

Figure 18-2. Comparison of Two Project Alternatives

statistical distributions associated with different projects on the same chart, as shown in figure 18-2. You can clearly see that the revenue for alternative A is lower (the mean is only $115,000), but the risk is also lower than that in alternative B. The distribution for alternative B is much wider than that for alternative A. Looking at this report, a decision-maker can easily compare the risk profiles of both projects.

The same type of chart is useful if you want to visualize the chance that revenue (or cost, duration, or other parameters) will be less or greater than a certain value. For example, draw a vertical line at $80,000 revenue, then compare areas of the chart to the left of the line. You will clearly see that the chance that alternative A would yield revenue below $80,000 is greater than that for alternative B.

Another useful tool is shown in figure 18-3. Look at its components:

- The vertical axis of this chart represents revenue, but it can also represent cost, duration, or other project parameters.

- The horizontal axis represents the risk associated with revenue as a result of quantitative analysis. If we have the statistical distribution, it will provide some statistical parameters, such as standard deviation and percentiles (P10, P90, P99). These parameters can be used as a measure of risk.

- Each circle represents a project alternative.

- The diameter of each circle represents an additional parameter for the alternative. For example, if the chart shows cost versus the risk associated with that cost, the diameter could represent the duration of the alternative.

To illustrate how you can evaluate a project alternative using this chart, split the area into three zones:

- **High revenue and low risk** (Alternative A). It is always nice to see one of the alternatives in this zone; unfortunately, often this is an indicator that some risk factors have not been accounted for in the alternative.

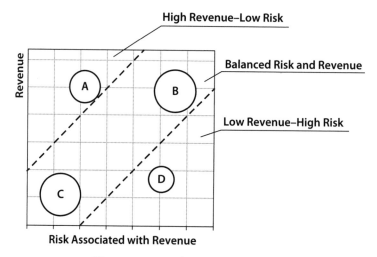

Figure 18-3. Risk vs. Return Chart

- **Balanced revenue and risk** (Alternatives B and C). High revenue is associated with high risk; low revenue is associated with low risk.
- **Low revenue and high risk** (Alternative D). The alternatives with this combination of risk and return should be the very first candidates for rejection.

This chart is also quite useful as a reality check. If an alternative seems too risky to be placed in the low-risk zone, it might mean that something is amiss with the data used in the quantitative analysis.

Another way to present alternatives is to combine them on a Gantt chart. Such a chart can also be used to represent the project schedule both with and without risks and uncertainties (figure 18-4). A project schedule without risks and uncertainties, even it is not realistic, creates a good reference point for the analysis. In this example, you can see that risk and uncertainties significantly extend the project duration.

Presentations Must Have Meaning

Have you ever been in a meeting where the presenter used a PowerPoint slide containing a table with hundreds of numbers? The presenter usually shows a tiny number (usually cost) somewhere in the middle of the table, which is then used to prove the point he wants to make. After pausing for only a moment, he moves quickly along to his next slide, believing that this dramatic use of numbers will impress upon his audience the thoroughness of his analysis. That quick transition might have left you a little befuddled, because you were not quite sure what that number actually indicated. But because everyone else was smiling and slowly nodding their heads, you remained silent—you did not want to be the only one in the meeting too dim not to grasp the significance of the numbers. So, you just nodded your head like the others. Well, guess what? No one else

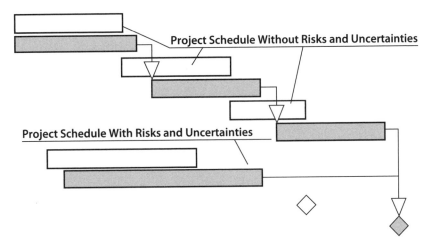

Figure 18-4. Gantt Chart that Combines Schedules with and without Risks

can understand those numbers, either. We all just nod our heads so we don't look foolish.

If you add quantitative analysis into the mix, the presentation can become even more obscure. The presenter might as well be speaking Greek with Latin subtitles on his slides. Everyone recognizes it as an impressive intellectual achievement, but no one has a clue as to what is being said. To avoid this scenario, here are few tips on how to present the results of decision analysis:

- Minimize the use of statistical terminology. If you say that the 95th percentile of the statistical distribution of duration is higher for the second alternative, you can be sure that you are speaking Greek to most of your audience; all that is missing is the subtitles. For the benefit of your audience, a better way of presenting your analysis is to show how one alternative is 50% more risky than the other one.

- Minimize the use of numbers in your presentation, especially those related to probabilities, correlation coefficients, percentiles, and other parameters. People understand numbers that have a reference point. Everybody understands dollars or days, but you cannot be sure that everyone in your audience understands standard deviation. You can test this assumption by simply asking your peers, "In what units is standard deviation measured?" The answers will be enlightening. Still, key numbers are very important.

- Use only a few statistical histograms. Quantitative analysis software tools can produce a wide array of different charts. Some of them are more intuitive, some less. For example, cumulative probability plots, as we already mentioned, are rather challenging to interpret. Even tornado and spider diagrams may cause some confusion. Thus, we recommend that you use only a couple of charts of the types shown in figures 18-2, 18-3, and 18-4.

- Finally, be creative! Use whatever you think is the most appropriate for your report.

Expressing Uncertainty

Probability is the relative frequency of an event, based on empirical evidence. If we have performed quantitative analysis, we can come up with some certain numbers (a 50% chance that the project will cost $100,000). In project management, however, we often do not have enough reliable data to assess probabilities. In these cases, people very often use verbal expressions of uncertainty, such as "possible," "probable," "may," "unlikely," and so on (Brun and Teigen 1988). One problem with these expressions is that people interpret these words differently. In his book *Psychology of Intelligence Analysis*, Richard Heuer (2016) gives the following example (see table 18-1).

Table 18-1. Example of the Report Table: Comparison of Revenue for Two Projects

	Project A	Project B
Deterministic (no risks and uncertainties)	$100,000	$120,000
With risks (low estimate)	$70,000	$100,000
With risks (mean)	$115,000	$150,000
With risks (high estimate)	$150,000	$200,000

Consider a report that there is little chance of a terrorist attack against the American embassy in Cairo at this time. If the ambassador's preconception is that there is no more than a 1-in-100 chance, she may elect not to do very much. If the ambassador's preconception is that there may be as much as a one-in-four chance of an attack, she may decide to do quite a bit. The term "little chance" is consistent with either interpretation, and there is no way to know what the report writer meant.

To illustrate the point, Heuer described an experiment with 23 NATO military officers working with intelligence reports. They were given a sentence beginning with "There is a little chance that. . . ." They were asked to assign a percentage to each verbal expression of uncertainty. The experiment showed a wide disparity in interpretation of these words. We did our own informal experiment with some engineers to see how their perception of uncertainty differed from that of the NATO officers. We asked 23 engineers involved in oil and gas projects to answer similar questions. Overall, our results were similar to Heuer's (figure 18-5).

Regardless of the area in which we work, our perception of uncertainty, when expressed in words, is very similar. The ranges associated with the answers are very high. To check it out, you can do this experiment in your organization.

Some industries have strict guidelines for what specific terms mean. For example, the oil and gas industries have well-defined classifications for both proven and possible reserves. In most industries, however, such guidelines are not available. If you are an analyst and need to express probabilities, try to use numbers rather than words. If you are a decision-maker who reads the reports, ask the analyst what "little chance" or "almost no chance" means.

The Power of Fear

In September 2006, the architect Nodar Kancheli gave an interview to a Moscow radio station. Shortly before the interview, he had been granted amnesty from

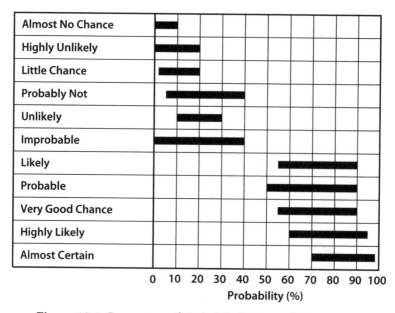

Figure 18-5. Perception of Verbal Definition of Uncertainty

charges of criminal negligence, stemming from mistakes he had made in the design of a large Moscow water park. In 2004 the roof of the water park collapsed and caused the deaths of 28 people. During the interview, Kancheli mentioned that there was a remote chance that the roof of Moscow's largest arena could also collapse during an upcoming Madonna concert because of the vibrations from the powerful speakers. We are sure that Kancheli was not trying to panic the public, but the media took his words out of context and broadcast them repeatedly over the next couple of days. Due to the engineer's notoriety from the previous collapse, he had some credibility (at least in the eyes of the public) as an expert in collaps-ing structures, which boosted this to become a major news story in Moscow. De-spite this "expert's" ominous warning, Madonna's concert merely "raised the roof" rather than collapsing it.

Sometimes we may report that there is a very small chance that a major or catastrophic event will occur. Some difficulties arise whenever we do this. First, we cannot actually comprehend probabilities on such a small scale. For exam-ple, if the chance of fire is 0.01% or 0.001%, what does that *mean*? Do you feel any more trepidation due to the higher probability of the former, compared to the latter? Probably not, because both probabilities are so small that they will have no significant impact upon your actions, although the first one is 10 times more likely than the second. On the other hand, you would surely appreciate the difference between a 6% chance and a 60% chance.

Let's assume that you have a report on your desk indicating a remote chance of some calamitous event. The report does not provide any concrete action plans, so it is your responsibility to furnish an action plan. The best way to determine your plan is to perform a reality check, based on its possible outcome. The simplest way to assess such an event is to create a rough estimate of its expected value. For example, an uninsured building that is under construction costs $200,000. The report tells you that of the 2,000 buildings that were constructed in the city over the past year, only one had a major fire. So, the chance of your building's suffering a major fire event is 1/2,000, and the expected loss would be $100.

In some cases, information about rare events is collected and used for guidelines or regulations. For example, most bridges can sustain extremely high floodwaters, but data indicates that once every thousand years there will be a flood high enough to collapse the bridge. We could build a bridge in such a way that it would sustain even the highest forecasted floods, but doing so would increase the costs so dramatically that it would make no economic sense.

Unfortunately, we usually lack sufficient historical data to make this type of assessment because there is no record of similar events. To use our example, how many times has an arena's roof collapsed during a rock concert because of sound waves? Scenarios like this make it very difficult to determine the probability of risk, but this is not the real problem you face.

Your main problem is that your judgment about the probability of these types of calamitous events can be tremendously influenced by emotions—particularly fear. In most cases, authors of an analytical report that includes a chance of a rare disastrous event are not trying to create a panic; they just want to ensure that the decision-makers are aware of all potential dangers to the project, regardless of how remote they are. Because people are prone to overreact to the threat of a disastrous event, quite often this psychological effect is taken advantage of by individuals who may want to promote a particular agenda. These individuals may be members of your project team, but often they are members of the media, politicians, local community activists, and other interested individuals and organizations. Their concerns cannot be discounted out of hand, for they often have valid points. For example, ecological considerations are frequently ignored unless one of these interested parties vividly demonstrates the destructive effect a project can have on, say, wildlife habitat.

How should you assess the probability and outcome of such rare events? If your own reality checks do not confirm the analytical assessment of the event, ask for more information. Has someone in your organization dealt with this type of event before? Can you look to any other organizations for accurate information? Do you have any information about analogous events? What is their probability? In cases of rare events with dramatic outcomes, intuition is generally *not* the preferred instrument for decision-making.

- Reporting the results of decision analysis is complicated by the fact that decision-makers have difficulties assessing information related to probabilities, risks, and uncertainties.
- When they interpret a report, decision-makers should take into an account that the authors of the report may have motivational biases.
- Presenting visualizations of the results of your decision analysis with a few intuitive charts will help decision-makers understand the report.
- To simplify interpretations of a report, analysts should avoid verbal definitions of uncertainties ("possible," "probable," "may," and others), minimize the use of statistical terminology, and present only the most important numerical results.
- Information about rare events with catastrophic consequences should be carefully presented to avoid biased assessment.

CHAPTER 19

Making a Choice with Multiple Objectives

Multi-criteria decision-making is a process that helps you incorporate conflicting objectives into your decision-making. The mental strategies we use to make choices with multiple objectives are the recognition, lexicographic, and elimination-by-aspect heuristics, among others. There are two approaches to multi-criteria decision-making: (1) convert all nonmonetary criteria to monetary equivalents, and (2) use special models and methodologies, such as a scoring model, to combine criteria of a different nature.

What Is Multi-Criteria Decision-Making?

In 2018, Dutch security services expelled Russian spies over a plot targeting the chemical weapons watchdog named the "Organisation for the Prohibition of Chemical Weapons (OPCW) in the Hague" (Harding 2018). Unlike James Bond, real-life spies need to submit an expense report. One of the expelled spies had retained his taxi receipt: he went by taxi from the Russian spy agency GRU's headquarters in Moscow to the city's international airport. He paid around $12. It is unknown if he was repaid, or if he left a tip. The taxi company later confirmed that receipt was real. The GRU has multiple objectives; among others, they need to ensure successful spying worldwide while managing expenses. Without controls in place, the entire Russian budget could possibly be spent funding the GRU's various capers. So, how can the GRU balance these objectives? In practical terms, how should the agency plan its spying projects to ensure high quality results, the physical safety of spying personnel, the lowest costs, and accountability?

Here is another example: global warming is one of the most complex, controversial, and highly political topics in the world today—which makes it a good subject to use as we examine the process of weighting different criteria in decision-making. As a society we see the benefits of economic growth, yet we also want to protect the environment. Measuring the effect that economic development has on climate change requires dealing with many uncertainties, since predicting economic processes and forecasting climate change are both inexact sciences. The main question is how to balance these conflicting criteria and make correct decisions. Similar types of problems, though not as complex, arise all the time in our projects as well as in our personal lives:

- A software company's dilemma: delivering software on time without jeopardizing quality
- A car manufacturer's dilemma: ensuring the durability of car parts without increasing the car's selling price
- A personal dilemma: determining the location of your home in either an expensive inner-city location close to work or an inexpensive location in the suburbs

In chapter 9 we discussed how to:

1. Determine project objectives and decision-making criteria.

2. Rank these objectives.

3. Identify potential trade-offs.

Eventually, we have to make a decision based on the criteria we have determined. In doing so, we need to understand how people make decisions with multiple objectives.

Here is a simple example: let's assume that you need to buy a new printer for your home office and you have three alternatives. Let's also assume that you need to use a single indicator for the analysis of these three alternatives—for example, cost, which is an indicator that captures all the positives and negatives of these alternatives. In this case, the decision is clear: select the printer with the lowest cost. Yet you will rarely come across criteria that allow for such an easy decision.

The problem is that in making decisions that contain multiple objectives, it is very difficult to put the different objectives into one equation. How do you translate quality-of-life issues (such as whether your chosen printer fits into your small home office, and how noisy it is) into monetary terms? In the same way, how does a corporation balance higher profits with a commitment to the environment? As a result, we tend to solve these problems intuitively, very often based on our emotions at a given moment.

Oil companies are not the cause of our ecological problems; rather, depending largely on the fossil fuels they produce has for a century been the way our economy operates. Businesses and commercial projects are basically concerned about a single criterion when they make decisions. This criterion has many different names: maximizing profit, improving NPV (net present value), maintaining cash flow. Essentially, they are all about money. Oil companies must weigh all their exploratory, production, and marketing decisions against this criterion.

In reality, in our economy if a company spends money on the environment, it is not a form of corporate altruism; it is doing so for the following reasons:

1. The company is going to make money out of it directly or indirectly. (For example, if a company invests in the environment to improve its public image, this should indirectly improve its profitability.)

2. The company is mandated to perform certain activities by government regulations.

Most projects are similar in that decisions are concerned with criteria that are directly associated with financial outcomes: scope, duration, and cost. Other parameters, such as quality and customer satisfaction, can also be associated with money, although the associations are less direct. But what about other criteria, such as safety, the environment, and community and employee relationships? If these criteria are not accounted for, major problems can arise. To address all these issues, we need to use multi-criteria decision-making methods.

> Multi-criteria decision-making helps incorporate multiple conflicting objectives formally into the decision-making process.

The Psychology of Balancing Multiple Objectives

As we have already learned, people make judgments about complex issues, using simplification strategies or heuristics. One of these rules of thumb is called the recognition heuristic (Goldstein and Gigerenzer 1999). Basically, if we have two alternatives, we usually make a choice based on the alternative we recognize. For example, if you are making choices between two components for your classic car, instead of analyzing all the pros and cons of the components, you will probably select the component that comes from a manufacturer you know. This explains why we often select a product based on brand name instead of performing a detailed analysis of features and benefits.

But what if both suppliers are equally recognizable? You may just make a random selection or go with your previous choice. Often your choice is affected by recent events, news, good presentations, or speeches—the availability heuristic we discussed in chapter 2. For example, you attended a presentation about the importance of quality management processes. The speaker presented examples of some successful projects where quality management processes were followed. But what impressed you most was a case study that showed the obverse: how the neglect of quality management led to disastrous consequences.

After that presentation, you will probably think that quality is the only criterion you need to consider. As a result, you may concentrate on quality improvement, to the detriment of cost, safety, and the environment. If you ignored the other competing objectives, you would deliver a high-quality but over-budget project and would possibly face lawsuits from workers' safety organizations and environmental groups.

Another mental strategy is called the lexicographic heuristic (Tversky 1969). In it, you rank criteria from the most to the least important. For example, the price of a component will be the most important, performance will be less important, and the country of manufacturing will be the least important. If all components have the same price, you make a selection based on performance. If all components have the same performance, you make a choice based on your preferred country of manufacturing.

This heuristic is called lexicographic because a similar algorithm is used to order words in dictionaries. For example, "dusk" will follow "desk" because when first letters are the same (d), second letters are used to order the word. This is called a ranking heuristic.

If one criterion is significantly more important than another, the lexicographic heuristic works well. However, if the relationship between various criteria is complex, this heuristic can cause problems. If you are basing your decision on a weighting of price, performance, and the manufacturer's delivery history, the ranking becomes much more complex, and the ability to make the correct choice becomes more difficult.

Another heuristic is called elimination by aspect (Tversky 1972). We already discussed the analytical formal method of creative thinking by using filters (see chapter 5), which is conceptually similar to this heuristic. Elimination by aspect is a mental strategy in which you eliminate a potential choice if it does not satisfy certain conditions. For example, you can eliminate all alternatives that have high prices, show low performance, and are manufactured outside your country. As a result, only a few potential alternatives (if any) will remain. The problem with this heuristic is that some potentially good alternatives can be eliminated because this approach does not include an analysis of trade-offs. For example, the price of a component may not be preferable; however, all other attributes may be very good. Alternatively, the price of a component may be very good, but the quality is poor. If you use the elimination-by-aspect heuristic, depending upon your ranking schema, you could unintentionally reject good alternatives and select alternatives that are less than optimal.

If you feel that intuitive strategies are not enough to help you make a choice with multiple objectives, you can use a variety of analytical methods to solve these puzzles.

Two Approaches to Multi-Criteria Decision-Making

Two approaches can help you make a decision when dealing with multiple objectives (Schuyler 2016):

1. **Convert all nonmonetary criteria to their monetary equivalents.**

With this approach, you convert all your criteria into dollar equivalents. The problem is that this type of accounting does not always work. For example, as of 2011, the Environmental Protection Agency set the value of a human life at $9.1 million. The Food and Drug Administration put it at $7.9 million, while the Department of Transportation figure was approximately $6 million (Partnoy 2012). These numbers are used in decision-making performed by these agencies, in particular deciding how much money they should be willing to spend to save a person from dying.

How much do you think your own life is worth? Are you worth more or less than your manager? Clearly, it is difficult to come up with some cost estimates, especially for criteria like the value we put on a human life that everyone will agree with.

2. Use special models and methodologies to combine criteria of a different nature.

Health, safety, environment, job satisfaction, corporate cultures—these are criteria that are used to make project decisions but are extremely difficult to convert to monetary equivalents. After you identify and rank these criteria, you must come up with a formula or algorithm to rank alternatives based on them. We will review one of the simplest methods: the scoring model.

Ranking Criteria with the Scoring Model

The scoring model is a relatively easy method for identifying the best alternative in a multi-criteria decision problem. Here is how it works:

1. Identify your decision-making criteria. This occurs during the identification of the project objectives (see chapter 9).

2. Assign a weight for each criterion, which is its relative importance in relation to the other criteria. An example is shown in table 19-1.

Table 19-1. Decision-Making Criteria and Their Relative Weights

	Criterion	Importance	Weight
1	Cost	Very important	10
2	Quality	Very important	10
3	Safety	Very important	10
4	Low maintenance	Important	6
5	Community relationship	Not very important	3
6	Customer satisfaction	Not very important	3

Table 19-2. Score Calculation for Two Alternatives

	Criterion	Weight	Alternative A		Alternative B	
			Rating	Score	Rating	Score
1	Cost	10	0.5	$0.5 \times 10 = 5.0$	0.1	$0.1 \times 10 = 1.0$
2	Quality	10	0.5	$0.5 \times 10 = 5.0$	1.0	$1.0 \times 10 = 10.0$
3	Safety	10	1.0	$1.0 \times 10 = 10.0$	0.8	$0.8 \times 10 = 8.0$
4	Low maintenance	6	0.2	$6 \times 0.2 = 1.2$	0.2	$6 \times 0.2 = 1.2$
5	Community relationship	3	0.5	$3 \times 0.5 = 1.5$	0.5	$3 \times 0.5 = 1.5$
6	Customer satisfaction	3	1.0	$1.0 \times 3 = 3.0$	0.8	$0.8 \times 3 = 2.4$
	Total Score			25.7		24.1

3. Assign a rating to each criterion that shows how well each decision alterative satisfies the criterion.

4. Compute the score for each alternative. The example is shown in table 19-2.

In this example, alternative A has highest score and should be selected.

A major flaw with this method should be obvious right away: weights for different criteria, as well as ratings, are highly subjective. In table 19-2, why, for example, does "cost" have a rank of 10 and "customer satisfaction" a rank of 3? These weights actually reflect an organization's decision policy, which is usually well established long before a ranking is done, and the selection of criteria and assigning of weights for all portfolios or projects is based upon that policy. The selection of criteria and assignment of weights can be the responsibility of a panel of experts that coordinates the decision analysis process while taking into account the organization's decision policies.

David Skinner (2009) recommends using a radar chart to visualize different strategies against multiple objectives. When you select multiple objectives and rank different strategies based on these objectives, you can display them on a chart similar to figure 19-1. The only limitation is that in this example the criteria have been assigned the same weight.

Advanced Methods of Multi-Criteria Decision-Making

If you can take only one key point away from this chapter, it is that the roots of many problems, such as global warming, lie in our inability to balance different objectives in our decision-making processes. A critical mistake that many project managers make is to base their decisions on a single criterion—usually

Figure 19-1. Radar Chart Used to Compare Strategies against Multiple Objectives

money—and then select the alternative that is the cheapest or has the most revenue potential.

In most cases, the simple scoring method and the radar chart will provide good solutions for problems involving multiple criteria. However, if you are dealing with large and complex projects, we strongly recommend that you engage the services of an independent consultant. Consultants have experience with many tools and methodologies to deal with multi-criteria decision-making. We include a list of these methods with references in appendix D.

- Many issues in project management are complex because they involve the selection of alternatives based on multiple and often conflicting criteria.
- People use simplified mental strategies when they make choices. Among these strategies are the recognition heuristic, the lexicographic heuristic, and the elimination-by-aspect heuristic.
- Using a single decision-making criterion, such as a monetary equivalent, can unwittingly cause some good project alternatives to be eliminated.
- Decision analysis methods, such as the scoring model, can help us select alternatives based on multiple criteria.

PART 5

Implementation, Monitoring, and Reviews

CHAPTER 20

Adaptive Project Management

Adaptive project management is a powerful method that incorporates constant learning and improvement. Quantitative analysis helps compare original assumptions with actual project data. Instead of making an irreversible major decision at the start of a project, it is important that project managers focus on making small sequential choices. Adaptive project management can be implemented only in a creative business environment, where potential issues and problems can be identified and corrected at an early stage.

Adaptive Management as Part of Project Decision Analysis

After the framing, modeling, and analysis phases of our work, we finally come to one of the important milestones in the project—the project launch. Why is that so monumental? It's primarily because many projects never make it to this stage. If the decision process is working correctly, the weakness in a project will be seen and the project will not be launched.

As we start to execute the project plan, we now have the opportunity to see how the project progresses in actuality—no longer just in theory—and can make necessary adjustments to our original plan. This process is called adaptive management. Adaptive management is a process of continually improving decisions by learning from the outcomes of decisions previously taken.

> Adaptive management is a process of continually improving decisions by learning from the outcomes of previous decisions.

Because of the many risks and uncertainties in a complex project, it is impossible to envision everything in the planning stage. We now have new inputs to our decision-making process: actual project performance.

The adaptive management concept was introduced by ecologists in the 1970s (Holling 2005; Walters 2002) and has become an effective tool in both ecological and environmental management. Environmental and project management have many things in common.

For one thing, both deal with multiple uncertainties. We believe that project managers can effectively apply adaptive management practices to their projects.

A key area of overlap between the two processes is the principle of continuity, which we discussed in chapter 3 as one of the key concepts for project decision analysis (along with consistency and comprehensiveness). Continuity is also a key principle of adaptive management. Look back at figure 3-3 in chapter 3. The arrows from the box "Implementation, Monitoring, Review" point to other phases of the decision analysis process. These arrows represent the iterative process of adaptive management. By analyzing the actual project performance, you can update the following:

- **Original assumptions made during decision-framing.** For example, you may add or retire certain risks. Sometimes you will have to update project objectives, assumptions about the business environment, and available resources.

- **Valuation models.** You can update the schedule or reassess the probability of certain risks. Active adaptive management may involve defining multiple models for different alternatives and testing them during the course of the project (Linkov et al. 2006b).

- **Quantitative analysis.** You can run a new analysis using Event chain methodology with an updated schedule model and risk breakdown structure.

Here is an example: when an oil company decides to start drawing oil from one of its reserves, it estimates the reserves in place using all available information: seismic surveys, exploratory data, and analogous information from nearby wells. If and when the well starts producing, the oil company can then use actual production data to refine its original estimates about the size of the reserve (Rose 2001). Although in some situations it is impossible to estimate precisely the volume of oil in the reserve until almost the entire field is produced, the company can reduce uncertainties and can update economic and production models based on new information obtained during the course of the project.

Principles of Adaptive Management

Adaptive project management consists of five basic principles that help you monitor the course of your project and refine your original decisions.

PRINCIPLE 1: USE ACTUAL PROJECT DATA IN COMBINATION WITH ORIGINAL ASSUMPTIONS

During the execution of a project, a manager might behave in either of two extreme ways:

1. Disregards the original assumptions made during the planning stage of the project.

2. Ignores the implications of the new data and adheres resolutely to the original forecast. This occurs because of differing motivational and cognitive biases, such as optimism or overconfidence, and because warning signs about the failing project are often ignored.

Neither extreme is desirable. Assuming that the original estimates were done using relevant historical data or expert opinion, both the original plan and the new data should come into play together. Let's say we have a project where we originally estimated that it would earn net revenue of $1 million by year-end, but by April net revenue is already $0.5 million. Should we readdress our estimate, and if so, how? If we simply multiply the current revenue by three to account for the remaining number of months, this may not account for expected slow summer sales. The solution is to perform an analysis and compare it with trends for current and previous years.

A number of techniques can help us forecast the future, based on actual and historical data. One such technique is regression analysis. Generally, regression analysis is a statistical technique for investigating and modeling the relationship between variables. If we know how a variable such as cost changes over time, we can come up with a forecast for future cash flows. Then, if we add actual data to the analysis, the quality of regression analysis improves.

When we deal with probabilities, the situation is much more complex. It is easy to ignore base-rate frequencies when trying to combine actual and historical data, especially if they are related to probabilities. Let's say we estimated that the chance of a certain risk occurring was 20%, but with the project only half completed the risk has already occurred twice. What is the chance that the risk will occur during the reminder of the project? We previously discussed this problem in the chapter on Event chain methodology, particularly in the section on performance tracking (see chapter 17). One of the solutions to this problem is to use a Bayes theorem to analyze the value of imperfect information. Using the Bayesian formula, you can combine original estimates of probabilities (prior probability or marginal probability) and data obtained as a result of actual project measurement. The actual formula is used in various analysis software (see appendix A).

PRINCIPLE 2: MINIMIZE THE COST OF DECISION REVERSALS ("TRY NOT TO KILL THE COW")

There is an old legend in which an elderly woman, having spent her last penny, decided to sell off her only cow to be slaughtered for meat. She called the local village butcher, who told her there were three pricing levels:

A. *The total weight of the live cow*

B. *The total weight of the dead cow after initial processing*

> C. *The total weight of the processed carcass, minus by-products that could
>   not be sold*

*The price per pound for B is greater than that for A, and for C is greater than that
for B. The problem is, the woman had to make her choice before the cow was
slaughtered. If she chose to kill the cow, she would get a higher price per unit of
weight, but would this be more or less than what she would receive for the live
cow? If she decided to kill the cow first, she would be faced with the same type of
decision when choosing between options B and C. However, she would be constrained by the fact that once she decided to forgo option A, her options would
then be limited to B and C. In other words, the decision to kill the cow is irrevocable. We are not experts in the cow-killing business, but we feel fairly confident
in saying that trying to resurrect a cow would not be a trivial process.*

*The old lady had the difficult task of estimating whether the cow would be worth
more dead or alive. Lacking any real data, she had to gamble. "Kill the cow," she
said. And she won: the dead cow was worth more than the live one. She also went
on to guess correctly when she agreed to the further processing of the cow. As a
result, she got the maximum possible price for her cow. The legend doesn't tell us
if she used her newfound money to buy milk.*

We do not recommend that you gamble with your projects—it is a bad idea, even
though a lot of project managers routinely do it. But what if your original decision
happened to be wrong? How much would it cost to go back and salvage the project? (That is, how much would it cost to bring your dead cow back to life?)

When you are performing a decision analysis, we recommend that you
consider the cost of decision reversal, meaning the cost associated with all the
expenses related to a wrong decision. In theory, the cost of a decision reversion
can be between zero and infinity for an irrevocable decision like killing a cow
(figure 20-1).

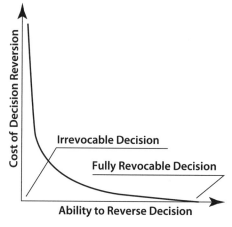

Figure 20-1. Cost of Decision Reversal

The idea behind this concept is that when you make a decision, you should also try to formulate an alternative that you can implement at minimum cost. For example, if you are an opera producer, you should always have the phone number of an easy replacement for your diva if she ends up in rehab after her fifteenth divorce. If you remember, in *The Phantom of the Opera*, the producers had a similar issue when they had to bring in a new star, Christine (the object of the Phantom's affection), after the original star was poisoned by the phantom. One never knows what goes on backstage.

Unfortunately, you cannot always make a U-turn in the middle of a project because it brings up a whole new set of risks: heavy traffic and slick roads.

PRINCIPLE 3: MAKE SMALL, SEQUENTIAL DECISIONS

The movie *Wag the Dog* is a good example of a project with multiple uncertainties and sequential decisions. Just two weeks before the presidential election, the president finds himself embroiled in a scandal that is threatening to escalate and ruin his chances at reelection. To divert attention from the scandal, the president's handlers and advisors decide to invent another crisis, a war with Albania (decision #1). With the help of a famed Hollywood producer, the president's advisor has several fake war scenes staged and distributed to the media. When they find themselves being undermined by other elements in the government, the advisors decide to add another twist to the tale by inventing a hero left behind enemy lines (decision #2), whose televised rescue will captivate the American audience. Unfortunately (for them), in an unexpected turn of events, "the hero" turns out to be a violent psychotic, and in the end he is shot. Still trying to make the best of a bad situation, the president's advisors decide to continue the charade by staging a state funeral for "the hero" (decision #3).

While this example is somewhat extreme (but very amusing), it shows how decisions can be made as a response to a constantly changing business situation. In other words, the advisors were using iterative decision-making.

In chapter 12 we discussed the use of the agile methodology in project management. We mentioned the benefits of an iterative approach, in which requirements are not completely defined up front and a working (and constantly redefined) project is delivered to the client on a regular basis.

Now we will prove to you mathematically that managing risks and uncertainties using an iterative project management process will save you both time and money. Let's assume that we have two scenarios affected by the same risk (figure 20-2):

- **Scenario 1.** There are three 20-day tasks, and each task has a risk "change of requirements" with a probability of 20%. If the risk occurs, the task will have to be restarted. The risks for each task are not correlated, so three small, separate decisions will be reviewed and, if necessary, corrected during the course of the project.

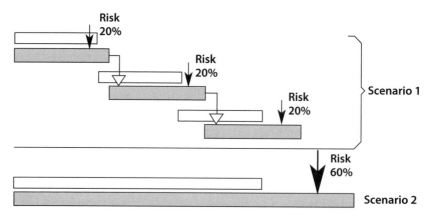

Figure 20-2. Quantitative Analysis of Two Project Scenarios

- **Scenario 2.** There is one 60-day task with the same risk, "change of requirements," but with a probability of 60%. If the risk occurs, the task will have to be restarted. This will require only one strategic decision, which will be strictly followed during the course of the project.

Which scenario will be completed first? An answer to these types of questions requires quantitative analysis. In this case, we will use Event chain methodology for the analysis. The original project schedule is shown on the event chain diagram as white bars. The project schedule with risks has gray bars. Table 20-1 shows the results of the analysis.

As you can see, the project scenario with the three 20-day tasks will be completed, on average, 17% faster than the project scenario with one large task. Moreover, if the risk "change of requirements" is most likely to occur at the end of the task, the difference between the two scenarios will be even more significant. In addition, the second scenario is also much riskier, because the range between low and high estimates of duration is much larger than that for the first scenario.

What this means is that projects with risks can be completed earlier if they are done iteratively. The iterative approach ensures faster feedback, which can be a result of testing, prototyping, demonstration to the client, and so on. Through this process, we can learn from actual experience and can then apply this learning to the next stage or iteration of the project.

PRINCIPLE 4: SUPPORT CREATIVE BUSINESS ENVIRONMENTS

If during a project you receive new information, you should be able to use it to steer the project in the right direction. At the same time, you do not want to create chaos by making

> Constraint learning and improvements can be implemented only in a creative business environment.

frequent U-turns as a response to small requests or small changes in the business environment.

Table 20-1. Results of Quantitative Analysis: Duration of Project in Days

	Risk most likely occurs at the end of the activity (triangular distribution for moment of risk)			Risk most likely occurs at the end of the activity (triangular distribution for moment of risk)		
	Risk			Risk		
	Low Estimate (P10)	Mean	High Estimate (P90)	Low Estimate (P10)	Mean	High Estimate (P90)
Scenario 1: 3 tasks, 20 days each	60	68	80	60	66	78
Scenario 2: 1 task, 60 days	60	84	115	60	78	110

Unfortunately, many organizations are not able to strike a balance between their ability to improve projects by using actual project information and their change-control process. Often, the change-control process is so vigorous that it suppresses any creative decision-making. For such organizations, the main problem is that necessary corrective actions will not be taken because of organizational pressure. If this is an issue, you will not be able to resolve it without major improvements occurring in the organization's culture.

PRINCIPLE 5: IDENTIFY AND FIX PROBLEMS EARLY (AVOIDING BEHAVIORAL TRAPS)

Suppose that during the project planning stage we made certain decisions that have been proven to be wrong during the execution of the project. However, we are reluctant to make necessary changes.

The longer we continue with an incorrect course of action, the more difficult it will be to reverse the course of action. This phenomenon has several different explanations, including technical and organizational. One of the most common explanations is related to behavioral traps. For example, the more money we invest in a failing project, the more money may be lost. This is the sunk-cost effect, which we discussed in chapter 2. The longer we continue to develop a software application with an unfriendly user interface, the more we get accustomed to it, and the more difficult it is to create a new interface. Therefore, it is very important to identify problems as soon as possible, perform an analysis, and try to fix them.

The PMBOK Guide *Approach to Project Executing, Monitoring, and Controlling*

The *PMBOK Guide* does not explicitly use the term "adaptive management." However, you will find important information related to adaptive management in two of the *Guide's* process groups: project executing and project monitoring and controlling.

The project monitoring and controlling process group includes the following project management processes:

1. **Monitor and control project work.** This includes collecting information, measuring project performance, and updating forecasts.

2. **Integrated change control.** This occurs when any changes made to the project scope through corrective and preventive actions need to be collected, analyzed, documented, and either approved or rejected. For example, as a result of testing, one component of the device does not meet specifications. While this issue needs to be addressed, this change may occur in the middle of the project and affect many other activities. This kind of impact must be carefully analyzed.

3. **Quality control.** This includes measurements, corrective and preventive action, recommended defect repairs, validation of deliverables, and other outputs. Good quality can be achieved not only by original design but also by constant testing and monitoring during the course of a project. It is very important to find a problem or a defect as early as possible; otherwise, the repair can be much more costly.

4. **Risk monitoring and control.** This includes tracking risks, monitoring residual risks (for which risk response is implemented), identifying new risks as early as possible, recommending preventive actions, and executing risk-response plans during the course of a project. The *PMBOK Guide* (chapter 11) recommends regularly reassessing risks based on actual project data. Risk audits can help to control the efficiency of risk responses. Reserve analysis helps to determine the amount of contingency reserves remaining at any time in the project.

Other processes included as part of the project monitoring and controlling process group include scope verification, scope control, schedule control, project team management (tracking the performance of team members and coordinating changes to enhance performance), performance reporting, stakeholders management, and contract administration.

One technique mentioned in the *PMBOK Guide* that can be used in adaptive management is a technical performance measurement, in which you constantly compare technical accomplishments during the course of a project with the project plan.

Adaptive Management and Changing Requirements

Let's assume that you are a famed British dressmaker and you are tasked with designing and making a wedding dress for a royal wedding. You know that the probability that the client's requirements for the dress will change over time is 100%. The question is what requirements and what changes will be required.

Changing requirements is one of the main uncertainties that project managers often face. There are two ways to manage this uncertainty:

1. Accept the changing requirements, and when they do change, use change management processes to address them.

2. Recognize that requirements may change, perform an analysis, and select the best course of actions, given the probability that requirements will change. If these acts are done properly, the value of the project can be significantly increased (Bordley et al. 2019). There are different ways to plan for changes in project requirement. One is risk-response planning, which we discussed in chapter 10. Change of requirements is a probabilistic event, which would trigger activity or group of activities as a response to the event.

So, what is the most effective way to manage requirements? It is difficult to plan projects in a manner that take into account all possible changes in requirements. Therefore, the solution is a hybrid approach: to plan a response to the most unstable requirements and then to implement change management processes when unplanned changes occur. If you are a dressmaker for royalty, you can probably anticipate some alterations, such as making longer sleeves that can be adjusted later. Yet some requests by your client will be difficult to anticipate and you will need to manage these changes according to adaptive process.

Adaptive project management is a process of constant learning, feedback, and improvement to the project management process. Adaptive project management is based on five main principles:

1. Combining original assumptions and actual project data through quantitative analysis
2. Minimizing the cost of a decision reversal
3. Using an iterative approach to decision-making
4. Having a supportive organizational culture
5. Identifying and resolving issues as early as possible

CHAPTER 21

Did You Make the Right Choice?
Reviewing Project Decisions

Post-project reviews of project decisions are important because they allow you to improve future decisions. However, these reviews can be influenced by a number of psychological biases. For example, management will often believe that project failures were more readily foreseeable than they actually were. A corporate knowledge base should provide a source of information about previous decisions and their outcomes.

Why Do We Need Post-Project Reviews?

Now that you have completed your project, you have reached the point where you need to review and understand any and all lessons learned from it. When you perform your project reviews, you need to address certain questions:

- Which choices were correct and incorrect? Why?
- Did you correctly identify risks and assign their probabilities and outcomes? Did you plan your risk responses properly?
- How do the results of your quantitative analysis compare with the actual data? If they are different, why?

Answering these questions during project review is one of the most important steps in the decision analysis process, because it will improve decision-making in the future. Most organizations perform these assessments, either formally or informally.

Unfortunately, not many organizations analyze how they selected their project plan from among the alternatives and determined the probabilities of the risk events. Moreover, few organizations have mechanisms in place to store this information where it can be easily retrieved. Often, the only record of this analysis is stored in the memories of the participants. Given normal staff turnover and the vagaries of human memory, this is a high-risk strategy in itself.

Before we explain how to set up a post-project review process in your organization, let's examine a number of psychological biases related to project reviews.

How Could We Not Foresee It?

Well before Hurricane Katrina struck New Orleans (figure 21-1) in August 2005, there were many predictions of how a hurricane would wreak disaster on the city (Wilson 2001; Fischetti 2001; Mooney 2005). In 2001, the *Houston Chronicle* published a story that predicted that if a severe hurricane hit New Orleans, it "would strand 250,000 people or more, and probably kill one of 10 left behind as the city drowned under 20 feet of water. Thousands of refugees could land in Houston" (Berger 2001).

Much of New Orleans sits below sea level. To prevent flooding, the city is defended by an extensive levee system. Parts of the system are quite old, and concerns had long been expressed about the system's ability to withstand the stress that a strong hurricane would impose upon it. Following Hurricane Katrina's landfall in August 2005, the levees failed in several places. Floodwater from Lake Pontchartrain inundated the city and caused many deaths and billions of dollars in damage. In the aftermath of Katrina, investigations have demonstrated that the levee failures were not caused by natural forces that exceeded the intended design strength. Rather, and alarmingly, the problem lay in the design of the structures, in addition to poor maintenance practices that exacerbated the condition of the levees. It is important to mention that the mechanism of potential levee failure was known years before Hurricane Katrina struck.

The question is, if so many warnings had been raised about potential problems with the levees and the risk of hurricanes, why weren't more resources invested to improve the levee system? Now, years after the event, these warnings are considered not to be probabilities, but absolute certainties. Before Hurricane Katrina struck, federal, state, and municipal governments and other organizations did not believe that major improvements to the levee system were a main priority. This was because the probability of an event as destructive as Katrina was underestimated, even though a number of experts had warned about the risk. Because the cost of protection against such an extreme event must be juggled with other public priorities, only a limited amount of work to improve the levees was done.

This psychological phenomenon occurs not only in major calamities but in project failures, as well. Often, as we look back at a failed project, we just cannot understand how we did not foresee a catastrophic event when we were given so many warnings. What caused us to ignore those warnings?

In reality, we are experiencing a common psychological phenomenon that occurs when reviewing the results of project decision analysis: *after the event, we tend to believe that project failures were more readily foreseeable than was in fact the case.*

Figure 21-1. Flooding in Northwest New Orleans and Metairie
after Hurricane Katrina (Credit: U.S. Coast Guard, 2005)

In any project there is a chance of failure or a major risk event that can significantly affect it. However, if the probability is deemed small, the project will proceed with risk mitigation in place. Risk mitigation does not mean that the risk will be completely removed, only that the probability of the risk's occurring and its potential impact will be reduced. Let's assume that an event occurred and caused major problems. In the aftermath of this event, management will believe that the wrong decision was made. But this is not necessarily true, for the decision could have been correct as long as decision analysis was performed using the most comprehensive information available at the time.

Situations are much more difficult when an unpredicted risk event occurs. Generally, these events were not foreseen because there was incomplete or imperfect data to perform an analysis. However, once an event has occurred, it is impossible to erase any knowledge of the event and to reconstruct the mental processes that occurred before the event.

During the decision process, a lot of irrelevant information must be sorted through (Wohlstetter 1962). Do you recall the movie *Tora! Tora! Tora!*, which dramatized the events leading up to and during the Japanese attack on Pearl Harbor? At the start of the movie, several scenes describe the warnings about an impending attack that the military and political leaders received and also the chain of events that led them to underestimate or disregard the threat. After watching this movie, you might wonder how all those people missed so many obvious signs of an impending attack and how so many could get it so terribly wrong. In reality, there were many, many other events occurring at the time that were not shown in the movie. Since we all have 20/20 hindsight, it always becomes clear to us after the fact which information was relevant and which was not. Because of this phenomenon, after a risk event occurs, management tends to believe that it should have been easy to foresee the risk and make the correct decision.

"I Knew It All Along"

Did the decision analysis process help us make better decisions for this particular project? How much more did we learn from the analysis than we already knew? These are very common questions raised by the members of management that approved the decisions.

"I knew it all along," referred to in psychology as the hindsight bias, is an extremely common psychological bias. Management usually underestimates how much they learned from the decision analysis process. As a result, management tends to undervalue the process—after all, they think, "Why bother with decision analysis if we already know the answer!"

At the project initialization phase, you presented a risk management plan to your manager. One of the risks was a major delay in the delivery of a component. Based on the analysis, you believed it was a critical risk, and in response you created a mitigation plan for it—purchase the component from another vendor. Your manager was not so sure, but agreed to include it in the project plan. Sure enough, this risk event occurred. Fortunately for the project, you had lined up another vendor in advance, and the project was completed as planned. When you have your project review, your manager (who now possesses 20/20 hindsight) notes that the fact that the component delivery risk was critical was obvious, regardless of your risk analysis. He goes further, questioning the value of your quantitative analysis, as this was something he says he intuitively knew. Next time, the manager may not give you an opportunity to do another analysis.

Once an event occurs, many people, not just decision-makers, tend to exaggerate how much probability they had lent to the event's occurring. Before it occurred, they might have thought the probability was 15%, but afterward they will probably confess that they were 99% sure that the event would occur.

Overestimating the Accuracy of Past Judgments

The two previous biases that we discussed affect managers when they try to evaluate project decisions. Yet project managers or analysts who perform the analysis are not immune from similar biases. In particular, both tend to overestimate the accuracy of past judgments.

Here is a small psychological experiment you can perform in your organization: ask a project manager to re-create, from memory, a risk list or risk breakdown structure he or she defined during a project initialization phase about a year ago. Now compare it with the original risk list. You will most likely find that in the new list the probabilities for risks that actually occurred are much higher than they were in the original list.

The knowledge of outcomes affects our memory of previous analyses. When analysts know the outcome, they will believe that they properly identified the event and assigned the correct probability. The more time that has passed since the original decision analysis was conducted, the greater the effect of this bias.

The Peak-End Rule

One curious heuristic is the peak-end rule, in which we judge our past experiences almost entirely on how they were at their peak (whether pleasant or unpleasant) and how they ended (Kahneman et al. 1999). When we do this, we discard other information, including net pleasantness or unpleasantness and how long the experience lasted. This heuristic affects project reviews because many project stakeholders remember only certain project details. You may recall the product launch itself (the first stage of the project) along with some highlights during the project (like the CEO's visit and a subsequent dinner in a good restaurant), but you probably don't remember why, how, and by whom certain choices were made.

The *PMBOK Guide* recommends identifying lessons learned at *any* point in the project. In other words, it recommends that you collect and record information about all major project decisions and events at all stages of the project. This helps to mitigate memory errors associated with the peak-end rule.

The Process of Reviewing Decisions

Actual project reviews or retrospectives are usually performed as part of other business processes. The *PMBOK Guide* recommends creating an organizational corporate knowledge base, which should include a "historical information and lessons learned knowledge base." This information is collected during the project execution. The Closing Project process includes the Updates of Organizational Process Assets procedure, where "historical information and lessons learned information are transferred to the lessons learned knowledge base for use by future projects." In practical terms, this means that the results of project reviews should be saved in an organization's knowledge base so they can be referenced when planning future projects.

In software development processes, such as the Rational Unified Process (RUP) (Kruchten 2003), reviews help to determine whether the established goal was achieved. Such reviews or retrospectives include people, processes, and tools and can be performed after each project iteration. A similar process of reviewing project decisions is called project retrospectives (Kerth 2001). In retrospective, the entire team meets to review what the project goals were, what actually happened during the project, why it happened, and how to improve related processes going forward.

Certain steps should be taken to capture information that is necessary to evaluate project decision-making:

1. Assess input information that was created at the project planning stage:
   * Project schedules
   * Risk-management plans, including risk breakdown structures with assigned probabilities of certain events
   * Strategy tables and other information used to select alternatives
   * Results of quantitative analysis

2. Compare input information with actual data:
   * Was the selected alternative correct?
   * Which events occurred, and which did not?
   * Were duration and cost estimates accurate?

3. Briefly document the conclusions, and store the document in a corporate knowledge base.

Corporate Knowledge Base

An organizational knowledge base is a repository, either paper or electronic, where one can find historical information about decisions, as well as lessons learned, in previous projects. How would a knowledge base work in reality?

In one engineering company, we met with a very interesting person. He was about 75 years old and had worked his entire life in the same organization. He probably had been working there for 50 years, serving in many different positions. Fresh out of college, he accepted a position as a junior engineer, and eventually he rose to become head of his department. For the last 20 years, he had worked as a full-time internal consultant to the various divisions in the company. Primarily, he himself was valued as the corporate "knowledge base."

Although he was not able to generate new engineering ideas, this individual's long-term memory was excellent. When asked, he analyzed each project to learn if there were any historical precedents that could be applicable. He looked to see if somebody had been faced with similar issues and what the results of their decisions were. By drawing on this knowledge, he was able to make some fairly accurate judgments about the actual probability of certain events.

While that human knowledge base seemed to work fine for the engineering company, human memory always has some limitations. First of all, it is hard to find a person or a group of people who have the capacity to remember and understand all relevant previous projects. Second, everyone has cognitive and motivational biases that can affect their judgment about previous decisions.

Fortunately, a number of computer tools are available to help establish a company's knowledge base. Some of them are specifically designed for organizational knowledge bases, and many portfolio management software products have document management functionalities, as well.

Not all companies have corporate portfolio management software, and not all companies would choose to store documents related to decision analysis, even if it had the software to do so. Here is a simple and effective way to establish a corporate knowledge base: save all your documents on a corporate intranet in such a way that they can be searched using search tools like Google. These tools can be used effectively in internal sites where you can search your internal archives. Just make sure you use proper keywords for your documents so that the search tool can return the most relevant documents.

- Review of project decisions is a very important step, for it will improve future decision-making.
- After an event, management will believe that project failures were more readily foreseeable than they were originally.
- After a project is complete, management will tend to underestimate the value of decision analysis.
- Project managers or analysts who performed the decision analysis tend to overestimate the accuracy of past judgments.
- The simplest way to establish a corporate knowledge base is to save documents related to completed projects on a searchable corporate intranet.

CONCLUSION

Does Decision Analysis Provide a Solution?

"It is our choices, Harry, that show what we truly are, far more than our abilities."

—DUMBLEDORE TO HARRY POTTER IN J. K. ROWLING'S
HARRY POTTER AND THE CHAMBER OF SECRETS

In this book we reviewed the multiple aspects of the formalized decision analysis process and its application in project management. Experience of various projects in different industries where decision analysis was used demonstrates its efficiency and usefulness. *It is always cheaper to perform analysis—including decision analysis—in advance, rather than having to fix problems when the project has started.* Still, there are a number of misconceptions related to the decision analysis process.

Common Misconceptions about Decision Analysis
MISCONCEPTION 1: THE DECISION ANALYSIS PROCESS IS NOT BENEFICIAL BECAUSE IT CANNOT ENSURE PROJECT SUCCESS

Failure of a project is simply *not* an indication that the decision analysis process did not work. As described at the start of this book, both NASA and Lockheed Martin took calculated risks and invested in new, unproven technologies. Without taking any risks at all, the research and development would have been impossible. To mitigate some of the risks, NASA and Lockheed Martin built a cheaper test vehicle instead of a full-scale spacecraft. In cases like this, decision analysis can help reduce the number of irrational project decisions and can significantly mitigate their negative outcomes.

MISCONCEPTION 2: DECISION ANALYSIS ADDS ADDITIONAL LEVELS OF BUREAUCRACY

Absolutely anything can devolve into a bureaucratic procedure. For example, when you go to the supermarket, you put your groceries on the conveyor belt and give the cashier your credit card, followed by the store's loyalty card, cards from affiliated loyalty programs, perhaps a gift certificate, coupons from the store, and so on. You get the picture. In return, the cashier gives you a receipt, your credit card receipt, and some coupons. In addition, you collect 30 coupons that will give you a 5% discount on various items on your next shopping trip. What used to be a quick exchange of goods for cash is now a web of mind-boggling transactions.

> Organizations should use a decision analysis process, provided that everyone feels it is helpful. If the process creates extra delay or introduces a paperwork burden, scrap it immediately.

Decision analysis does not necessarily imply additional administrative overhead. It is more a way of thinking than a documentation management process, and it should be made as simple as possible. We have stressed throughout the book that a decision analysis process can be tailored to meet specific organizational needs. For example, if you do not think that quantitative analysis is going to add any benefit to your project, no problem—don't use it.

Remember that the main purposes of decision analysis are to:

- Come up with real alternatives
- Analyze which alternative will bring the most value
- Select a course of action and monitor its progress (most organizations already do this in one way or another)

Organizations spend huge amounts of resources establishing business processes, usually for business software, training, consulting, and such. And in most cases, that is a good investment for the right causes. Sometimes such processes do not work as planned and do, in fact, create a bureaucracy that leads to more spending. If this occurs, it is important to freeze the implementation and make necessary adjustments; or if things are really dire, scrap the process altogether. It is like an investment in the stock market: if you see a stock tumbling, don't wait until it hits bottom. Sell it now and limit your losses.

MISCONCEPTION 3: ONLY ORGANIZATIONS WITH MATURE PROJECT MANAGEMENT PROCESSES CAN BENEFIT FROM DECISION ANALYSIS

Any company should be able to benefit from the decision analysis process in the same way that any person would benefit from knowing how to think rationally. For example, if you have received a bonus at work, you probably have a few options:

A. Pay down your mortgage (apparently, this is not a very popular alternative).

B. Buy 10 new pairs of shoes from Oscar de la Renta.

C. Gamble everything at the local casino.

You will select an alternative based on your preferences (your risk profile) and on which one will give you maximum value. The point is that you do not need to hire a consultant, create a sophisticated mathematical model, and produce a large amount of paperwork to make this decision. The only thing you need to do is make a logical, rational choice based on the alternatives, perhaps using something that you have learned from this book.

If you want to establish a decision analysis process, do it step-by-step. For example, start by identifying your success criteria, which should be consistent over multiple projects, and then specify who will evaluate the alternatives. If you feel that you are benefiting from these activities, you may continue adding additional stages of the process: modeling, quantitative analysis, and review. Once you are comfortable and even happy with your process, you may then want to invest in a software system that will help you with your project decision analysis.

Why Do We Believe that the Decision Analysis Process Is So Important?

The age of amateur tinkers working away in their garages and developing state-of-the-art technology has passed. Technical innovations in our modern world have become extremely expensive and take a much longer time to develop. But marshaling all the money, engineers, and managers still does not ensure success. Here are just several examples:

- After the first satellite launch in 1957 and the first manned space flight in 1961, people started dreaming about building cities on the Moon and Mars. Well, we all know how far we have gotten with that effort! Despite having flown to the moon and back, humanity has not made any more significant strides in human space exploration. This is certainly not what was prognosticated in the early excitement of the 1960s. In reality, the design of SpaceX and other new generations of launch vehicles that promise to replace the old *Space Shuttle* is conceptually very similar to what we had over 60 years ago.

- For several decades people have been trying to build a thermonuclear reactor to produce electric power using fusion. Despite significant progress in the research, a working fusion reactor remains a distant dream. The international community, including the European Union, Japan, China, Russia, the Republic of Korea, and the United States, were originally planning to invest $5 billion over next 10 years in the ITER project (ITER 2018), an experiment aimed at proving that fusion can be used to generate electric power). In June 2005 this group decided that a 500 megawatt

Figure Concl. Aerial View of ITER Site in 2018 (Credit: Oak Ridge National Laboratory, 2018)

reactor would be built at Cadarache, in the south of France, with the first plasma ITER reactors planned to be online at the end of 2016. Cost estimates made in 2015 were approximately $15 billion, and today the first plasma reactor is expected to be operating in 2025.

Often, when engineers are unable to solve a technical problem, they say that the technology is "not mature." What does that mean? It means that they have not spent enough time and resources to solve the problem.

Because we global citizens, wherever we live, are always faced with scarce resources, where can we find the additional ways to solve these problems? Perhaps the solution to scarce resources lies in a more efficient use of the resources we *do* have. One way to do that is to use data analysis, along with better management practices. Decision analysis is one of such technologies. In particular:

- Good decision analysis processes can reduce the burden of wrong decisions and allow us to spend resources more efficiently, and also to improve organizational performance.
- Changes in corporate culture and the elimination of FES (Frustrated Employee Syndrome) will reduce the inefficient allocation of resources and increase productivity.

In conclusion, while resources will always be limited, we exacerbate resource scarcity through poor decision-making. If decision-makers throughout business and government can learn and practice proper decision analysis processes, that alone will lead to a major acceleration in technological innovation and productivity.

Appendix A:
Risk and Decision Analysis Software

The following risk and decision analysis software products widely used in project management can help you implement the processes described in this book. Please note that we did not perform detailed evaluations of each software and therefore cannot make specific recommendations. Each product has its unique set of the features, and every customer has its unique set of requirements. We also do not guarantee that this list is comprehensive, as we did not include all available software.

All software within a category is listed in alphabetical order.

Quantitative Project Risk Analysis Software

	Software	Company	Comment
1	Deltek Acumen Risk	Deltek www.deltek.com	Monte Carlo cost and schedule risk analysis; includes risk register and integration with other scheduling software
2	Full Monte	Barbecana www.barbecana.com	Monte Carlo cost and schedule risk analysis for Microsoft Project and Oracle® Primavera
3	Primavera Risk Analysis	Oracle www.oracle.com	Monte Carlo cost and schedule risk analysis for OraclePrimavera
4	RiskyProject	Intaver Institute www.intaver.com	Monte Carlo risk analysis; includes advanced risk register and integration with other scheduling software

(*cont.*)

(continued)

	Software	Company	Comment
5	Safran Risk	Safran www.safran.com	Monte Carlo cost and schedule risk analysis; includes risk register and integration with other scheduling software
6	Tamara	Vose Software www.vosesoftware.com	Monte Carlo cost and schedule risk analysis

Enterprise Risk Management Software

	Software	Company	Comment
1	Active Risk	Sword Active Risk www.sword-activerisk.com	Comprehensive enterprise risk management focused on project risk management
2	BWISE	Bwise www.bwise.com	General purpose enterprise risk management
3	Enablon	Wolters Kluwer www.enablon.com	General purpose enterprise risk management
4	ETQ Enterprise Risk Management	ETQ www.etq.com	General purpose enterprise risk management
5	Intelex Enterprise Risk Management	Intelex www.intelex.com	General purpose enterprise risk management
6	IRIS Intelligence	IRIS Intelligence www.irisintelligence.com	Enterprise risk management focused on project risk management
7	LogicManager Enterprise Risk Management	LogicManager www.logicmanager.com	General purpose enterprise risk management
8	MetricStream Enterprise Risk Management	MetricStream www.metricstream.com	General purpose enterprise risk management
9	Resolver Enterprise Risk Management	Resolver www.resolver.com	General purpose enterprise risk management
10	RiskyProject Enterprise	Intaver Institute www.intaver.com	Enterprise project risk management; includes project scheduling, plus advanced quantitative and qualitative risk analysis

Other Decision and Risk Analysis Software Used in Project Management

	Software	Company	Comment
1	@RISK	Palisade www.palisade.com	Monte Carlo simulation to Microsoft® Excel. Can be used for project management, as well
2	Analytica	Lumina Decision Systems www.lumina.com	Visual tool for creating, analyzing, and communicating decision models; created using influence diagrams.
3	CrystalBall	Oracle www.oracle.com	Monte Carlo simulation software for Excel
4	Decision Frameware	Decision Frameworks www.decisionframeworks.com	Set of decision analysis software tools
5	DPL	Syncopation Software www.syncopation.com	Desktop tool for decisions; includes influence diagrams, decision tree analysis, Monte Carlo simulation, and sensitivity analysis
6	SmartOrg	www.smartorg.com	Modeling, evaluating, forecasting, and managing the business opportunities in projects and portfolios
7	TreeAge	TreeAge Software www.treeage.com	Decision tree and influence diagram, sensitivity analysis, Bayes's revision, Monte Carlo simulation, and multi-attribute analysis

Microsoft® is a registered trademark of the Microsoft Corporation in the United States and/or other countries. Oracle® is a registered trademark of Oracle Corporation. All other names and trademarks are the property of their respective owners.

Appendix B: Heuristics and Biases in Project Management

The following is not a comprehensive list, although it does include the most relevant heuristics and biases that apply to project management. Some psychological effects mentioned in this book, such as the creativity block, are not included, to avoid repetition. If you glance through the list from time to time, that will refresh your memory and give you some ideas about how you should think while you manage your projects.

The discipline of psychology helps us look at our actions from a fresh point of view. When we showed this list to managers who were not familiar with cognitive biases, most recognized the mental pitfalls that had tripped them up in the past. We hope this list will help you avoid some of these pitfalls.

It is difficult to come up with definitive classifications for heuristics and biases in project management. Many biases are related to each other and may affect our behavior in various ways. Nevertheless, we have grouped all the biases into a few logical categories. Within each category, the biases are presented in alphabetical order. Note that a few fundamental psychological concepts, such as selection perception, and some heuristics have a number of biases associated with them.

Behavioral Biases and Biases Related to Perception

Ascription of Causality—The tendency to ascribe causation even when the evidence suggests only correlation. Managers may think that a project succeeded because they created and managed a risk list. Correlations between a project's success rate and the presence of a risk list are not enough to conclude that a risk list led to the positive result.

Bias Blind Spot—The tendency not to see your own cognitive biases (Pronin et al. 2002). Even if people know their own cognitive biases, they do not invariably compensate for them. Knowledge of this bias is important for both project management training and education.

Biased Covariation Assessment—The tendency not to examine all the possible outcomes when making a judgment regarding a correlation or an association. We may focus on only one or two possibilities, while ignoring the rest. This bias affects a project manager's ability to analyze correlation and causation in a project.

Choice-Supportive Bias—The tendency to remember positive attributes as having been part of the chosen option rather than of the rejected option. For example, research participants were asked to make a choice between two options. Later, in a memory test, participants were given a list of positive and negative features. Positive features were more likely to be attributed to the chosen option, while negative features were more likely to be attributed to the rejected option (Mather and Johnson 2000). This bias is related to the selection of project alternatives and reviews of the results of decision analysis.

Congruence Bias—A bias that occurs as a result of a decision-maker's reliance on direct testing of a given hypothesis while neglecting indirect testing. Hampered by this bias, decision-makers are often unable to consider alternative hypotheses. This bias is related to generation and evaluation of creative project alternatives.

Elimination-by-Aspect Heuristic—A heuristic in which people eliminate a potential choice from a plurality of choices if it does not satisfy certain conditions (Tversky 1972). It manifests itself when project managers select project alternatives based on multiple criteria.

Escalating Commitment—The tendency to invest resources in failing projects with a very small chance of recovery (McCray et al. 2002). This behavioral trap is related to the sunk-cost effect.

Experiential Limitations—Inability or unwillingness to look beyond the scope of past experiences or rejection of the unfamiliar. This bias serves as a creativity block that occurs when project managers may discard good ideas because they do not fit into a familiar pattern.

Failure to Consider Alternatives—A tendency to evaluate and consider only a single course of action. It occurs when project managers attempt to reduce efforts during the evaluation of alternatives. It is often the result of sufficient information about one particular suggested course of action along with insufficient information about alternatives. This bias is related to the congruence bias.

Focusing Effect—A bias that occurs when decision-makers place too much importance on a single aspect of an event or process. For example, a software project manager believes the software's quality is associated only with the number of software defects. In reality, though, the notion of software quality, along with the quality of the software code, involves the quality of the documentation, user interface, packaging, and support.

Hyperbolic Discounting—The tendency to prefer smaller payoffs to larger ones when the smaller payoffs come sooner in time than the larger. For instance, a project manager may prefer a $500,000 NPV project now to one with a $1 million NPV several years from now. However, given the choice of the same $500,000 NPV project five years from now and the $1 million NPV six years from now, most project managers would choose $1 million in six years.

Illusion of Control—The tendency of decision-makers to believe they can control or influence outcomes over which they in fact have no influence. For example, when rolling dice in craps, people tend to throw stronger for high numbers and softer for low numbers. Similarly, sometimes project managers plan projects under the assumption that they can control most processes, which in reality they cannot.

Impact Bias—The tendency of a decision-maker to believe that if a negative event occurs, it takes longer to recover emotionally from the event than it actually does. In project management this is related to the analysis of risk impacts.

Inconsistency—The inability or unwillingness to apply the same decision criteria in similar situations. Consistency is one of the fundamental principles of the project decision analysis process.

Inertia—An unwillingness to change thought patterns that we have used in the past, when faced with new circumstances. Project managers often follow the same practices in a new environment, such as project size, industry, organizational structure, and so on. In many cases, this can be inappropriate and may lead to problems.

Information Bias—The tendency to seek information even when it cannot possibly affect a decision. In organizations, management sometimes requires more reports and analysis than strictly necessary. Value-of-information analysis will help to mitigate a negative effect of this bias.

Invisible Correlations—The inability to see correlations because they are not expected to be related. In project management, this inability is often related to a correlation between an individual's motivation, beliefs, experience, and preferences and the ultimate project results.

Lexicographic Heuristic—The tendency of people to apply the following process to make a choice between alternatives strategies: (a) rank the order attributes; (b) select the option rated highest on the most important attribute; (c) if a tie, go to the next attribute (Tversky 1969). This heuristic is called lexicographic because a similar algorithm is used to order words in dictionaries. The heuristic manifests itself when project managers select project alternatives based on multiple criteria.

Omission Bias—The tendency to judge potentially harmful actions as worse than equally harmful inactions (omissions). Project managers may believe that new product development is riskier than continuing to maintain an existing product that is losing sales, even if the costs of both project alternatives are the same.

Outcome Bias—The tendency to evaluate a decision by its final outcome instead of the quality of the decision at the time it was made. If a decision results in a negative outcome, this does not mean that decision was wrong, because the decision was made based on the best possible information at the time. This bias manifests itself in the review of project decisions.

Planning Fallacy—The tendency to underestimate the duration of project activities. Project managers may eliminate factors that they perceive are not related to the project. Moreover, they may discount multiple improbable high-impact risks because each one is so unlikely to happen. The planning fallacy is one of the fundamental biases related to estimations in project management.

Post-Purchase Rationalization—A bias that occurs when people have invested a lot of time, money, or effort in something and try to convince themselves that the expenditure must have been worth it. It may affect the analysis of projects during reviews.

Prospect-Theory-Related Biases:

- **Endowment Effect**—The tendency of decision-makers to place a higher value on objects they own than on objects they do not. It explains why people rarely exchange a product they have already purchased for a better product. It can manifest in project management in choices related to replacing existing products, tools, and services (Kahneman et al. 1990).
- **Loss Aversion**—The tendency of decision-makers to prefer avoiding losses versus acquiring gains. In project management this bias is associated with risk aversion and risk tolerance which may occur when decision-makers evaluate possible project gains and loses.
- **Pseudocertainty Effect**—The inclination to make risk-averse choices if the expected outcome is positive, but to make risk-seeking choices to avoid negative outcomes (Tversky and Kahneman 1981; Slovic et al. 1982). Actual choices can be affected by simply reframing the descriptions of the outcomes. Project managers will prefer to take a risk and buy a component if they receive a free unit for every three purchased instead of buying all four components with a 25% discount.

- **Zero-Risk Bias**—The preference for reducing a small risk to zero over a greater reduction in a larger risk. Individuals may prefer small benefits that are certain to large ones that are uncertain. Project managers sometimes prefer to avoid a small risk completely rather than significantly mitigate a larger one.

Recognition Heuristic—When making a judgment between two items when only one of the items is recognized, the recognized item will be considered to have a higher criterion value (Goldstein and Gigerenzer 1999). This heuristic manifests itself when project managers select project alternatives based on multiple criteria.

Repetition Bias—A willingness to believe what we have been told most often and by the greatest number of different sources. Repetition bias is related to the exposure-memory effect and can lead to wrong assessments of business situations in project management.

Selective Perception—The tendency for expectations to affect perception. Sometimes selective perception is referred to as "What I see is what I want to see." These are several biases related to selective perception:

- **Confirmation Bias**—The tendency of decision-makers to seek out and assign more weight to evidence that confirms a hypothesis, and to ignore or give less weight to evidence that could discount the hypothesis. This can lead to statistical errors. This bias is related to estimations and evaluations of alternatives in project management.

- **Disconfirmation Bias**—The tendency for decision-makers to extend critical scrutiny to information that contradicts their prior beliefs (Lord et al. 1979). This bias is also related to the confirmation bias.

- **Premature Termination of Search for Evidence**—The tendency to accept the first alternative that looks as if it might work.

- **Professional Viewpoint Effect**—The tendency to look at things according to the conventions of a decision-maker's profession, forgetting any broader point of view. For example, project management professionals may not fully apply methodologies and tools that originated from operations research.

- **Selective Search of Evidence**—The tendency to gather facts that support certain conclusions while disregarding other facts that support different conclusions.

Similarity Heuristic—Relates to how people make judgments based on similarity. Thinking by similarity is one of the fundamental mental strategies of project managers, who usually analyze project issues by comparing them with previously corrected problems. Over time, a project manager's past experiences will allow his or her use of the similarity heuristic to be highly effective, quickly choosing the corrective actions that will likely reveal the problem's source. Similar approaches are used by software programmers, doctors, police investigators, and other professionals.

Source Credibility Bias—The tendency to reject information if a bias exists against the person, organization, or group that is the source of the information. The opposite effect is the tendency to accept information uncritically from trusted sources. In project management this can lead to a sampling bias, when too much faith is placed in certain information while other information is rejected (Skinner 2009).

Status Quo Bias—The inclination of decision-makers to prefer that things stay relatively the same (Samuelson and Zeckhauser 1988). This bias is similar to the omission bias and is related to the endowment effect. It explains why ineffective project management procedures often are not changed and why outdated technology is not replaced.

Student Syndrome—The tendency of people to wait until a deadline is near to start to fully apply themselves to a task (Goldratt 2002). The bias is named after the way many students tend to put off doing their papers until the night before they are due. The bias is related to estimation of project activity duration. A similar effect is Parkinson's Law, which states that the demand upon a resource always expands to match the supply of the resource (Parkinson 2018). Particularly, work expands to fill the time available for its completion. It is also strongly related to procrastination.

Sunk-Cost Effect—The tendency to make a choice considering the cost that has already been incurred and cannot be recovered (sunk cost). Sunk costs affect the decisions made due to the loss-aversion effect. Sunk costs may cause cost overruns and may also lead to investment in a project that now has no value. This effect is related to the escalating commitment bias.

Wishful Thinking—The formation of beliefs and decision-making according to what might be pleasing to imagine instead of by appealing to evidence or applying rationality. For example, a project manager often makes estimates based on positive results he or she wants to achieve instead of what is possible to achieve. Wishful thinking is related to the optimism bias.

Biases in Estimation of Probability and Belief

Ambiguity Effect—The tendency to prefer options with known probabilities and to avoid options in which missing information makes the probability seem unknown. In project management is it important to collect information for all selected alternatives.

Anchoring Heuristic—The tendency to rely on one trait or piece of information when making decisions. The following are biases related to the anchoring heuristic:

- **Insufficient Adjustment**—The tendency of decision-makers to "anchor" on a current value and make insufficient adjustments for future effects. In project management this bias often manifests itself in the estimation of uncertainties. A project manager frequently does not allow for sufficient adjustment after making three-point estimates of an activity's duration or cost.

- **Overconfidence in Estimation of Probabilities**—A tendency to provide overly optimistic estimates of uncertain events. Decision-makers tend to set the ranges of probability too low and to remain overconfident that these ranges will include true values. Overconfidence is most likely after a series of project successes, and it can lead to risk-taking.

- **Overestimating the Probability of Conjunctive Events**—If an event is composed of a number of elementary events, the probability of the elementary events should be multiplied to come up with the probability of a main event. For example, say the probability of task completion is 80%. If the project consists of three tasks, the probability of project completion will be $(0.8 \times 0.8 \times 0.8)$, or 51.2%. People tend to overestimate the probability of the main event because the probability of elementary events serves as an anchor.

Availability Heuristic—The tendency to make judgments about the probability of events' occurring by how easily these events are brought to mind. The following are biases related to the availability heuristic:

- **Illusory Correlations**—The tendency to overestimate the frequency with which two events occur together. In project management the bias manifests itself in the analysis of relationships between two or more parameters—for example, whether the geographic location of a supplier is related to the quality of its products.

- **Vividness**—The tendency of people to recall events that are unusual or rare, vivid, or associated with other events such as major issues, successes, or failures. As a result, assessment of probabilities for project risks can be wrong.

Optimism Bias—The tendency to be overly optimistic about the outcome of planned actions. This bias manifests itself in project planning and forecasting. Project managers often overestimate the probability of successful project completion and underestimate the probability of negative events. The optimism bias is also related to wishful thinking.

Representativeness Heuristic—A heuristic according to which people estimate probability by judging how representative the object, person, or event is of a certain category, group, or process. The following are biases related to the representativeness heuristic:

- **Conjunction Fallacy**—An unwanted appeal to more detailed scenarios. This fallacy can lead to a "preference for details." If, for example, a project manager must select one project from a number of proposals, he or she may tend to pick those proposals with the most detail, even though they may not have the best chance of success.

- **Gambler's Fallacy**—The belief that a successful outcome is due after a run of bad luck (Tversky and Kahneman 1971). In project management, corrective actions as a response to certain issues and problems are often not taken because project managers believe that the situation will improve itself.

- **Ignoring Base-Rate Frequencies**—The tendency of people to ignore prior statistical information (base-rate frequencies) when making assessments about probabilities. In project management this bias can manifest itself in the estimation of probabilities and forecasting. For example, what is the probability that a new component from a supplier is defective? Project managers can make estimates based on recent testing where most components were defective. However, they may ignore the fact that historically 99% of the components from this supplier have been problem-free.

- **Ignoring Regression to Mean**—The tendency to expect extreme events to be followed by similar extreme events. In reality, extreme events most likely will be followed either by an extreme in the opposite way or by an average event. Project managers should not expect extraordinary performances from a team or individuals for every project because of the regression to mean, or the tendency to be average.

Memory Biases and Effects

Context Effect—Memory is dependent on context of the environment. Out-of-context memories are more difficult to retrieve than in-context memories. For example, the recall time and accuracy for a project-related memory will be lower when a manager is at home, and vice versa.

Exposure Effect—People can express an undue liking for things merely because they are familiar with them. The more often we read about a certain method or principle, the more we like it. This effect is used in the advertisement industry. For example, a project manager may like certain project management software just because it is advertised more often in an industry journal.

False Memory—A memory of an event that did not happen or a distortion of an event that did occur, as influenced by externally corroborated facts. Often, project managers simply forget important information and lessons learned.

Generation Effect—People will recall information better if it is generated rather than simply read. If a project manager experienced a certain issue and actually dealt with it, he or she will remember it better than if he or she merely read about it. The generation effect can be a strategy for learning.

Hindsight Bias (the "I Knew It All Along" effect)—The tendency to see past events as being more predictable than they actually were. The possible explanation of this bias is that events that actually occur are easier to recall than possible outcomes that did not occur. This bias manifests in the review of project decisions.

Misinformation Effect—A memory bias that occurs when misinformation affects people's reports of their own memory. If people read an inaccurate report about a project and are asked to recall their own experience about the project, the report will distort their memory about the project (Roediger et al. 2001).

Peak-End Rule—The heuristic according to which people judge their past experiences almost entirely on how they were experienced at their peak (pleasant or unpleasant) and how they ended. Other information is discarded, including net pleasantness or unpleasantness and how long the experience lasted. In project management this heuristic is important in project reviews because project stakeholders may not remember all necessary project details (Kahneman et al. 1999).

Picture Superiority Effect—Concepts and ideas are more likely to be remembered if they are presented as images rather than as words (Paivio 1971; 2006). This effect is important for presentation and interpretation of project information, as for example in the results of project decision analysis.

Zeigarnik Effect—Project managers may remember tasks in progress better than recently completed ones (Zeigarnik 1967).

Social and Group Biases

Attribution Biases—Biases that affect attribution, or the way we determine who or what was responsible for an event or action. Understanding of attribution biases is important for project human resource management. Attribution biases include:

- **Egocentric Bias**—The tendency of people to claim more responsibility for the results of a joint action than an outside observer would.

- **False Consensus Effect**—The tendency of decision-makers to overestimate the degree to which others agree with them. If members of a group reach a consensus and it is not disputed, they tend to believe that everybody thinks the same way. Therefore, if nobody expresses a contrary opinion in a team meeting, project managers will believe that everybody agrees on the course of action.

- **Fundamental Attribution Error** (also called the Correspondence Bias or Overattribution Effect)—The tendency of people to overemphasize personality-based explanations for behaviors observed in others while underemphasizing the role and power of situational influences on the same behavior. People tend to judge what a person does based more on what "kind" of person he or she is than on the social and environmental forces at work on that person.

- **Outgroup Homogeneity Bias**—People see members of their own group as being relatively more varied than members of other groups.

- **Self-Fulfilling Prophecy**—A prediction that, once made, actually causes itself to become true. In other words, a false statement may lead people to take actions that will ultimately result in fulfillment of the prophecy. For example, a project manager expresses a concern that resources are not sufficient for the project. When resources are not given to him, he perceives all problems with the project as a result of limited resources. In J. K. Rowling's novel *Harry Potter and the Order of the Phoenix*, a prophecy was made shortly before Harry's birth that the one with the power to destroy Voldemort would be born shortly. To protect himself, Voldemort attempted to kill Harry while he was an infant, but his curse backfired on him, transferring some of his powers to Harry. In fact, this power transfer is a response to the prophecy. The prophecy was only "true" because Voldemort believed it.

- **Self-Serving Bias**—The tendency to claim responsibility for successes rather than failures. The self-serving bias results in the better-than-average effect and also in overconfidence. For example, project managers of a successfully completed project might say, "I did it because I am highly experienced." Project managers of a failed project might say, "The clients did not provide good specifications, and we did not have the necessary resources."

- **Trait-Ascription Bias**—The tendency of people to view themselves as relatively variable in terms of emotion, personality, and behavior while viewing others as much more predictable. This may be because people are able to observe and understand themselves better than others. This bias may lead to stereotypes and prejudice. The bias manifests itself in project team communication. This bias is similar to outgroup homogeneity bias on the group level.

Bandwagon Effect (Groupthink)—The tendency to do (or believe) things because many other people do (or believe) the same. The effect manifests itself in project teams when project managers and team members feel reluctant to express different points of view.

Ingroup Bias—The tendency of people to give preferential treatment to people they perceive to be members of their own groups, even if the group they share is random or arbitrary (such as having the same birthday). Ingroup bias is an important factor related to communication within project teams.

Polarization Effect—The tendency for group discussions to lead to amplified preferences or inclinations of group members. If a project team member already has an opinion about a certain issue (e.g., new product design), as a result of the meeting he or she may hold a much stronger opinion about this issue. People on both sides can move farther apart, or polarize, when they are presented with the same mixed evidence.

Appendix C:
Risk Templates

Generic Risk Template #1

This is the basic set of risks in this Risk Breakdown Structure, adopted from the *PMBOK Guide* (Project Management Institute 2018). We recommend using as a very generic risk template when you identify risks in all types of projects.

Risk	Examined
Technical	
Requirements	☐
Technology	☐
Complexity and interfaces	☐
Performance and reliability	☐
Quality	☐
Safety	☐
External	
Subcontractor	☐
Components	☐
Legal and regulatory environment	☐
Market	☐
Customer relationship	☐
Site specific issues	☐
Weather and other environmental factors	☐
Organizational	
Project dependencies	☐

(cont.)

(continued)

Risk	Examined
Resources	
Personnel resources	☐
Material resources	☐
Funding	☐
Prioritization	☐
Project Management	
Estimating	☐
Planning	☐
Controlling	☐
Communication	☐

Generic Risk Template #2

Here is another generic risk template, which has separate external and internal issues. It can be useful for construction projects where external issues play very big role.

Risk	Examined
External	
Environment	
Weather	☐
Natural environment	☐
Site specific issues such as facility and infrastructure availability	☐
Local services and support	☐
Political environment	☐
Legal environment	☐
Community and social environment	☐
Cultural environment	☐
Market	
Competition	☐
Demand	☐

(cont.)

(*continued*)

Risk	Examined
Labor conditions such as labor cost and availability	☐
Material and fuel cost, quality, and availability	☐
Financial conditions such as interest rates and inflation	☐
Vendor and supplies availability	☐
Seasonal and cyclical factors affecting the market	☐
Internal	
Organization	☐
Organizational culture	☐
Decision profile including attitude toward risk	☐
Organizational experience in the project area	☐
Overall organizational stability, including financial situation	☐
Organizational structure	☐
Organizational ownership and management	☐
Organizational performance related to particular projects	☐
Public relationship	☐
Labor relationship	☐
Vendor/Subcontractor Relationship	
Quality of supplies and materials	☐
Issues related to delivery, installation, and implementation of supplies and materials	☐
Subcontractor relationship	☐
Acquisition and procurement process maturity	☐
Customer Relationship	
Level of requirement definition	☐
Requirement uncertainties	☐
Requirement complexity	☐
Level of customer involvement	☐

(*cont.*)

(continued)

Risk	Examined
Technology	
Technology availability and maturity	☐
Technology limits	☐
Technology complexity	☐
Resources (Personnel)	
Personnel skill set	☐
Personnel performance	☐
Personnel experience for specific project	☐
Personnel availability, including availability of business experts	☐
Project Management	
Project management process maturity	☐
Project manager experience	☐
Issues related to project schedule development	☐
Issues related to estimation of project activities	☐
Issues related to project scope definition	☐
Quality and Safety	
Overall quality objectives	☐
Issues related to quality standards	☐
Safety policy, standards, and procedures	☐

Risk Template for Software Development Project

Here is another risk template, which can be useful for IT related projects, particularly for the software development projects. Risk categories in this template are associated with Rational Unified Process workflows (Kruchten 2003).

Risk	Examined
Business Modeling and Requirements	
Clear business objectives	☐
Requirements gathering	☐

(cont.)

(continued)

Risk	Examined
Requirements review	☐
Requirements changes	☐
Requirements acceptance	☐
Contract	☐
Analysis and Design	
Architecture	☐
Technology capability	☐
New technology	☐
Requirements interpretation and analysis	☐
Design	☐
Implementation	
Coding	☐
Unit testing	☐
Integration	☐
Modification	☐
Quality Control	
Evaluation	☐
Testing	☐
Acceptance testing by the client	☐
Deployment and Maintenance	
Deployment	☐
Maintenance	☐
Installation and packaging	☐
Upgrade and growth	☐
Configuration and Change Management	
Configuration management, including build process	☐
Change management process	☐
Changing scope or objectives	☐

(cont.)

(continued)

Risk	Examined
Project Management	
Project management process maturity	☐
Senior management commitment	☐
Client involvement	☐
Technical performance	☐
Cost management	☐
Environment	
Development environment	
Software and tools	☐
Hardware	☐
Organizational environment	
Management skills	☐
Organizational stability	☐
Organizational experience in the particular project	☐
External relationship	☐
Subcontracting and outsourcing	☐
Resources	
Resource availability	☐
Resource usage	☐
Resource performance	☐
Resource turnover	☐
Other environment	
Natural environment	☐
Site specific issues such facility and infrastructure availability	☐
Political and legal environment	☐
Community, cultural, and social environment	☐

Appendix D: Multi-Criteria Decision-Making Methodologies

This appendix lists some methods for multi-criteria decision-making that can be useful in project and portfolio management. These methods are employed mostly for selecting projects within a portfolio, as well as for making important project decisions. Each of these methods has its own strengths and weaknesses (see Linkov et al. 2006a).

Selecting methodologies and tools for multi-criteria decision-making should be part of the decision analysis process within your organization. It would be better to use this approach for many problems within a portfolio rather than for one particular problem. A number of off-the-shelf software tools can be used for the various methods. In particular, some methodologies are implemented as part of project portfolio management software.

Method	Short Description	References
Analytic Hierarchy Process (AHP)	• Develop a hierarchy that includes decision alternatives and criteria. • Perform pair-wise comparison to establish consistent priorities for different criteria. Input data for pairwise comparison is an expert judgment. • Calculate overall score for different alternatives and rank them according to score.	Anderson et al. 2015; Saaty and Vargas 2014
Goal Programming	A linear programming approach to multi-criteria decision problems whereby the objective function is designed to minimize deviation from goals	Anderson, et al. 2015; Schniederjans 2012
Multi-Attribute Utility Theory	1. Derive single-attribute functions for project parameters, such as project duration and cost. 2. Combine single-attribute utility functions to create multi-attribute utility function. 3. Perform consistency check to verify that multi-attribute utility function actually represents decision-maker's preferences.	Goodwin 2014; Keeney and Raiffa 1993
Simple Multi-Attribute Rating Technique (SMART)	1. Construct value trees, which represent decision-making criteria. 2. Define value functions, which represent relationships between criteria (e.g., project cost vs. project value). 3. Determine weights for all criteria. Compute overall value (score) for each alternative. 4. Perform sensitivity analysis to determine how sensitive value is to the selected weights.	Goodwin 2014

Glossary

3C Principles of Project Decision Analysis Three most important rules of decision analysis process: continuity, comprehensiveness, and consistency.

Adaptive Management A systematic process for continually improving decisions, management policies, and practices by learning from the outcomes of decisions previously taken.

Agile Process A conceptual framework for the undertaking of different projects. Originally conceived for the software development projects, agile approaches are a family of methods used in different industries.

Anchoring and Adjustment Heuristic A heuristic according to which people rely on one trait or piece of information ("anchor") when making decisions.

Attribution Theory A theory concerned with how people explain (or attribute) the behavior of others, or themselves (self-attribution).

Availability Heuristic A heuristic according to which people judge the probability of the occurrence of the events by how easily these events are brought to mind.

Bayes Theorem A formula that revises probabilities based on new information.

Behavioral Trap A psychological phenomenon that occurs when rational activity later becomes undesirable and difficult to escape from.

Best Fit A process of identification of statistical distribution that would better approximate a given empirical distribution.

Beta Distribution A bounded statistical distribution that uses a mathematical formula that includes two coefficients. By changing these coefficients, beta distribution can take variety of shapes; it can be symmetrical or non-symmetrical.

Bias The discrepancy between somebody's judgment and reality.

Bounded Rationality A behavior that is rational within the parameters of a simplified model that captures essential features of a problem.

Brainstorming A problem-solving technique that involves creating a list that includes a wide variety of related ideas.

Change Control A process of controlling changes to the original project plans. The process involves identification, analysis, documenting, and approving or rejecting changes during the course of a project.

Cognitive Bias A bias that is introduced by the way the expert processes the information. In other words, it is a distortion in the way humans perceive reality.

Contract Administration A process of managing contracts as well as relationship between buyers and sellers.

Controllable Input See *Deterministic Input.*

Corporate Culture Company View A company's values, beliefs, business principles, traditions, ways of operating, and internal work environment. Corporate culture significantly affects decision-making in the company.

Corporate Culture Employee view The basic assumptions and beliefs held by employees about the enterprise they work for. Corporate culture refers to a company's values, beliefs, business principles, traditions, ways of operating, and internal work environment.

Cost-Benefit Analysis A technique used to compare the various costs associated with a project with the benefits that it proposes to return.

Cost of Decision Reversal A cost associated with paying for all expenses associated with a wrong decision. Can be between zero and infinity of irrevocable decisions.

Creativity Block A factor that prevents decision-making from finding creative solutions to problems.

Creativity Theories A set of psychological theories that try to explain the phenomenon of creativity.

Critical Chain Method A schedule network analysis technique that modifies the project schedule to account for limited resources.

Critical Events or Critical Event Chains In Event chain methodology, the single events or the event chains that have the most potential to affect the projects. Critical events or critical event chains can be identified using sensitivity analysis.

Critical Path A sequence of activities that determines the completion time for the project.

Critical Path Method A schedule network analysis technique that determines the amount of float on different network paths. Critical path method is also used to determine project duration.

Crucial Task (crucial activity) A task (activity) that affects uncertainty in a main project parameter, such as cost and duration, at most. Crucial tasks can be determined as a result of sensitivity analysis.

Decision A conscious allocation of resources for the purpose of achieving desirable objectives.

Decision Analysis A structured way of thinking about how the action taken in a current decision would lead to a project result.

Decision Analysis Manifesto Basic principles why decision analysis should be adopted in the organization.

Decision Analysis Process An integrated set of procedures and tools that help project managers to make a rational choice.

Decision Board See *Decision Committee.*

Decision Committee A panel of experts that coordinates the decision analysis process in the organization for the particular project. Also called Review Board, Decision Board.

Decision Conferencing A face-to-face 1- to 3-day meeting of experts moderated by a decision analyst. Decision analyst acts as a neutral observer, who applies decision analysis methods and techniques during this meeting. Decision analyst creates a computer-based model that incorporates judgment of the experts.

Decision Criteria Indicators that are used to determine which alternative should be taken.

Decision Framing A step of the decision analysis process which helps decision-makers identify potential problems or opportunities, assess business situations, determine success criteria, and identify uncertainties.

Decision Policy A set of principles or preferences used for selection alternatives. Risk policy is a component of decision policy.

Decision Theory Theory of decision making under uncertainties.

Decision Tree A graph that represents a decision problem. Includes chance, decision, and end (terminal) nodes.

Delphi Technique A group discussion technique, according to which group members don't meet with each other face-to-face. Instead they provided their opinions anonymously in a series of rounds until consensus is reached.

Descriptive Decision Theory A branch of decision theory that describes how people actually make decisions. See also *Normative Decision Theory*.

Deterministic Input (Controllable Input) Input to a simulation model that was selected by the decision-maker.

Discounted Cash Flow Techniques for establishing the relative worth of a future investment by discounting (at a required rate of return) the expected net cash flows from the project.

Elimination by Aspect Heuristic A heuristic in which people eliminate a potential choice from a plurality of choices if it does not satisfy certain conditions.

Emotion A mental state that arises automatically in the nervous system rather than through conscious effort. It can evoke either a positive or a negative psychological response.

Enterprise Project Management See *Project Portfolio Management*.

Enterprise Resource Management (ERM) A methodology and software program that manages a company's assets and resources, including accounts payable and receivable, as well as manufacturing, inventory, and human resources.

Event An instantaneous occurrence that changes the state of the system in the simulation model.

Event Chain In Event chain methodology, a series of single events linked to each other.

Event Chain Diagram A diagram that shows the relationships between events and tasks and indicates how the events affect each other.

Event Chain Methodology An uncertainty modeling and schedule network analysis technique that is focused on identifying and managing both events and event chains that affect project schedules.

Expected Utility Theory The family of theories of rational behavior. Expected utility theory is intended to describe how people should behave if they make rational choices.

Expected Value Expected value is probability-weighted average of all outcomes. It is calculated by multiplying each possible outcome by the probability of occurring and then adding the result.

Filter In creative decision-making, it is a set of conditions used to test a proposed solution. If the solution does satisfy these conditions, it does not pass through the filter and will not be considered in later stages of the analysis.

Filter Diagram A diagram that can be used for selection project alternatives through applying filters.

Fluctuation In Event chain methodology, a small deviation in activity's cost or duration that cannot be attributed to any specific risk events.

Framing A psychological effect according to which decision-makers respond differently to the problem because of different norms, habits, preferences, and characteristics of the decision-maker as well as different formulations of the problem.

Free Float (Slack) An amount of time the activity can be delayed without delaying any other immediately following activity.

Frustrated Employee Syndrome (FES) A "disease" that can afflict a corporate culture, particularly aspects such as decision-making, efficiency, and productivity. FES is a problem because frustrated project team members will not produce good projects.

Frequency Chart (Frequency Histogram) A histogram that shows the number of samples or probability versus the value of the variable. Frequency charts allow you to analyze the risk associated with a variable.

Fundamental Objectives Primary project objectives or goals that need to be accomplished during the course of a project.

Game Theory A mathematical theory of human behavior in competitive situations. Game theory studies situations where players choose different actions in an attempt to maximize their returns.

Gantt Chart A bar chart that depicts activities as blocks over time. The beginning and end of the block correspond to the beginning and end dates of the activity. The chart was developed as a production control tool in 1917 by Henry L. Gantt, an American engineer and social scientist.

Global Event In Event chain methodology, an event affecting all tasks or all resources in the project.

Heuristics (in psychology of judgment and decision-making) Simplified mental strategies or rules of thumb that people rely on to come up with judgments. In many cases, heuristics lead to rational solutions. However, heuristics can often cause inconsistencies and predictable biases.

Impact See *Risk Impact.*

Influence Diagram A graphical tool that shows the relationship among decisions, chance events, and consequences for a decision problem.

Intuitive Thinking A direct perception of meaning or truth, without conscious reasoning. Intuitive thinking is a mental activity that is validated by the thinker's belief systems.

Irrevocable Decision A decision that can be reversed. See also *Cost of Decision Reversal.*

ISO 9000 A family of ISO (the International Organization for Standardization) standards for quality management systems.

Lag A delay between a predecessor and successor activity. For example, in a finish-start logical relationship, a five-day lag means the successor will start five days after the predecessor is finished.

Lens Model In psychology, a conceptual framework to deal with our judgment and expectations concerning events and outcomes of possible courses of actions. The framework was developed by Egon Brunswik.

Lessons Learned A learning obtained from performing a project. The learning may be gained at any stage of the project.

Lessons Learned Knowledge Base A depository of lessons learned and historical project information.

Local Event In Event chain methodology, an event affecting a particular task or resource.

Lognormal Distribution A statistical distribution of a random variable whose natural logarithm is normally distributed. The lognormal distribution is often used to model data that is positively skewed.

Mean A statistical parameter. Mean is calculated as the sum of variable values on each simulation divided by the number of simulations.

Means Objectives Project objectives that help to achieve fundamental objectives.

Method of Relative Heights A method of eliciting judgment about continuous statistical distribution using a frequency histogram.

Milestone A reference point indicating a major event in the project. Milestones are used to monitor the project's progress.

Mind Map A diagram used to represent ideas, activities, risks, or other items linked to a central theme. In a mind map, the ideas related to the main theme radiate from that central image as "branches."

Mitigation Plan See *Risk Mitigation Plan.*

Model See *Valuation Model.*

Moment of Event In Event chain methodology, the moment when a particular event occurs during the course of an activity.

Monte Carlo The mathematical method used in risk analysis. Monte Carlo simulations are used to approximate the distribution of potential results based on probabilistic inputs. Each trial is generated by randomly pulling a sample value for each input variable from its defined probability distribution. These input sample values are then used to calculate the results. This procedure is repeated until the probability distributions are sufficiently well represented to achieve the desired level of accuracy.

Motivational Bias A bias that is caused by the personal interest of the expert expressing the judgment.

Multi-Criteria Decision-Making The study of methods and procedures by which concerns about multiple conflicting criteria can be formally incorporated into the decision-making process.

Nash Equilibrium In game theory, a solution to a game in which no player has anything to gain by unilaterally changing only his or her own strategy.

Net Present Value (NPV) The present value of a series of future net cash flows that will result from an investment, minus the amount of the original investment.

Normal Distribution A statistical distribution that describes situations where values are distributed symmetrically around the mean.

Normative Decision Theory A branch of decision theory that describes how people should make a decision. See also *Descriptive Decision Theory*.

Objective Probability A probability that is based of comprehensive assessment of the evidence, including understanding of all random properties of the system. See also *Subjective Probability.*

Opportunity A favorable situation that will have a positive impact on project objectives if it occurs. The opposite situation is a threat.

Overconfidence A psychological bias according to which people tend to overestimate the accuracy of their predictions. Overconfidence is one of the most common biases in project management.

Parameters Numerical values that appear in the mathematical relationship of a model.

Percentile A value on a scale of 0 to 100 that indicates what percent of a distribution is equal to or below it. A value in the 95th percentile is a value equal to or better than 95% of other values.

PERT See *Program Evaluation and Review Technique.*

Precondition of Event In Event chain methodology, a precondition is a state of an activity or environmental factor. Some events can occur only if there is a certain precondition.

Probability The relative frequency of the event based on some evidence. The word "probability" derives from the Latin *probare* (to prove, or to test). Synonyms: likelihood, odds, chance.

Probability and Impact Matrix A tool to prioritize risk based on probability and impact. The probability and impact matrix is presented as a two-dimensional table with distinct areas associated with high, medium, and low risks.

Probability Method A method of eliciting expert judgment about continuous statistical distributions.

Probability Wheel A graphic tool used to elicit expert judgment related to discrete probabilities.

Program Evaluation and Review Technique (PERT) A network-based project scheduling procedure. Developed between 1956 and 1958 by consulting firm Booz Allen Hamilton for the U.S. Navy's Special Project Office.

Project Life Circle A collection of sequential project phases.

Project Objective *PMBOK Guide* describes project objective as "something towards which work is to be directed, a strategic position to be attained, or purpose to be achieved, a result to be obtained, a product to be produced, or a service to be performed" (Project Management Institute 2018).

Project Portfolio Management (Enterprise Project Management) A methodology and tool that organizes a series of projects into a single portfolio consisting of reports that capture project objectives, costs, timelines, accomplishments, resources, risks, and other critical factors. Executives can then regularly review entire portfolios, spread resources appropriately, and adjust projects to produce the highest departmental returns.

Project Schedule A detailed plan of major project phases, milestones, activities, tasks, and resources allocated to each task. The most common representation of the project schedule is in a Gantt Chart.

Project Success Rate A chance that a project will be successfully completed

Prospect Theory A theory of behavior developed by D. Kahneman and A. Tversky as an alternative to expected utility theory.

Qualitative Risk Analysis A process that determines the probability and impact of the risks on the project. Qualitative risk analysis includes ranking of risk according to their impact on the project schedule.

Quantitative Risk Analysis A process of assigning numerical probabilities to the risks and uncertainties and then applying quantitative methods to determine the impact of those risks on the project schedule.

Radar Chart A chart used to visualize different strategies against multiple objectives.

Rate of Return (ROR) A measure of profitability of an investment. It is an increase in the value of the investment, expressed as a percentage.

Rational Choice An alternative that leads to maximum value for the decision-maker.

The Rational Unified Process (RUP) An iterative software development process created by the Rational Software Corporation, now a division of IBM.

Reality Check A method of assessing results of analysis by comparing it with results, obtained from different analyses or from subjective assessments.

Regression Analysis A statistical technique for investigating and modeling the relationship between variables.

Repeated Activity A previous activity that needs to be executed again due to an event. Repeated activities can be modeled using Event chain methodology.

Representativeness Heuristic A heuristic according to which people estimate probability by judging how representative the object, person, or event is of its category, group, or process.

Reserve Analysis A technique to establish reserves for schedule duration, budget, estimated cost, or funds for a project.

Resource Leveling A schedule network analysis technique in which project schedule is calculated, given resource constraints such as resource availability.

Review Board See *Decision Committee*.

Risk A stochastic event that can be applied to tasks or resources and that affects project schedules. The effect can be positive (opportunity) and/or negative (threat). Risks in Event chain methodology are defined by name, chance of occurrence, outcome, and moment of occurrence. Risks can be global (for all tasks or resources in project) and local (for a particular task or resource in the project).

Risk Audit A technique that helps to control efficiency of risk responses as well as efficiency of risk-management process.

Risk Breakdown Structure (RBS) A hierarchical structure of risks created during risk identification. Event chain methodology uses Risk Breakdown Structure and project schedule together to perform quantitative risk analysis.

Risk Identification A process of determining and identifying properties of potential threats and opportunities.

Risk Impact Consequences (outcome) of risk event on the activity and project. In Event chain methodology, impact is one of the properties of the event.

Risk Mitigation Plan A proactive risk-response strategy that reduces the probability of a risk event and its impact.

Risk Monitoring and Control A process of tracking identified risks, monitoring residual risks, identifying new risks, and executing risk-response plans during the course of a project.

Risk Policy Individual's or organization's risk preferences. Individuals or organizations can be risk averse or risk-taking. Risk policy can be expressed using utility function.

Risk Register A document that includes information about risks: risk name, description, category, cause, probability, impact on project objectives, responses, owner, current status, and other related information.

Risk-Response Planning A formalized process of planning options and activities to reduce threats and enhance opportunities to project objectives.

Risk Tolerance A level of risk that an organization or individual is willing to accept.

Rule of Pi A bias that affects estimations: actual duration (cost) of an activity will be pi (3.1415 . . .) bigger than the original estimate, even if the estimator was aware of this rule.

Sampling In Monte Carlo simulations, a process of retrieval of the value from the statistical distribution.

Scenario Analysis See *What If Scenario Analysis.*

Schedule Consolidation An algorithm that is used to reduce the number of activities presented on a decision tree as a result of schedule-to-decision-tree conversion.

Schedule Control A process of monitoring changes to the project schedule.

Schedule Model A model used to perform schedule network analysis and to generate the project schedule.

Schedule Network Analysis A technique used to identify start and finish times for the uncompleted activities of a project schedule.

Schedule-to-Decision-Tree Conversion An algorithm used to convert a project schedule with multiple alternatives for the decision tree.

Scope Control One of the project scope management processes related to controlling of changes in project scope.

Scope Verification A process of formalizing acceptance of the completed project deliverables (Project Management Institute 2018).

Scoring Model An approach to multi-criteria decision-making that requires the user to assign weights to each criterion that describes the criterion's relative importance. The user also assigns a rating that shows how well each decision alternative satisfies each criterion. The output of the model is a score for each decision alternative.

Selective Perception A psychological term that describes either the conscious or unconscious increase in attention to stimuli and information consistent with a person's attitudes or interests, or a conscious or unconscious discounting of inconsistent stimuli ("What you see is what you want to see").

Self-Actualization A psychological term to describe the motivation to fulfill somebody's potential. The notion of self-actualization is used in theories of creativity.

Sensitivity Analysis A type of probabilistic analysis that determines how sensitive results of the analysis are to uncertainties in input variables. Sensitivity analysis determines which uncertainty has the greatest potential for the impact.

Simulation A method of learning about a real system by experimenting with a model that represents the system.

Six Sigma A rigorous and disciplined methodology that utilizes data and statistical analysis to measure and improve a company's operational performance, practices, and systems. Six Sigma identifies and prevents defects in manufacturing and service-related processes.

Slack See *Free Float.*

Spearman Rank Order Correlation Coefficient A nonparametric (distribution-free) rank statistic proposed by Spearman in 1904 as a measure of the strength of the associations between two variables.

St. Petersburg Paradox A game that leads to a random variable with infinite expected payoff, which is considered to be worth only a small amount of money. The St. Petersburg paradox is a classical situation where expected value approach would recommend a course of action that no rational person would be willing to take.

Standard Deviation A statistical parameter: a measure of how widely dispersed the values are in a distribution. Equals the square root of the variance.

Statistical Distribution An arrangement of values or variables showing their observed or theoretical frequency of occurrence.

Student Syndrome A psychological bias related to project scheduling: many people will start to fully apply themselves to a task just in the wake of a deadline.

Subjective Probability A probability that is based on a person's judgment of the likelihood of an event. See also *Objective Probability.*

Success Rate The chance that a task or project will be completed. A task success rate of 56% means that there is a 56% chance that this task will be completed and a 44% chance that the task will be canceled.

SWOT Analysis A technique (noting strength, weaknesses, opportunities, and threats) used for risk identification and strategic planning.

Theory of Constraints A management approach that focuses on identifying and relaxing the constraints that limit an organization's ability to reach a higher level of goal attainment. Theory of constraints was developed by Eliyahu Goldratt.

Threat An unfavorable situation that will have negative impact of project objectives if it occurs. The opposite situation is opportunity.

Tornado Diagram A diagram presenting results of sensitivity analysis. Input parameters, which affect output parameters at most, are shown at the top of the diagram.

Trial In Monte Carlo simulations, a single run of the calculation.

Triangular Distribution A statistical distribution in which the parameter is estimated using minimum, maximum, and most likely estimates.

Uncertainty Any event or group of events with an uncertain outcome.

Uniform Distribution A statistical distribution that represents an equal probability that the parameter will be within certain range.

Util Arbitrary units used to measure utility scale.

Utility A measure of total worth of the particular outcome. It reflects decision-maker's attitude toward a collection of factors, such as profit, lost, and risk.

Utility Function A chart of mathematical equations that represent the relationship between objective measures, such as money and utility. Utility function is used in quantitative analysis.

Valuation Model An approximation of the problem or project. Valuation consists of input and output variables as well as mathematical formulas.

Value Measure An outcome measure used for decision analysis. Examples of value measures are NPV, ROI, project duration, and cost.

Variable Parameter in a model that has a value. Examples of variables can be task cost or duration.

Verbal Expressions of Uncertainty Words used in the decision analysis report such as "possible," "probable," "may," and "unlikely" that are intended to express uncertainties.

What If Scenario Analysis A schedule network analysis technique that includes generating and assessing multiple project scenarios under different conditions.

WITI Test A way to separate means and fundamental objectives by answering a question: <u>W</u>hy <u>I</u>s <u>T</u>hat <u>I</u>mportant?

Work Breakdown Structure A hierarchical set of project activities. Each Work Breakdown Structure level has more detailed information than the previous level.

Future Reading

Decision Analysis (Including Psychology of Judgment and Decision-Making)

Belton, V., and T. Stewart. 2002. *Multiple Criteria Decision Analysis: An Integrated Approach*. 2002 edition. Springer.

Clemen, R. T., and T. Reilly. 2013. *Making Hard Decisions*. 3rd ed. Cengage Learning.

Goodwin, Paul. 2014. *Decision Analysis for Management Judgment*. 5th ed. Wiley.

Hammond, J., R. Keeney, and H. Raiffa. 2015. *Smart Choices: A Practical Guide to Making Better Decisions*. Harvard Business Review Press.

Hastie, R., and R. Dawes. 2009. *Rational Choices in an Uncertain World*. 2nd ed. Thousand Oaks, CA: Sage Publications.

Heuer, R. J., Jr. 2016. *Psychology of Intelligence Analysis*. Center for the Study of Intelligence—Central Intelligence Agency.

Schuyler, J. 2016. *Risk and Decision Analysis in Projects*. 3rd ed. Planning Press.

Skinner, D. 2009. *Introduction to Decision Analysis*. 3rd ed. Probabilistic Publishing.

Popular Books on the Psychology of Judgment and Decision-Making

Ariely, D. 2010. *Predictably Irrational, Revised and Expanded Edition: The Hidden Forces That Shape Our Decisions*. Harper Perennial.

Christian, B., and T. Griffiths. 2017. *Algorithms to Live By: The Computer Science of Human Decisions*. Picador.

Gardner, P. E., and D. Tetlock. 2015. *Superforecasting: The Art and Science of Prediction*. Crown.

Gigerenzer, G. 2015. *Calculated Risks: How to Know When Numbers Deceive*. Simon & Schuster.

Gilbert, D. 2007. *Stumbling on Happiness*. New York: Vintage.

Gladwell, M. 2007. *Blink: The Power of Thinking Without Thinking*. New York: Little, Brown and Co.

Kahneman, D. 2013. *Thinking, Fast and Slow*. Farrar, Straus and Giroux.

LeGault, M. 2006. *Think! Why Critical Decisions Can't Be Made in the Blink of an Eye*. New York: Threshold Editions.

Plous, S. 1993. *The Psychology of Judgment and Decision Making.* New York: McGraw-Hill.

Rosling, H., A. Rosling Rönnlund, and O. Rosling. 2018. *Factfulness: Ten Reasons We're Wrong About the World—and Why Things Are Better Than You Think.* Flatiron Books.

Schwartz, B. 2009. *The Paradox of Choice: Why More Is Less.* New York: Harper Perennial.

Singer, M. 2007. *The Untethered Soul: The Journey Beyond Yourself.* New Harbinger Publications/ Noetic Books.

Thaler, R. H., and Cass Sunstein. 2015. *Misbehaving: The Story of Behavioral Economics.* W. W. Norton.

———. 2009. *Nudge: Improving Decisions About Health, Wealth, and Happiness.* Updated ed. New York: Penguin.

Project Management (Including Project Risk Management and Decision Analysis)

Cretu, O., R. B. Stewart, and T. Berends. 2011. *Risk Management for Design and Construction.* RSMeans.

Ghantt, T. 2012. *Project Risk Management: Using Failure Mode Effect Analysis for Project Management.* Plumbline Publishing Group.

Hillson, D. 2009. *Managing Risk in Projects (Fundamentals of Project Management).* Gower Publishing.

———. 2012. *Practical Risk Management: The ATOM Methodology.* 2nd ed. Management Concepts Press.

———. 2014. *The Risk Doctor's Cures for Common Risk Ailments.* Management Concepts Press.

Hillson, D., and Ruth Murray-Webster. *A Short Guide to Risk Appetite (Short Guides to Business Risk).* Gower Publishing.

Hulett, D. 2011. *Integrated Cost-Schedule Risk Analysis.* Ashgate Publishing.

———. 2009. *Practical Schedule Risk Analysis.* Gower Publishing.

Jordan, A. 2013. *Risk Management for Project Driven Organizations: A Strategic Guide to Portfolio, Program and PMO Success.* J Ross Publishing.

Jutte, B. 2009. *Project Risk Management Handbook: The Invaluable Guide for Managing Project Risks.* Mantaba Publishing.

Kendrick, T. 2015. *Identifying and Managing Project Risk: Essential Tools for Failure-Proofing Your Project.* 3rd ed. AMACOM

Pritchard, C. 2014. *Risk Management: Concepts and Guidance.* 5th ed. Auerbach Publications.

Raydugin, Y. 2013. *Project Risk Management: Essential Methods for Project Teams and Decision Makers.* Wiley.

Virine, L., and M. Trumper. 2017. *Project Risk Analysis Made Ridiculously Simple.* World Scientific–Now Publishers Business.

———. 2013. *ProjectThink: Why Good Managers Make Poor Project Choices.* Gower Publishing.

Warren, R. 2013. *Project Risk Management: The Most Important Methods and Tools for Successful Projects.* CreateSpace Independent Publishing Platform.

References

Anderson, David R., Dennis J. Sweeney, Thomas A. Williams, Jeffrey D. Camm, James J. Cochran, Michael J. Fry, and Jeffrey W. Ohlmann. 2015. *Quantitative Methods for Business*. 13th rev. ed. South-Western College Publishing.

Arkes, H. R., and C. Blumer. 1985. "The Psychology of Sunk Cost." *Organizational Behavior and Human Decision Processes* 35, no. 1 (February): 124–40.

Aviation Safety Network. 2019. ASN Safety Databases. https://aviation-safety.net/database/record.php?id=19770327-0. Accessed May 22, 2019.

Berger, E. 2001. "Keeping its Head Above Water: New Orleans Faces Doomsday Scenario." *Houston Chronicle*, December 1, 2001.

Bier, V., and F. Kosanoglu. 2015. "Target-Oriented Utility Theory for Modeling the Deterrent Effects of Counterterrorism." *Reliability Engineering & System Safety* 136 (April): 35–46.

Bordley, R. F. 2017. "Elicitation in Target-Oriented Utility." In *Elicitation. The Science and Art of Structuring Judgement*, edited by Luis C. Dias, Alec Morton, and John Quigley, 265–86. Springler International.

Bordley, R. F., J. Keisler, and T. Logan. 2019. "Managing Projects with Uncertain Deadlines." *European Journal of Operational Research* 274, no. 1 (April): 291–302.

Bordley, R. F. and Craig W. Kirkwood. 2004. "Multiattribute Preference Analysis with Performance Targets. *Operations Research* 52, no. 6 (November/December): 823–35.

Bordley, Robert, and Marco LiCalzi. 2000. "Decision Analysis Using Targets Instead of Utility Functions." *Decisions in Economics and Finance* 23, no. 1 (2000): 53–74.

Bordley, Robert, Luisa Tibiletti, and Mariacristina Uberti. 2015. "A Target-Oriented Approach: A 'One-Size' Model to Suit Humans and Econs Behaviors." *Applied Mathematical Sciences* 9, no. 100: 4971–78.

Brown, D. 2003. *The Da Vinci Code*. New York: Doubleday.

Brun, Wibecke, and Karl Halvor Teigen. 1988. "Verbal Probabilities: Ambiguous, Context Dependent, or Both?" *Organizational Behavior and Human Decision Processes* 41, no. 3 (June): 390–404.

Buehler, R., D. Griffin, and M. Ross. 1994. "Exploring the 'Planning Fallacy': Why People Underestimate Their Task Completion Times." *Journal of Personality and Social Psychology* 67, no. 3: 366–81.

Cabanatuan, M. 2005. "Bay Bridge Construction Delay Cost $81 Million." *San Francisco Chronicle*, December 7.

Castagnoli, E., and M. L. Calzi. 1996. "Expected Utility Without Utility." *Theory and Decision* 41, no. 3: 281–301.

Centers for Disease Control (CDC). 2018. "Disease Burden of Influenza." https://www.cdc.gov/flu/about/burden/index.html. Accessed December 1, 2018.

Chapman, L. J., and J. P. Chapman. 1971. "Test Results Are What You Think They Are." *Psychology Today* (November 18–22): 106–10.

Clemen, Robert T., and Terence Reilly. 2013. *Making Hard Decisions with Decision Tools.* 3rd ed. Cengage Learning.

Coombs, C. H. 1975. "Portfolio Theory and The Measurement of Risk." In *Human Judgment and Decision Processes in Applied Settings*, eds. Martin F. Kaplan and Steven Schwartz, 63–85. New York: Academic Press.

Crocker, J. 1982. "Biased Questions in Judgment of Covariation Studies." *Personality and Social Psychology Bulletin* 8, no. 2: 214–20.

Davis, G. 2004. *Creativity Is Forever.* 5th ed. Dubuque, IA: Kendall Hunt Publishing.

Delbecq, Andre L., Andrew H Van de Ven, and David H. Gustafson. 1975. *Group Techniques for Program Planning.* Glenview, IL: Scott, Foresman.

Dijksterhuis, A., M. W. Bos, L. F. Nordgren, and R. B. van Baaren. 2006. "On Making the Right Choice: The Deliberation-Without-Attention Effect." *Science* 311, no. 5763 (February): 1005–7.

Feynman, R. P. 1988. "An Outsider's Inside View of The Challenger Inquiry." *Physics Today* 41, no. 2: 26–37.

Fischetti, Mark. 2001. "Drowning New Orleans." *Scientific American*, October.

Fishburn, P. C. 1984. "SSB Utility Theory and Decision-Making Under Uncertainty." *Mathematical Social Sciences* 8, no. 3 (December): 253–85.

Flyvbjerg, B. 2003. "Delusions of Success: Comment on Dan Lovallo and Daniel Kahneman." *Harvard Business Review* (December 2003): 121–22.

———. 2006. "From Nobel Prize to Project Management: Getting Risks Right." *Project Management Journal* 37, no. 3 (August): 5–15.

Flyvbjerg, Bent, Mette Skamris Holm, and Soren Buhl. 2002. "Underestimating Costs in Public Works Projects: Error or Lie?" *Journal of the American Planning Association* 68, no. 3: 279–95.

Fortune. 2018. "100 Best Companies to Work For." http://fortune.com/best-companies/list/. Accessed November 29, 2018.

Gigerenzer, Gerd. 2015. *Calculated Risks: How to Know When Numbers Deceive You.* Simon & Schuster.

Gladwell, Malcolm. 2007. *Blink: The Power of Thinking Without Thinking.* New York: Little, Brown and Co.

Goldratt, Eliyahu M. 2002. *Critical Chain.* Great Barrington, MA: North River Press.

———. 2014. *The Goal: A Process of Ongoing Improvement.* 30th anniversary ed. North River Press.

Goldstein, D. G., and G. Gigerenzer. 1999. "The Recognition Heuristic: How Ignorance Makes Us Smart." In *Evolution and Cognition: Simple Heuristics That Make Us Smart*, eds. G. Gigerenzer and P. M. Todd, 37–58. New York: Oxford University Press.

Goodwin, Paul, and George Wright. 2014. *Decision Analysis for Management Judgment*. 5th ed. Wiley.

Grinshpun, Michael. 2018. "Tesla Model 3 = #1 Best Selling Car in the US (In Revenue)." September 9th, 2018. https://cleantechnica.com/2018/09/09/tesla-model-3-becomes-1 -best-selling-car-in-the-us/. Accessed November 22, 2018.

Grossman, Karl. 1997. *Wrong Stuff: The Space Program's Nuclear Threat to Our Planet*. Monroe, ME: Common Courage Press.

Hall, D. 2005. "Lessons Discovered but Seldom Learned or Why Am I Doing This If No One Listens." In *Proceedings of Space Systems Engineering and Risk Management Symposiums*. October 26–28, pp. 170–78. Los Angeles.

Hammond, Kenneth R., and Thomas R. Stewart, eds. 2001. *The Essential Brunswik: Beginnings, Explications, Applications*. New York: Oxford University Press.

Harding, L. 2018. "How Russian Spies Bungled Cyber-Attack on Weapons Watchdog." *The Guardian*. October 4, 2018. https://www.theguardian.com/world/2018/oct/04/how -russian-spies-bungled-cyber-attack-on-weapons-watchdog. Accessed December 5, 2018.

Hastie, R. 1986. "Experimental Evidence on Group Accuracy." In *Information Pooling and Group Decision Making: Proceedings of the Second University of California, Irvine, Conference on Political Economy*, eds. Bernard Grofman and Guillermo Owen, 129–57. Greenwich, CT: JAI Press.

Hastie, Reid, and Robyn M. Dawes. 2009. *Rational Choice in an Uncertain World: The Psychology of Judgment and Decision Making*. 2d ed. Thousand Oaks, CA: Sage Publications.

Heuer, Richards J., Jr. 2016. *Psychology of Intelligence Analysis*. Center for the Study of Intelligence–Central Intelligence Agency.

Highsmith, Jim Robert. 2009. *Agile Project Management: Creating Innovative Products*. 2nd ed. Addison-Wesley Professional.

Hill, Gayle W. 1982. "Group Versus Individual Performance: Are N+ 1 Heads Better Than One?" *Psychological Bulletin* 91, no. 3: 517–39.

Hillson, David, and Ruth Murray-Webster. 2007. *Understanding and Managing Risk Attitude*. 2nd ed. Aldershot, UK: Gower Publishing.

Holling, C. S., ed. 2005. *Adaptive Environmental Assessment and Management*. Blackburn Press.

Howard, R. A., and J. E. Matheson. 1984/2005. "Influence Diagrams." In *Readings on the Principles and Applications of Decision Analysis*, eds. Ronald A. Howard and James E. Matheson, vol. 2 (1984), 719–62. Menlo Park, CA: Strategic Decisions Group. Reprinted in *Decision Analysis* 2, no. 3: 127–43.

ITER. 2018. https://www.iter.org/. Accessed December 6, 2018.

Johnson, J. 2016. *My Life Is Failure*. James Johnson.

Kahneman, Daniel. 2013. *Thinking, Fast and Slow.* Farrar, Straus and Giroux.

Kahneman, Daniel, Edward Diener, Norbert Schwarz, eds. 1999. "Objective Happiness." In *Well-Being: The Foundations of Hedonic Psychology*, 3–25. New York: Russell Sage.

Kahneman, Daniel, Jack L. Knetsch, and Richard H. Thaler. 1990. "Experimental Tests of Endowment Effect and The Coase Theorem." *Journal of Political Economy* 98, no. 6 (December): 1325–48.

Kahneman, D., and D. Lovallo. 2003. "Response to Bent Flyvbjerg." *Harvard Business Review* (December): 122.

Kahneman, Daniel, and Amos Tversky. 1979. "Prospect Theory: An Analysis of Decisions Under Risk." *Econometrica* 47, no. 2 (March): 263–91.

Karmarkar, U. 1978. "Subjective Weighted Utility: A Descriptive Extension of the Expected Utility Model." *Organizational Behavior and Human Performance* 21, no. 1 (February): 61–72.

Keeney, Ralph L. 1982. "Decision Analysis: An Overview." *Operations Research* 30, no. 5 (September/October): 803–38.

———. 1996. *Value-Focused Thinking: A Path to Creative Decisionmaking.* Rev. ed. Cambridge: Harvard University Press.

Keeney, Ralph L., and Howard Raiffa. 1993. *Decisions with Multiple Objectives: Preferences and Value Tradeoffs.* Cambridge University Press.

Keisler, Jeffrey M., and Robert F. Bordley. 2015. "Project Management Decisions with Uncertain Targets." *Decision Analysis* 12, no. 1.

Kendrick, Tom. 2015. *Identifying and Managing Project Risk: Essential Tools for Failure-Proofing Your Project.* 3rd ed. New York: AMACOM.

Kerth, Norman L. 2001. *Project Retrospectives: A Handbook for Team Reviews.* Dorset House.

Kruchten, Philippe. 2003. *The Rational Unified Process: An Introduction.* 3rd ed. Addison-Wesley.

Lambert, F. 2018. "Elon Musk says Tesla will be out of 'production hell' in a month as they start ramping up to 10,000 Model 3s per week." *Electrek.* https://electrek.co/2018/07/12/elon-musk-tesla-production-model/. Accessed December 4, 2018.

Ledoux. Joseph. 2015. *The Emotional Brain: The Mysterious Underpinnings of Emotional Life.* New York: Simon & Schuster.

LeGault, Michael R. 2006. *Think! Why Crucial Decisions Can't Be Made in the Blink of an Eye.* New York: Threshold Editions.

Linkov, I., F. K. Satterstrom, G. Kiker, T. P. Seager, T. Bridges, S. L. Benjamin, and D. A. Belluck. 2006b. "From Optimization to Adaptation: Shifting Paradigms in Environmental Management and their Application to Remedial Decisions." *Integrated Environmental Assessment and Management* 2, no. 1 (January): 92–98.

Linkov, I., F. K. Satterstrom, G. Kiker, T. P. Seager, T. Bridges, K. H. Gardner, S. H. Rogers, D. A. Belluck, and A. Meyer. 2006a. "Multicriteria Decision Analysis: A Comprehensive Decision Approach for Management of Contaminated Sediments." *Risk Analysis* 26, no. 1 (February): 61–78.

Lord, C., L. Ross, and M. Lepper. 1979. "Biased Assimilation and Attitude Polarization: The Effects of Prior Theories on Subsequently Considered Evidence." *Journal of Personality and Social Psychology* 37, no. 11: 2098–2109.

Luce, R. Duncan. 1959. *Individual Choice Behavior: A Theoretical Analysis*. New York: John Wiley & Sons.

Makary, Martin A., and Michael Daniel. 2016. "Medical Error—The Third Leading Cause of Death in the US." *BMJ*, 353: i2139.

Manifesto for Agile Software Development. 2006. Available at http://agilemanifesto.org. Accessed December 1, 2018.

Maslow, Abraham H. 1987. *Motivation and Personality*, edited by Robert Frager, James Fadiman, Cynthia McReynolds, and Ruth Cox. 3rd ed. New York: Harper Collins.

Massey, C., D. Robinson, and R. Kaniel. 2006. "Can't Wait to Look in the Mirror: The Impact of Experience on Better-Than-Average Effect." Paper presented at *INFORM Annual Meeting*, Pittsburgh, PA, November 5–8.

Mather, M., and M. K. Johnson. 2000. "Choice-Supportive Source Monitoring: Do Our Decisions Seem Better to Us As We Age?" *Psychology and Aging* 15, no. 4 (December): 596–606.

McAllister, Brian. 1997. *Crew Resource Management: Awareness, Cockpit Efficiency and Safety*. Shrewsbury, England: Airlife.

McConnell, S. 1996. *Rapid Development*. Redmond, WA: Microsoft Press.

McCray, Gordon E., Russell L. Purvis, and Colleen G. McCray. 2002. "Project Management Under Uncertainty: The Impact of Heuristics and Biases." *Project Management Journal* 33, no. 1 (March): 49–57.

Mooney, Chris. 2005. "Thinking Big About Hurricanes." *The American Prospect*, May 23.

Moscovici, Serge, and Marisa Zavalloni. 1969. "The Group as a Polarizer of Attitudes." *Journal of Personality of Social Psychology* 12, no. 2: 125–35.

Myers, David G., and Martin F. Kaplan. 1976. "Group-Induced Polarization in Simulated Juries." *Personality and Social Psychology Bulletin* 2, no. 1 (January): 63–66.

National Aeronautics and Space Administration (NASA). 2018. Space Shuttle Flights by Orbiter. http://www.nasa.gov/mission_pages/shuttle/launch/orbiter_flights.html. Accessed November 23, 2018.

Nisbett, Richard E., and Lee Ross. 1980. *Human Inference: Strategies and Shortcomings of Social Judgment*. Englewood Cliffs, NJ: Prentice-Hall.

Paivio, Allan. 1971. *Imagery and Verbal Processes*. New York: Holt, Rinehart & Winston.

———. 2006. *Mind and Its Evolution: A Dual Coding Theoretical Approach*. Psychology Press.

Parkinson, C. N. 2018. *Parkinson's Law, and Other Studies in Administration*. Blurb.

Partnoy, F. 2012. "The Cost of a Human Life, Statistically Speaking." *The Globalist*. https://www.theglobalist.com/the-cost-of-a-human-life-statistically-speaking/. Accessed December 5, 2018.

Payne, J. W. 1973. "Alternative Approaches to Decision Making Under Risk: Moments versus Risk Dimensions." *Psychological Bulletin* 80, no. 6: 439–53.

Pfizer. 2018. "Pfizer Pipeline as of January 30, 2018." Available from https://www.pfizer.com /sites/default/files/product-pipeline/01302018_PipelineUpdate.pdf. Accessed November 26, 2018.

Plous, Scott. 1993. *The Psychology of Judgment and Decision Making.* New York: McGraw-Hill.

Plumer, Brad. 2017. "U.S. Nuclear Comeback Stalls as Two Reactors Are Abandoned." *New York Times,* July 31.

Project Management Institute. 2018. *A Guide to the Project Management Body of Knowledge (PMBOK Guide).* 6th ed.

Pronin, Emily, Daniel Y. Lin, and Lee Ross. 2002. "The Bias Blind Spot: Perceptions of Bias in Self versus Others." *Personality and Social Psychology Bulletin* 28, no. 3 (March): 369–81.

Raiffa, Howard. 1968. *Decision Analysis: Introductory Lectures on Choices under Uncertainty.* New York: McGraw-Hill.

Roediger, Henry L., Michelle L. Meade, and Erik T. Bergman. 2001. "Social Contagion of Memory." *Psychonomic Bulletin & Review* 8, no. 2 (June): 365–71.

Rombout S., and D. Wise. 2007. "Failure to Launch: Has Poor Estimating Compromised Your Project?" In *Proceedings of the 2007 PMI College of Scheduling Conference,* April 15–18, Vancouver, BC.

Rose, P. 2001. "Risk Analysis and Management of Petroleum Exploration Ventures." *AAPG Methods in Exploration Series,* number 12. Tulsa, OK: American Association of Petroleum Geologists.

Rosental, B. 2017. "The Most Expensive Mile of Subway Track on Earth." *New York Times.* December 28.

Saaty, Thomas L., and Luis G. Vargas. 2014. *Models, Methods, Concepts & Applications of the Analytic Hierarchy Process.* 2nd ed. Springer.

Samuelson, W., and R. J. Zeckhauser. 1988. "Status Quo Bias in Decision Making." *Journal of Risk and Uncertainty* 1: 7–59.

Savage, Leonard. J. 1954. *The Foundation of Statistics.* New York: John Wiley & Sons.

Schelling, Thomas. 1971. "On the Ecology of Micromotives." *Public Interest* 25: 61–98.

Schkade, David A., and Daniel Kahneman. 1998. "Does Living in California Make People Happy? A Focusing Illusion in Judgments of Life Satisfaction." *Psychological Science* 9, no. 5 (September): 340–46.

Schlaifer, Robert. 1969. *Analysis of Decisions under Uncertainty.* New York: McGraw-Hill.

Schniederjans, Marc. 2012. *Goal Programming, Methodology and Applications.* New York: Springer.

Schuyler, John R. 2016. *Risk and Decision Analysis in Projects.* 3rd ed. Planning Press.

Shachter, Ross D. 1986. *Evaluating Influence Diagrams. Operations Research* 34, no. 6 (November/December): 871–82.

Simon, H. A. 1956. "Rational Choice and the Structure of the Environment." *Psychological Review* 63, no. 2: 129–38.

Simons, J. 2006. Risky Business. *Fortune* (September 4): 131–38.

Skinner, David C. 2009. *Introduction to Decision Analysis: A Practitioner's Guide to Improving Decision Quality.* 3rd ed. Probabilistic Publishing.

Slovic, Paul, Baruch Fischhoff, and Sarah Lichtenstein. 1982. "Facts and Fears: Understanding Perceived Risk." In *Judgment Under Uncertainty: Heuristics and Biases*, eds. Daniel Kahneman, Paul Slovic, and Amos Tversky, 463–89. Cambridge, UK: Cambridge University Press.

Sniezek, Janet A., and Rebecca A. Henry. 1989. "Accuracy and Confidence in Group Judgment." *Organizational Behavior and Human Decision Processes* 43, no. 1 (February): 1–28.

———. 1990. "Revision, Weighting, and Commitment in Consensus Group Judgment." *Organizational Behavior and Human Decision Processes* 45, no. 1 (February): 66–84.

Statista. 2018. "Insured Losses Caused by Natural Disasters Worldwide from 1995 to 2017." https://www.statista.com/statistics/281052/insured-losses-from-natural-disasters-worldwide/. Accessed December 1, 2018.

Sveriges Riksbank Prize in Economic Sciences in Memory of Alfred Nobel. 2002. http://nobelprize.org/nobel_prizes/economics/laureates/2002/ Accessed November 22, 2018.

Tetlock, Philip E., and Dan Gardner. 2015. *Superforecasting: The Art and Science of Prediction.* Crown.

Thaler, Richard H., and Cass R. Sunstein. 2009. *Nudge: Improving Decisions About Health, Wealth, and Happiness.* Updated ed. New York: Penguin.

Tversky, A. 1972. "Elimination by Aspects: A Theory of Choice." *Psychological Review* 79, no. 4: 281–99.

———. 1969. "Intransitivity of Preferences." *Psychological Review* 76, no. 1: 31–48.

Tversky, A., and D. Kahneman. 1971. "Belief in the Law of Small Numbers." *Psychological Bulletin* 76, no. 2: 105–10.

———. 1981. "The Framing of Decisions and the Psychology of Choice." *Science* 211, no. 4481 (January): 453–58.

———. 1982. "Judgment Of and By Representativeness." In *Judgment Under Uncertainty: Heuristics and Biases*, eds. Daniel Kahneman, Paul Slovic, and Amos Tversky, 84–99. Cambridge, UK: Cambridge University Press.

Ulam, S. M. 2002. *Adventures of a Mathematician.* Reprint ed. Berkeley: University of California Press.

von Neumann, John, and Oskar Morgenstern. 1947. *Theory of Games and Economic Behavior.* Princeton, NJ: Princeton University Press.

Virine, Lev, and Michael Trumper. 2017. *Project Risk Analysis Made Ridiculously Simple.* World Scientific–Now Publishers Series in Business.

———. 2013. *ProjectThink: Why Good Managers Make Poor Project Choices.* Routledge.

Walters, Carl. 2002. *Adaptive Management of Renewable Resources.* Blackburn Press.

Williams, T. 2004. "Why Monte Carlo Simulations of Project Networks Can Mislead." *Project Management Journal* 35, no. 3 (September): 53–61.

Williams-Byrd, J., D. Arney, et al. 2016. "Decision Analysis Methods Used to Make Appropriate Investments in Human Exploration Capabilities and Technologies. NASA Technical Report Server." Available at https://ntrs.nasa.gov/search.jsp?R=20160012013. Accessed November 24, 2018.

Wilson, Jim. 2001. "New Orleans is Sinking." *Popular Mechanics*, September 2001.

Wohlstetter, Roberta. 1962. *Pearl Harbor: Warning and Decision*. Stanford, CA: Stanford University Press.

Wong, Ernest Yat-Kwan, and Rod Roederer. 2006. "Should the U.S. have Attacked Iraq? Can Decision Theory Shed Light on Polarizing Debate?" *OR/MS Today* 33, no. 6: 42–45.

Zeigarnik, Bluma. 1967. "On Finished and Unfinished Tasks." In *A Sourcebook of Gestalt Psychology*, ed. Willis D. Ellis, 300–14. New York: Humanities Press.

Acknowledgments

Writing a book about project decision is a big project itself involving many decisions. In any project, whether designing software, constructing buildings, shooting reality TV shows, or catching criminal masterminds, you have to rely on help from others to move it to a successful conclusion. We would like to thank our reviewers who helped us by providing ideas and suggestions: Robert Bordley, Linda Rising, and Erik Gfesser. We were lucky to come across a very talented artist, Alex Alexeev, who produced the cartoons you will find in this book. Special thanks to Charlotte Ashlock and the highly professional staff and editors at Berrett-Koehler Publishers who guided us through the complex process of publishing our work.

Index

About the Authors

Lev Virine has more than 30 years of experience as a structural engineer, software developer, and project manager. Over the past two decades he has been involved in a number of major projects performed by Fortune 500 companies and government agencies to establish effective decision analysis and risk-management processes, as well as to conduct risk analyses of complex projects. He also has significant experience in the information technology, manufacturing, pharmaceutical, and oil and gas industries.

Lev is the author of more than 50 scientific papers and patents as well as three books. His current research interests include decision analysis and risk management, particularly their applications in project management. He writes and speaks to conferences around the world on project decision analysis, including the psychology of judgment and decision-making, modeling of business processes, and risk management. He received his doctoral degree in engineering and computer science from Moscow State University. Lev can be reached at lvirine@projectdecisions.org.

Michael Trumper has worked in the fields of technical communications, marketing, and software development for the past 25 years. He has long been involved in projects involving economic valuation as well as risk and project life-cycle modeling. Michael has authored several papers and articles on project risk management. He holds a bachelor's degree from the University of Victoria, Canada. Michael can be reached at mtrumper@projectdecisions.org.

Berrett–Koehler
Publishers

Berrett-Koehler is an independent publisher dedicated to an ambitious mission: *Connecting people and ideas to create a world that works for all.*

Our publications span many formats, including print, digital, audio, and video. We also offer online resources, training, and gatherings. And we will continue expanding our products and services to advance our mission.

We believe that the solutions to the world's problems will come from all of us, working at all levels: in our society, in our organizations, and in our own lives. Our publications and resources offer pathways to creating a more just, equitable, and sustainable society. They help people make their organizations more humane, democratic, diverse, and effective (and we don't think there's any contradiction there). And they guide people in creating positive change in their own lives and aligning their personal practices with their aspirations for a better world.

And we strive to practice what we preach through what we call "The BK Way." At the core of this approach is *stewardship,* a deep sense of responsibility to administer the company for the benefit of all of our stakeholder groups, including authors, customers, employees, investors, service providers, sales partners, and the communities and environment around us. Everything we do is built around stewardship and our other core values of *quality, partnership, inclusion,* and *sustainability.*

This is why Berrett-Koehler is the first book publishing company to be both a B Corporation (a rigorous certification) and a benefit corporation (a for-profit legal status), which together require us to adhere to the highest standards for corporate, social, and environmental performance. And it is why we have instituted many pioneering practices (which you can learn about at www.bkconnection.com), including the Berrett-Koehler Constitution, the Bill of Rights and Responsibilities for BK Authors, and our unique Author Days.

We are grateful to our readers, authors, and other friends who are supporting our mission. We ask you to share with us examples of how BK publications and resources are making a difference in your lives, organizations, and communities at www.bkconnection.com/impact.

Dear reader,

Thank you for picking up this book and welcome to the worldwide BK community! You're joining a special group of people who have come together to create positive change in their lives, organizations, and communities.

What's BK all about?

Our mission is to connect people and ideas to create a world that works for all.

Why? Our communities, organizations, and lives get bogged down by old paradigms of self-interest, exclusion, hierarchy, and privilege. But we believe that can change. That's why we seek the leading experts on these challenges—and share their actionable ideas with you.

A welcome gift

To help you get started, we'd like to offer you a **free copy** of one of our bestselling ebooks:

www.bkconnection.com/welcome

When you claim your **free ebook**, you'll also be subscribed to our blog.

Our freshest insights

Access the best new tools and ideas for leaders at all levels on our blog at ideas.bkconnection.com.

Sincerely,

Your friends at Berrett-Koehler